huckleberry

HUCKLEBERRY

STORIES, SECRETS, AND RECIPES FROM OUR KITCHEN

ZOE NATHAN

WITH JOSH LOEB AND
LAUREL ALMERINDA

PHOTOGRAPHS BY MATT ARMENDARIZ

CHRONICLE BOOKS
SAN FRANCISCO

Library of Congress Cataloging-in-Publication Data available.
ISBN 978-1-4521-2352-3

Manufactured in China

Design by Alice Chau

10 9 8 7 6 5

Chronicle Books LLC
680 Second Street
San Francisco, California 94107
www.chroniclebooks.com

Being part of a restaurant is the same as being part of a large, complicated, supportive, sweet, and sometimes not-so-sweet family. I dedicate this book to my family—both blood and restaurant. Without you, I have no reason and no way to do all of this.

Love, Zoe

contents

josh's foreword

Yes, I'm biased. I'm married to Zoe, plus share a family and several businesses with her, so I don't blame you if you're a bit skeptical about my ability to write objectively about her culinary skills. But the truth is I fell in love with Zoe's cooking and baking even before I fell in love with her (though the two were not very far apart).

Zoe came into my life when my first restaurant, Rustic Canyon, was just a six-month-old baby. My mom, Shirley, desperate for me to meet the right girl, met Zoe's mom, Jesse, a fellow Santa Monica resident, and after hearing about Zoe and her passion for food decided that the two of us should meet. Now, granted, I wasn't looking for a wife at the time, Zoe had plenty of other job offers, and the last thing I wanted was to be set up with someone by my mom; we met.

Zoe came to Rustic Canyon and did a tasting for me, and it was amazing. Up until then I didn't really know what Rustic Canyon's pastry program should be, I just knew that it wasn't there yet. Zoe had a vision and her execution was perfect. She wowed me with moist and buttery Warm Blueberry Cornmeal Cake and a beautiful assortment of cookies including her glorious Kouign

Amanns, a cookie she picked up during her travels through France. She made homespun ice cream and chocolates the way they should be made, not too sweet and with enough salt to bring out the true flavors without tasting salty.

She was everything I was looking for professionally and personally, but until then I didn't know I was looking for either. After I wrestled her away from more lucrative jobs and more prestigious restaurants with a promise that she could "make her own mark at Rustic," she finally took the job. That was when my restaurant and my life changed forever.

Zoe is a baker and chef in the same way that I imagine most great sculptors work. She has an amazing instinct for food, gets an idea, and works and works at it until it is exactly as it should be, which usually looks painfully simple yet delicious in a way that is unparalleled. While many people refer to her as a natural, she debunks the myth that "naturals" at anything even exist. Instead—as she says and teaches her staff—she just cares more and will not compromise anything in the creating of a dish and certainly will not serve it if it's not perfect. As she tells her girls every day,

"Make mistakes, throw things away, just don't put anything out unless you know it's perfect. Remember, we're trying to fool these people into thinking we're perfect!"

Zoe and I officially started dating just a couple short months after we began working together. I vividly remember one of the first moments I knew she was the one. My dad underwent an emergency heart procedure and I spent the night with my family in the hospital down the street from Rustic Canyon while they operated on him. It was touch and go, but around 6 A.M. we got news that it was all going to be okay, and I headed out relieved and completely emotionally spent. I needed to be out of the hospital but I also needed a little warmth and something to take my mind off the difficult night before. I headed to Rustic Canyon because I knew that at 6 A.M. the one person who would be there was Zoe, and I wanted to see her in a way I couldn't explain. I walked in the door and it turned out she knew already (my brother, who left shortly before me, had already come through for his hug). She gave me a big hug and a chocolate chip cookie and both were the best of their kind.

The early stages of our relationship moved at lightning speed. Within two months we were living together, four months later we were engaged, and early the next year we were married. Along the way she wowed me with freshly baked croissants out of our home oven (still my favorite). I put on a very happy extra thirty pounds, because everything she made, from her baked goods to braised chicken at night, tasted so good I couldn't stop eating it. Every time I saw a friend that I hadn't seen in a while, they would pat my expanding belly, give me a smirk, and say, "You look so happy." While I've since learned to eat her delicious cooking in moderation, she still makes me happier than ever; Zoe has that effect on people.

In April of that year, Zoe told me that she wasn't satisfied just being a pastry chef of a restaurant and wanted to do more. She wanted to open her own bakery and restaurant, a place where she could serve all her favorite pastries alongside heaping breakfast plates, freshly baked breads, rotisserie chickens, and more. We tested out the breakfast portion of her dream place on Saturday mornings at Rustic Canyon, and it turned into a huge

hit. For a few hours every Saturday morning, our dinner-only restaurant was transformed into a breakfast oasis, with a bar heaped with fresh fruit crostatas, prosciutto-Gruyère and chocolate croissants, stone fruit tarts and galettes, scones, savory flatbreads, cakes, and much more. It became clear that we had something special on our hands. People asked when we would open Zoe's place, how much they could invest, and the rest was history.

We came across a soon-to-be vacant Chinese fast-food restaurant across the street from Rustic where we saw potential, and Zoe told me if I could get if for us, she would make it special. Mine was the easy part, and she more than delivered.

Huckleberry opened in February of 2009, three weeks after we got married. It was a hit from the very beginning, with people flocking to everything she put out. Huckleberry offers a lot: great artisan coffee, freshly baked breads, sandwiches, salads, soups, dinner entrées to take home, plus desserts and of course great breakfast items and pastries. When it came time to write this book, Zoe said that she didn't want to tackle it all at once,

but that she loved breakfast and felt there weren't enough great breakfast cookbooks.

Zoe is a cookbook aficionado. One of the many bonuses I got when she moved into my house and my life were hundreds of great cookbooks. She reads them, flips through recipes, scribbles notes all over the pages, but mostly just gets inspired. This book comes not only from a chef but also a true cookbook lover. So enjoy it, get inspired, make notes in the margins, rip out pages, make delicious stuff, and occasionally eat more than you should because it just tastes so good. It's worth it, I promise.

laurel's foreword

If I didn't have a very good sense of humor and love Zoe with every fiber of my being, I'd probably want to strangle her most days. In fact, at this moment I want to strangle her. We are right up against our deadline for this book, and she is creating new recipes like a mad scientist. Of course, few of them will make any sense when she hands them to me to flesh out. Most will have at least three measurements wrong, and the bake times will only be vaguely in the ballpark. But after years of working side by side at all hours of the night and day, in all states of body and mind, including her at nine months pregnant or me with my jaw wired shut after major surgery, all I need is a sketch to know what she means. To me that is one of the most precious things about our partnership.

Before meeting Zoe, I had been a filmmaker, with a little film of mine screening at Sundance. But after I poured my heart and soul into a screenplay that struggled to get financing, and my writing partnership grew impossible to navigate, I became downright miserable. The only thing that grounded me at the end of the day was standing by my stove stirring risotto and sipping wine.

Around that time, while listening to KCRW's *Good Food*, I heard that it was to be Rustic Canyon's very last Saturday Morning Breakfast. So I dragged my then-boyfriend to the car, barely out of his pajamas, for one last bread pudding experience.

We ordered far too much food. Numerous pastries, brisket hash; it was silly. Needless to say, a to-go box was required. We gave up our table and I loaded up my box by the coffee station. But I didn't know what to do with our dirty dishes; I didn't want to leave a gross mess next to the cream and sugar. I was looking around at a loss and said over my shoulder to my honey, "I need a busser."

Zoe in her apron appeared beside me saying, "You need me," and took the plates from my hands with an easy grin.

I know it was a simple thing, but it floored me. She was so humble, warm, and generous. She and her food made total sense to me, and I thought, "I think I do need you."

The next day, I knocked on the kitchen door and handed my resume to Josh. A few days later when Zoe called me I just squealed into the phone with uncontrollable joy at the sound of her voice. Fortunately, this made her laugh and I think it gave us both the sense that we could probably work together.

I started to intern in the Rustic kitchen. Shortly after, our little pastry operation moved from a tiny corner of that kitchen to a bakery kitchen all our own. I was sure there had been a scheduling error when I saw I was to work as Morning Baker on Huck's opening day.

For days before, we made what we thought were big batches of anything that could be prepared ahead, and filled our freezer with raw biscuits, scones, and crostatas. We thought we were set up for a week.

We went through it all on opening day.

In the beginning, we scrambled to keep up. All the while, things seemed to be falling apart around us. The prep girl we counted on to set us up would blow it, and we would start the morning wildly behind. Or our bread baker would just not show up, and we would have to tackle her station at the same time as our own. Misfires on the line would force Zoe to help fry eggs until the guys were out of the weeds. And our purveyors would sometimes simply forget to deliver something crucial like milk.

For a good two months it was madness. We worked six-day weeks, fourteen-plus-hour days, growing more and more tired. Laughing was the only way we got through it all. We love to laugh. And we love to laugh at each other, perhaps the most. God forbid I have a new work ensemble, because I will be ridiculed all day for my palazzo pants or macramé cap.

When I think back on it now, I wonder how I did it. Why I did it.

Through it all, every batch of biscuits had to be perfect, even if she had to make them herself. Every time I saw her kick a new dent in the freezer, destroying another pair of kitchen clogs and disappearing into the office for a long while, I got scared. I would think, "This is finally it; that was the last straw. She can't handle anymore; now I'm alone in this chaos." But before too long, she would always emerge. Maybe her eyes were a little puffy, but she would go right back to her station and start her next task. And all it would take was one ridiculous customer modification to get us laughing again.

I think I hung in there with Zoe because I could see how determined she was. How passionate, and strong. I did not want to let down someone like that. Zoe was teaching me that yes, you can have your meltdowns in life; in fact, you are going to have them. But then you pull yourself together and you pick up where you left off, undeterred.

I cannot thank Zoe enough for all the countless lessons she has taught me over time and look forward to many more to come.

zoe's introduction

I wear a lot of different hats in my professional life. I'm a chef in charge of savory and pastry at Huckleberry, plus a restaurateur in charge of running several neighborhood businesses with my husband, but when people ask me what I do for a living, the answer is simple. I'm a baker.

Some people run, meditate, or do yoga to find their peace of mind. I bake. I have always loved baking, ever since I was a kid making scones with my mom, but especially since that morning when I walked by the window of Tartine Bakery in San Francisco and saw Chad Robertson and Liz Prueitt and a bunch of tough girls with tattoos shaping croissants, making scones, and filling lemon tarts that would soon be topped with fresh flowers and essentially begged them to take me on and teach me what they knew.

I love the process of baking, of working with just a handful of ingredients, and losing myself in my hands while working to transform these ingredients into something beautiful and delicious. I love taking a box of perfect peaches back to the restaurant from the farmers' market and turning them into sheet pans of whole-wheat peach squares, or peach crumble, or fresh peach preserves. When I'm

baking, the finished product almost doesn't matter; once I get into the simple peaceful acts of scaling, mixing, and scooping, I'm satisfied. When I get stuck doing management stuff and get too far away from the kitchen, I become agitated and grumpy, and I begin to deeply crave getting my hands in some dough and making something. I'm generally not okay again until I do so.

Huckleberry started from the Saturday Morning Breakfasts we used to do at Rustic Canyon. I began doing these because I wasn't satisfied just being the pastry chef at Rustic Canyon and I wanted to do more. I came from Tartine Bakery, which was always crazy-busy and where baked goods were the focus, to a restaurant where dessert was a complement to the rest of the meal, which people ordered only if they had managed to "save room." I craved early mornings, high-volume baking, and the mad push to get dozens of baked goods out and beautifully displayed by 8 A.M.

One day I was out taking a walk with Josh and I told him about my desire to hijack his nighttime restaurant and turn it into a full-scale bakery one morning each week. I could tell he wasn't very into the idea at the

time but he loved me, so he was in a pretty tough spot. Josh can be pretty headstrong, but he also gets a really big kick out of a challenge, so we compromised: He agreed to do it and help as long as we didn't hire anyone who wasn't family and wouldn't work for free and that I buy all the platters and supplies out of our own money.

A couple of Saturdays later, I arrived at the restaurant at 2:30 A.M. and started baking. Josh came with me and buttered the ring molds for crostatas and kept me company. My father, not only one of my favorite people on Earth but also incredibly talented and free labor, arrived at around 6:30 to prep his contribution, making pancakes, eggs, and fritattas, which he was famous for at our house but had certainly never done in a professional kitchen. Josh's brother Gabe worked the front with Josh and made coffee. This was our team.

The first couple of weeks weren't that busy and would end with my father and me sitting at a table, exhausted, sharing a super-sized mimosa, wondering if anyone would ever show up the following week. Those were famous last words. Pretty soon the word got out and the place was full. We screwed up so much because we

couldn't handle the volume, but the pastries looked great and I felt so good getting in there each morning super-early and working to put out an even bigger display of treats than the week before.

Josh finally realized that we had a good thing going and let me hire my friend Alice Park, who ended up helping me open Huckleberry, as well as one of our sassy line cooks, Renee Garcia, and my opening savory sous at Huckleberry, Tad Weyland. My dad stayed on, of course, and as we built this new family, which was a combination of my blood family and our restaurant family, all of whom we loved so much, we realized that it was time to find a real home for this motley crew.

We opened Huckleberry in February of the next year. Growing up, I always wanted to own a shop. Which kind wasn't that important to me; I just wanted a place where everyone knew they could find me at any hour of the day and visit me while I'm doing what I love. Huckleberry is my shop. When I think of Huckleberry I think abundance, slightly organized chaos, amazing early morning gossip, lots of blood, sweat, tears, and laughter. It's a place where I can pull a tray of

cinnamon rolls or a blueberry corn-meal cake out of the oven and walk one over to my mom or a regular who just sat down so they can eat it when it's hot and perfect. I don't get to do this every day, but I've gotten to do it a lot, and it makes me so happy when I do.

The display case at Huckleberry is the essence of abundance. It's full to the brim with heaping platters of pastries, stacked high. At Huckleberry you order at the counter, but as you move toward the front, you pass all the goodies: bowls of farmers' market salads; the abundant pastry case full of scones, muffins, crostatas, cookies, and doughnuts; and then the dessert case full of puddings, cream pies, and caramels. This is on purpose! We want you to come in with the best of intentions and then decide to be naughty and get something sweet. Then we want to make sure it's so good that you leave feeling that it was well worth it.

When I told people that I wanted to open a bakery in West Los Angeles, I was informed over and over again that it wouldn't work because people don't eat bread and pastries anymore. Well, luckily the naysayers were wrong. When someone comes into

Huckleberry for breakfast and tries to abstain from pastries because they are trying to be "healthy," I constantly want to yell (and those who know me know that sometimes I do), "Get off your juice fast! This *is* healthy; sitting down for a few moments and slowly eating a homemade muffin with a beautiful latte is good for you. Yoga is not the only place you should slow down and breathe!"

I don't think one needs to eat pastry every day, but I do think that pastry when eaten and enjoyed properly slows life down. I know, for me, baking slows life down. And I know for my son waiting for banana muffins to bake in the oven can feel like a month, a very slow-moving month.

Huckleberry does a lot of things other than breakfast. We offer a full-scale lunch with dozens of sandwiches and farmers' market–inspired salads. We make thousands of turkey meatballs and mounds of brisket each week, roast off dozens of organic chickens each day, and run a full-scale catering operation. I'd love to write a bunch of books about Huckleberry, but I started with breakfast because to me breakfast is where it all started. From those crazy Saturday mornings at Rustic where we got half of everyone's orders wrong to the bakery girls being the first ones in at 3 A.M. every day to filling the bakery case so it's abundant and impossible to refuse first thing in the morning to satisfying a groggy regular with his perfect cappuccino—this is the heart and soul of Huckleberry.

Of course, breakfast is more than just pastries. I may be a baker first, but when I wake up I want eggs and bacon (with a little maple syrup), and I want them done right. I purposely chose to make Huckleberry more than just a bakery because I wanted to offer more. I wanted Huck to be an experiment in overabundance: big heaping bowls of brisket with perfectly cooked sunny-side-up eggs beside a blueberry muffin and a latte. I wanted a place where everyone could come and find something they truly loved, be it a pastry or a bowl of quinoa with eggs. I wanted to give people a crazy moment of plenty as the first experience of their day. You will never experience stinginess at Huck, that's a promise.

I love cookbooks and I've always wanted to write one, but until now it wasn't the right time. I had enough recipes, had people who

were interested in publishing it, but mainly I just wanted to be in the kitchen at work and not be bothered with the logistics of converting big recipes to home batches or recipe testing in a home kitchen or any of that. I baked all day at work; when I came home I wanted a glass of wine and a good movie, not to get in the kitchen and start baking again.

Then Josh and I had our son, Milo, and he began to eat and love food as much as his dad and I do, and all of a sudden everything changed. I started working way less, preferring to be home chasing him around. He started to want cookies, doughnuts, and other treats in my house, and I began to fall in love again with working in my own kitchen and giving him freshly baked goodies straight out of the oven. My counter at home now has freshly baked pastries on it, pumpkin muffins, and homemade granola. We go over to a friend's house and I bring a plate of cookies, baked with Milo as my assistant, rather than just something from Huckleberry. And I love it. I found my love of baking at home again, and that's what I want to share with you.

My love of breakfast began in a busy professional kitchen at 3 A.M. listening

to loud music and cranking out as many pastries as our hands would allow. It continued as I watched customer after customer come into Huckleberry and enjoy a messy fried egg sandwich, and now it continues in my home when I wake each morning with excitement and anticipation as I wonder what I will make for Milo to start his day. I look forward to sharing all this with you, and hopefully you in turn share it with the people you love, because giving something you made with love to someone you love is just about the best feeling in the world.

tips, secrets, and rules we live by

Because I am a professional baker, people make plenty of incorrect assumptions about me. They assume that I'm organized, good at math, precise with measurements, and, at the very least, good at following a recipe. The truth is I'm awful at all these things, but somehow I've managed to open a successful bakery and restaurant. I think I survive as a baker and chef in spite of my shortcomings because I trust my taste and intuition when it comes to making something good. Plus I'm not afraid to make dozens of batches of the same item until I get it just right.

There are two ways to use this book. You can find recipes that look good to you and follow them to the letter: If you choose to wake up at 6 A.M. to surprise your family with muffins made by exactly following one of our recipes, I promise you will be successful and get a lot of extra love and appreciation from your family.

You can also use these recipes to give you guidance, messing around with them, inserting your own ideas, until you get it exactly as you want it. I will certainly not be offended if you tell me that you took one of my recipes and substituted one type of flour for another, tried using coconut oil instead of butter because you wanted to make it for your vegan friend, or even switched fruit for chocolate or ginger for lemon.

Please remember baking is supposed to be fun, so don't take yourself too seriously while you're doing it. Also remember that no one is a "natural"; there is just the willingness to make mistakes, learn from them, and still love what you're doing. That makes you "good."

The same goes for the following tips and guidelines. I live by this list in my home and restaurant kitchens, but use them only if they ring true to you.

INGREDIENTS

GENERAL NOTES

In this book the eggs are large, the sugar is always granulated, except when indicated otherwise, and when measuring ingredients we don't pack tightly.

USE GOOD INGREDIENTS

Try to buy organic and from suppliers that you know and trust. Not to sound like a total dork, but I do think this makes a huge difference both in baking and our impact on the world. Plus, the better the fruit you use, the less sugar you need, which means you can eat more!

SEASONAL PRODUCE

Don't make a fresh tomato dish in the winter. It simply won't turn out great. Use good seasonal produce from your local farmers' market and let the produce inspire and dictate what you cook.

SECONDS

If you want to feel like you're really in the know and get a great deal, in the peak summer months go to the farmers' market super-early and ask your favorite farmers if they have any "seconds." Seconds are bruised, overripe, and often ugly-looking fruit that the farmers don't feel they'll be able to sell at full price. This fruit is ideal for jams, jellies, cobblers, and galettes, basically any dish where you cook down the fruit and want as much ripe flavor as possible. My favorite two items to get seconds on are tomatoes and stone fruit. If you want to make the best tomato soup you've ever made in your life, make it with seconds. It's also perfect for recipes like the Cherry Tomato–Goat Cheese Cobbler (page 157) and Blueberry Nectarine Crisp (page 159). Don't use seconds for anything where you want the fruit to hold its shape. It's not great for recipes like the Vanilla Apricot Tart (page 146) or the Roasted Peaches with Nut Crumble (page 154). When it comes to overripe berries, those farmers generally freeze their seconds and bring them only on request, so you'll need to plan a week ahead for those. It's a way to make great berry jams and jellies without breaking the bank.

BREAD

Support your local artisanal baker! Of course, we encourage you to make your own bread, but we also understand that it can take a fair amount of time and not everyone has that. But just because you are short on time doesn't mean you should eat sandwiches on mass-produced, thoughtless bread. There is almost always an amazing baker either at your local farmers' market or in your town that woke up at 2 A.M. that day to bake fresh bread. It may be slightly more expensive or a little out of your way, but it will always be worth it. There are few things people actually create start to finish with their own two hands, bread being one of them, and we have to make sure to support that.

SALT

I know this is going to offend a few cookbook writers (and, honestly, most bakers) but when following a recipe from most cookbooks, double the salt. It'll make the recipe taste one million times better and will actually make your baked goods taste like something other than sugar. Almost every time someone who works for me forgets the salt, I'll ask them what they think the pastry needs and they will generally say, "More sugar." No! It needs salt to bring out the sweetness from the sugar. In baking, salt should be used as a flavor enhancer and only occasionally and intentionally as a flavor. We use only kosher salt to bake and cook with, and fleur de sel to finish because the rougher-cut,

larger granules really make your food sparkle. Please buy both; they are game changers.

EGGS

On the Huckleberry menu you will mostly see eggs done two ways: sunny-side up and poached soft (but of course we always have scrambled eggs for the kids). Why? Because I very strongly believe those are the most delicious ways to eat eggs. I like them sunny-side up because I like my yolk very runny and I think the yolk is breathtakingly beautiful on top of just about anything. I never like color on the whites because I think they are hard to cut through with a fork and I just simply don't think they taste better that way. I love poaching eggs because they feel light and you still get that awesome runny yolk. All that said, at Huckleberry we also realize everyone grew up eating and loving eggs differently, so we are always flexible, within reason, and the same goes for this book. Make your eggs how you like them—scrambled, over-easy, over-hard, basted, etc. All I care about is that you take the time to make yourself a beautiful breakfast.

BUTTER

At Huckleberry we use a good European-style butter. We think that the low water content and high fat make for much better-tasting baked goods. Always use unsalted butter so that you can control the salt in your dish. More expensive butter generally tastes better, so on pastries that should really taste like butter, such as flaky dough, don't skimp; use the good stuff.

VANILLA

As with salt, when using recipes from other cookbooks I recommend doubling the vanilla because in most recipes, the vanilla is called for in such small amounts that it's pointless. You don't want it to be the dominant flavor, but you do want to taste it. So when you see the measurements for vanilla in this book please rest assured they are not misprints. Use good vanilla extract, it makes a difference. And lastly, we often call for whole vanilla beans in this book because I love to bake with them. Try to get your hands on them; they'll give a richer, cleaner vanilla flavor than extract. If you can't find vanilla beans, substitute 2 tsp of vanilla extract per vanilla bean.

CHOCOLATE

As always, use good ingredients, especially with chocolate. I like Valrhona 66% cacao, but find what you like and buy it in bulk so you're never stuck using inferior stuff. As we wrote this book, we had a hard time figuring out how to express chocolate amounts using a cup measure. We found that unless we were using chocolate chips, which we never do at Huckleberry, it was difficult to quantify in that way, because depending on how someone chops their chocolate you can fit very different amounts in a cup. We did the best we could for our cup measurements, but we really encourage you to either use a scale or buy the baking bars that are scored into 1 oz portions, or the like, so you're not stuck using a measuring cup.

BUTTERMILK AND CRÈME FRAÎCHE

At Huckleberry we go through cartons of buttermilk each day. But at home, when I was recipe testing, I was floored that I could never get through the entire carton, since most recipes call for only 2 or 3 tbsp. So if you need just a little buttermilk, make it yourself by combining 1 tsp lemon juice with 1 cup/235 ml milk, and allow it to sit for about 20 minutes at room temperature. The same is true for crème fraîche. Some of our testers were annoyed with the price of crème fraîche. If you don't want to buy it, you can make your own by mixing 1 cup/235 ml heavy cream, with 1 tbsp buttermilk. Whisk them together, wrap tightly, and allow to rest at room temperature in a slightly warmer spot of your kitchen for 24 to 48 hours until thickened: the warmer the kitchen, the faster it'll go. Once it's thickened, refrigerate and use as needed.

GRAINS

I love cooking with lots and lots of different grains. Not even half of those that I enjoy working with are represented in this book. I can't push you enough to play with and learn about grains like bulgur, cracked wheat, quinoa, barley, and millet. To me they are often so much more flavorful than white-flour pastas, white rice, or couscous.

COOKING WINE

For the most part, my rule of thumb is cook with the kind of wine you'd like to drink that dish with. But I will be honest with you: When cooking for this book, if a dish called for white but I had only a lighter red kicking around, I used it. You should feel free to do the same. There's no need to stress yourself out about it. With beer it's key that you do not use a bitter beer like an IPA in these recipes because once you start cooking it down, all you'll be left with is the bitterness.

BACON

We tried as much as possible while writing this book to use ingredients that were easily accessible at your local supermarket. One item we found that you need to search a little harder for is good, thick-cut bacon. Most packaged stuff is so thin it cooks down to almost nothing. Luckily most supermarkets now have good slab bacon at the meat counter. At

Huckleberry we always serve nitrate-free bacon because pregnant women and kids can eat it, and I know that when I was pregnant it's all I really wanted to eat.

GRUYÈRE

At Huckleberry we go through 50 lb/ 23 kg of Gruyère every week. It's the perfect cheese for baking and great for most hot sandwiches. It's got the right amount of "stink," melts beautifully, and has a really great depth of flavor. I love the way it browns when it gets really hot, and in pastries it's the perfect complement to butter.

AIOLI

It's not that hard to make. It's much more flavorful than mayonnaise. Just do it. Use our recipe on page 224.

TOOLS

VESSELS

Most batters can be dropped into different vessels to feel like an entirely different dish. Blueberry cornmeal cake in a muffin tin can become blueberry muffins. Zucchini muffins can be thrown into a cake pan and become a teacake. But remember, smaller things bake faster and larger things take more time.

ON POTS AND PANS

Using the right pan is really important in getting the most out of your cooking. If you use too small a pan when sautéing mushrooms, they'll get too watery and never get a good sear. If you use too big a pan when sautéing cherry tomatoes, they'll burn before they get a chance to get tender and burst. So if the recipe calls for a small pan, please try to use a small pan and vice versa. Pan size is just as integral to the execution as adding the right amount of salt or cooking your onions for the right amount of time. Also it's especially important when frying eggs to use a nonstick pan, or you will curse, curse, and curse as you try to slide your eggs out of the pan.

BUY A SCALE

Another way to make baking go quicker and have less dishes to do is to use a scale. I know it seems like just another thing to buy and clutter your kitchen with, and it takes a little getting used to, but it really will make baking a lot easier.

THE FREEZER IS YOUR FRIEND

Keep unbaked scones, packets of flaky dough, unbaked cookies, and much more in your freezer. That way when you're going to a potluck or having friends over or it's a rainy day and your five-year-old has a craving for something sweet, you can bake something off in a matter of moments. Just be sure to tightly double wrap when storing in the freezer. You should be able to turn it upside down or drop it on the floor without anything spilling out.

CALIBRATE YOUR OVEN

Before you begin baking, check your oven and make sure it's calibrated properly. You can do everything in these recipes correctly but if your oven is off you are going to feel like a really crappy baker. When we were doing Saturday Morning Breakfast at Rustic Canyon we had awful ovens. They were lopsided, the temperatures were inaccurate, and the pilots went out all the time, always at the worst possible moment. I would do everything as close to perfect as I could but I still wound up with burnt, lopsided, underbaked, or overbaked muffins without the right color on top. It was rough. At Rustic Canyon, I dealt with this by choosing a wall in the kitchen and hurling the crappy muffins at it, which is not something I recommend. But I had to figure out how to get out my aggression and move on, and that was my way. So unless you want to decorate one of the walls in your home with muffins, I suggest you check your oven with a basic oven thermometer at both 350°F/175°C and 500°F/260°C.

TECHNIQUES

TOASTING

When I tell someone in the Huckleberry kitchen to toast nuts or wheat germ, they all know what I mean: I want some deep, dark color on them, and I want to really be able to smell them when they come out of the oven. When you toast nuts and wheat germ properly, you give them a much stronger, nutty flavor that is imperative when you are baking with them. If you don't toast properly, they can easily get lost in all the butter, white flour, and anything else you have in there. So please toast your nuts and wheat germ deep, dark, and fragrant.

CRUMBLE TOPPING

If you're exhausted and desperate for dessert or have a bunch of fruit that is about to die or your husband is grumpy and needs something sweet, turn your oven on; toss your fruit in sugar, salt, and maybe a touch of cornstarch; and top it with crumble (see page 152). Bake it and voilà! You are Martha Stewart and you didn't even take out the mixer.

HOMEMADE BREADCRUMBS

You should make your own bread-crumbs. I don't know one person on Earth that doesn't have bread going stale around their house. Instead of

throwing away that loaf that's past its prime, slice it, spread it out on a sheet pan, and bake it in a 300°F/150°C oven until it's incredibly dry and beginning to brown. Cool, then break it up in a food processor or with a knife if necessary for larger pieces. Unseasoned breadcrumbs like these will last in an airtight container in your pantry for up to a month. If you want to make a seasoned version, before toasting the bread, drizzle with olive oil and sprinkle with kosher salt, black pepper, and whatever other spices you want. If you want to add herbs, do so after toasting. Seasoned breadcrumbs will last at room temperature for at least a week. If you choose to buy breadcrumbs for any of these recipes, buy them unseasoned, because all our recipes are based on unseasoned breadcrumbs.

GLUTEN-FREE BAKING

I can't stress enough how important it is to make your own gluten-free flour mix. Most store-bought gluten-free mixes have bean flours in them, which I find really off-putting. I originally wrote off gluten-free baking as just another diet trend; then I met some people who loved good pastries but got really sick after eating them. I realized then that gluten-free and

vegan didn't need to go hand-in-hand, so I got excited about the challenge of making delicious buttery pastries that could not only be made without gluten, but that also actually tasted better without it. The key was making my own gluten-free mix, which I happily share with you in this book (see page 55). Feel free to adjust it based on your own taste.

CARAMELIZING ONIONS

I believe slow and low is not the way to do this. I know many will disagree, but I like to turn up the heat and stir frequently. I want my onions caramelized but to still have texture and not be completely mushy.

STOCK

A good homemade stock makes food so much more flavorful. Whenever we're done eating a roast chicken for dinner at home, the first thing I do is throw the carcass into a large stock pot with a couple of unpeeled carrots, a whole unpeeled onion, fennel, a couple of unpeeled garlic cloves, and any herbs I might have in the fridge or garden, plus any other vegetables that might be on their last days in my refrigerator. Sometimes if I have a bottle of white wine that we didn't quite finish, I'll pour that in, too. Simmer on medium, allow it to cook down by half; it will take 4 to 5 hours. If you want to let this go overnight, put it in a 275°F/135°C oven, uncovered, for 8 to 10 hours and let it get delicious while you sleep. Strain it and refrigerate if you think you're going to use it soon, or freeze for some future day. Never add salt or pepper, so you have the freedom to season whatever dish when you make it. Another option is to buy a few chicken bones or legs at the market and roast with whatever veggies you love, a little olive oil and salt at 500°F/260°C for about 20 minutes, and then throw them in water like the chicken carcass, adding herbs if you like. Having your own stock on hand is another game changer.

SOUS VIDE

I have never had a piece of sous vide meat that is better than a properly grilled steak or a properly braised brisket. Sue me, shoot me, burn me at the stake, but that is what I believe.

TIPS AND SECRETS

COLOR IS FLAVOR

Don't be scared of color when baking or cooking. Embrace it. Color is flavor. Treat it as another ingredient to be measured properly. It is often the difference between something good and something remarkable. This is true whether you're roasting off a tray of bacon, cooking a pot of caramel, or baking a cobbler. When I train someone new on how to bake a cobbler, they are always so scared of it getting too dark that they pull it out way too early. Invariably, the fruit's not cooked and the dough just tastes doughy. If you flirt with disaster, and really allow the biscuits to caramelize on top of the cobbler and the fruit to cook until it's sweet and jammy, the people who eat it will appreciate it and be blown away that a simple cobbler can taste so complex.

PARBAKING

Yuck! Don't do it. Ever. Breads and pastries are not green beans. Parbaking just messes up the texture and flavor.

PANCAKES

Make sure your griddle is nice and hot and always throw out your first pancake—that one's always a mess.

If it kills you to throw out food, you can always roll it up with some jelly and eat it yourself while you're cooking the rest of the pancakes.

THE STEALTH CHECK

You're worried that you forgot an ingredient or weighed the wrong amount of something, but you're not sure. Don't risk cutting into a cake that might actually be good before you're ready to serve it. Instead, when you're turning out your cake, rip a little taste off the bottom, put it aside, let it cool for a few minutes, and then taste it. If it's good, no one will ever know that you doubted it at some point. If it's bad, throw it away, start again, and don't beat yourself up. I've done it plenty of times.

BAKE WITH YOUR EYES, NOSE, AND INTUITION

Don't be a slave to a timer. The times I give in these recipes work at my house in my oven. But maybe your oven is different, or your fruit has more or less liquid. When you start to smell your baked good, it is getting close. If you see it has no color, don't hesitate to crank up the oven temperature and keep an eye on it. Sometimes to make something

perfect, you have to adjust. Using all your senses is truly the only way to bake well.

BRUSH OFF YOUR FLOUR

When dealing with any dough you're rolling out, such as flaky dough, you will always have to use extra flour to dust the table and dough. When you are done, be sure to brush all excess flour off of your pastry. It will not miraculously dissolve into the pastry and it will not taste good at all; it will simply still taste like raw flour after it is baked. I always like to have a dry brush on hand for this exact purpose when I'm rolling anything out.

PLATING (AND LIGHTING) FIXES EVERYTHING

Pretty plates, dim lighting, and powdered sugar can often save the day. Did you bake something a little too dark? Is it kind of lopsided? Did the fruit sink? Don't panic; put it on a pretty plate, dust the whole thing with powdered sugar, and lower the lights. Trust me.

SIFTING

Sifting is annoying and only sometimes do we feel it actually makes any sort of real difference. So if we say to sift, then you really need to. If we don't, then don't waste your time.

MUFFIN TOPS (THE KIND YOU WANT)

Huckleberry muffins, when they are not made in a convection oven, will not look super-high like a traditional domed muffin. I chose to put our actual recipes in this book even though they bake up slightly less domed when baked in a traditional home oven, because I wanted you to have the best flavor and texture. I could have added flour to get the look, but I didn't think it was worth the compromise.

SALT AS YOU GO

When you're making a dish that has multiple stages of cooking, salt each one as you go as opposed to just trying to salt the dish as a whole at the end. A dish tastes better when everything is seasoned correctly. You'll also see in these recipes I give pretty exact measurements for salt, which is something most recipe books don't do when it comes to savory food. One of the biggest pitfalls of a home cook is not putting enough salt in your food, and I want to make sure that your food comes out tasting bright and beautiful.

HEAT

The thing I find most annoying about cooking with anyone who is not a professional is that the flame is never high enough. When my husband is cooking, I literally spend half the time behind his back turning things up, poor guy. Go against your instincts and turn it up. Don't be afraid to cook with heat; it's what gives your food life. Just pay attention so you don't burn stuff.

BÉCHAMEL

I love béchamel. I like to think of it as my savory pastry cream. It's obviously great on a Traditional Croque Monsieur (page 242), but it's also perfect used on the bottom layer in savory crostatas, bread puddings, lasagna, macaroni and cheese, enchiladas, and much more. Just remember it is very important to cook the flour well before adding the milk so the floury raw taste is cooked out.

FRESH GREENS

I love a good, heavy breakfast dish like brisket, braised pork, or a fried egg sandwich but feel that they all benefit from a little lightening up with a handful of fresh greens. I don't toss the greens with anything, because once the yolks break it becomes a dressing in and of itself. I love arugula and use it all the time, but you can really use anything like watercress, red leaf lettuce, or butter lettuce, but nothing hard or overly chewy like raw kale.

PLAN AHEAD FOR BREAD (AND OTHER THINGS THAT RISE)

Plan ahead when making bagels or brioche from this book. Almost all these recipes take two days to make, so be sure to plan accordingly and read the whole recipe the day before you want to eat it. Generally, dough that has more time to ferment and build flavor, either by sitting overnight or with the addition of a poolish, will have much better flavor than one that is just mixed, proofed, and baked quickly.

MEASURE THE NIGHT BEFORE

This will make your life so much easier. At Huckleberry, we're in by 3:30 A.M. and by 7:30 A.M. we have produced a full pastry spread. How do we make this happen? We do a lot of the time-consuming stuff the day before, such as gathering ingredients and measuring them. This also eliminates a lot of early morning, foggy brain, incorrect weighing. Ideally all you should have to do the morning of is drink coffee, listen to music, and dump, mix, scoop, and bake. If you want to be really prepared, you can even set out your tools and prepare your pans. Then, in the morning, your items will come together in minutes.

PREP AHEAD

There are a number of things you can entirely prepare ahead—one more step toward a calm breakfast. Cakes and muffins like the Chocolate Chunk Muffins (page 36), the Chocolate Almond Muffins (page 38), the Old-Fashioned Coffee Cake (page 91), and the Pear Whole-Wheat Crumb Cake (page 88) you can make, pan up, then refrigerate overnight and just pop right into the oven. A few cakes and muffins hold up so well overnight that you can mix and bake them off the day before you want to serve them, such as the Pear Ginger Muffins (page 44), Zucchini Muffins (page 49), and Banana Poppy Seed Muffins (page 39). Cobblers can be put together the night before and placed in the fridge ready to be baked in the morning. Things that are frozen, like biscuits, scones, galettes, crostatas, and turnovers can be made days, even weeks, ahead. Just transfer to your refrigerator the night

before to defrost and bake from that very-cold-but-no-longer-frozen state. With savory dishes and sandwiches, you can cook a lot of the elements the night before. Then in the morning it's simple to throw something wonderful together in much less time. Use these tricks, and you can easily throw together an insane spread without having to wake up at 3 A.M.

BRAISE AHEAD

Braising the day before not only saves time in the morning and ensures that your guests will eat their breakfast before 2 P.M., but also makes meat taste so much better; it allows the meat to soak up all the wonderful flavors in the braising liquid, and it just gets better and better, so don't be afraid to braise even two or three days ahead.

DINNER FOR BREAKFAST

Okay, I'm going to let you in on a little secret: Even with all the savory recipes in this book, some of the best breakfast plates are when you simply turn last night's dinner into breakfast. Pull your meat, heat it up, and put an egg on it—and if you really feel creative, top it with some fresh bread-crumbs, chopped herbs, or arugula.

BREAKFAST FOR DINNER

In order to recipe test everything in the book, and spend time with my husband, I had pretty much every savory breakfast dish in this book for dinner. Guess what? These were some of the best dinners ever. So feel free to eat these dishes for dinner, too.

3:30 A.M.

muffins

It's 3:30 A.M., which is definitely more night than morning. I often drive into work and pass rowdy girls and guys my age who are wrapping up their nights while I'm just beginning my morning. It can honestly make you feel like a real dork sometimes.

I'm half asleep. I move through my morning routine on autopilot. I turn on the ovens, flip the retarder from "retard" to "proof," and I make myself tea. Next, I text Josh to let him know I'm in the kitchen all safe and sound. I know he won't be able to fall back to sleep until he gets it. I press SEND and take half a minute to long for my warm bed and my sweet husband, then shake it off and get to work. Before long I'm at the sheeter, rolling out the yeasted flaky dough I made the day before. I have no plan, so once it's rolled out I scour the walk-in for what's ripe.

My pastry sous chef, Laurel Almerinda, is the next one in after me. She mumbles, "Hi," grabs an apron, and turns Pandora to Dolly Parton radio and blasts it. I don't say a thing; it's what wakes her up and I need her awake, so I keep my mouth shut.

It takes a lot of people to run a place like Huckleberry, but no one is more important to it or to me than Laurel. I first met her when she was a regular at our Saturday Morning Breakfasts at Rustic Canyon. She had zero experience but she talked me into giving her an internship. She did a lot of prep work around the pastry kitchen, and I don't want to sound like a jerk but between planning my wedding, recipe testing, going over construction documents for Huckleberry, and making all Rustic Canyon's desserts every night, I didn't pay much attention to her. But she hung in there, kept learning, came over to Huckleberry with me as a baker, and pretty quickly moved up to being my sous chef.

All of a sudden we were spending five or six mornings a week working next to each other trying to figure out how to actually run this monster of a place. She didn't have the confidence yet but she had the passion, strength, and excitement to learn, and, most important, we made each other laugh.

I'm not always the easiest person to work beside. I make a mess, change my mind halfway through making something, and throw your stuff out if it looks crappy in any way, no matter how long you've been working on it. But Laurel gets me, she doesn't take things personally, and when I don't like something, she makes it again and again until it's right. I trust Laurel because she is not only incredibly talented and caring but also crazy in the way I'm crazy. She's a hard-nosed perfectionist who still manages to be a sweet person. Like me, she can cry in the middle of the kitchen when something goes wrong, then pull it together and make some of the most delicious things you've ever tasted.

Choosing Laurel to help run Huckleberry's sweet side was truly the best decision I've ever made besides marrying my husband and having Milo. She knows me, almost too well. I can walk by something and barely glance at it thinking that something's not right and all of a sudden I hear from around the corner, "I know. We're remaking it." Without Laurel, a lot of this doesn't happen.

Back in the bakery, my team continues to trickle in silently, hoodies over their heads. One girl goes right to the coffee grinder. Another girl loads chocolate chunk muffins into the oven before she's even taken her jacket off. No one says much, except for Dolly, of course.

These started out as olive oil–cocoa nib muffins that were good but not great. Slowly I began to work on them and tweak little things here and there, but they still just weren't right. I was about to throw in the towel when I thought I would try adding just a little butter, who would know? Well, my love of butter runs deep. Real deep. So a little became a little more, until I could no longer justify calling them olive oil muffins. So here we have our rich Cocoa Nib Muffins. Please serve these as a fun treat at your next brunch.

cocoa nib muffins with dark chocolate glaze

MAKES 12 MUFFINS

MUFFINS

2 eggs

2 egg yolks

½ cup + 2 tbsp/130 g sugar

7 tbsp/100 ml extra-virgin olive oil

5 tbsp/70 g unsalted butter, melted

2 tbsp dry white wine

1½ tbsp maple syrup

1 tbsp vanilla extract

¾ tsp kosher salt

¾ cup/90 g all-purpose flour

¼ cup/40 g cornmeal

1 tsp baking powder

¼ cup/45 g cocoa nibs

GLAZE

⅔ cup/165 ml heavy cream

⅔ cup/120 g chopped dark chocolate, 60 to 70% cacao

Cocoa nibs for sprinkling (optional)

1. To make the muffins: Preheat your oven to 350°F/180°C. Line one 12-cup muffin pan with 12 paper liners.

2. In the bowl of a stand mixer fitted with the paddle attachment, combine the eggs, egg yolks, and sugar and beat on medium-high speed until thick and ribbony, 2 to 3 minutes.

3. Meanwhile, in a separate bowl, combine the olive oil, melted butter, wine, maple syrup, vanilla, and salt. Whisk together.

4. Slowly pour the olive oil mixture into the egg mixture with the mixer on low. Pause mixing and add the flour, cornmeal, baking powder, and cocoa nibs. Mix until just incorporated.

5. Pour the batter into the muffin cups, filling them almost all the way to the top. Bake for about 20 minutes, until the muffins slightly spring back to the touch. Please do not overbake! Allow the muffins to cool for about 10 minutes.

6. To make the glaze: Bring the cream to a boil in a small pan over medium-high heat, then immediately pour it over the chocolate in a small bowl. Allow the mixture to sit undisturbed for about 1 minute to melt. Then stir with a wooden spoon until homogenous.

7. Spoon glaze over each muffin, allowing a little to drip down the sides, and sprinkle with nibs, if you like.

These keep nicely, tightly wrapped, at room temperature, for up to 2 days.

These chocolate chunk muffins are hands down my husband's favorite muffin I make. He loves them so much that for his birthday last year I made mini chocolate chunk muffins to go along with his chocolate cake and homemade Twix bars. He was a happy man.

If you are looking for one batter you can do almost anything with, you have finally found it. It's awesome with the chocolate chunks but it's also really amazing with almost any kind of fruit mixed in, from blueberries to sliced peaches. For another great variation add 1 tbsp cinnamon and top it with any of the crumble toppings from the Baked in a Dish chapter. The possibilities are endless.

Another thing I love about these muffins is that they can be mixed and assembled in the muffin tins the night before and thrown in the oven in the morning. Just remember to add a few minutes to the bake time because the batter will be cold.

chocolate chunk muffins

MAKES 12 MUFFINS

¾ cup/170 g unsalted butter, at room temperature

¾ cup + 2 tbsp/165 g sugar, plus more for sprinkling

1 tsp kosher salt

2 eggs

1¼ cups/160 g all-purpose flour

¼ cup/25 g almond flour

1½ tsp baking powder

½ tsp baking soda

¾ cup/180 ml plain whole yogurt

1½ tsp vanilla extract

2¼ cups/210 g chopped dark chocolate, 60 to 70% cacao

1. Position a rack toward the top of your oven and preheat to 350°F/ 180°C. Line one 12-cup muffin pan with 12 paper liners.

2. In the bowl of a stand mixer fitted with the paddle attachment, cream the butter, sugar, and salt on medium-high speed until nice and fluffy, 1 to 2 minutes. Incorporate the eggs, one at a time, beating well after each addition. Be sure to scrape the sides of the bowl well with each addition. Pause mixing. Add the all-purpose flour, almond flour, baking powder, baking soda, yogurt, vanilla, and chocolate. Mix cautiously, just until incorporated.

3. Fill the muffin cups with batter all the way to the top, even a little over. Sprinkle the tops with a little sugar.

4. Bake for 22 to 25 minutes, until the muffins are brown and just spring back to the touch. Please do not overbake!

These keep perfectly, tightly wrapped, at room temperature, for up to 3 days.

These muffins are always the first to go. People love a dessert disguised as a muffin. The most important thing about this recipe is to make sure the almond paste is very finely broken up with the cocoa powder so you don't see clumps of almond paste when you bite into the muffin. If you happen to get a few clumps of almond paste, don't worry, they'll taste perfect but won't look as pretty as they should.

   I don't use almond paste often because it has such an intense flavor, but when it's used properly and coupled with chocolate it tastes amazing and adds a moistness that butter alone can't achieve. When testing these muffins at home we were amazed by the extreme differences in cocoa powders. At the bakery we use a Dutch Valrhona–process cocoa powder, which is very dark in color and rich in flavor. Try to get your hands on a good dark cocoa powder for this recipe, but if you can't, still make these muffins—they will be delicious, just lighter in color and with a slightly stronger almond flavor.

chocolate almond muffins

MAKES 16 MUFFINS

¾ cup/200 g almond paste

1 cup/200 g granulated sugar

1 tsp kosher salt

⅓ cup/30 g Dutch process cocoa powder

1 cup + 1 tbsp/240 g unsalted, cubed butter, at room temperature

6 eggs

2 tsp vanilla extract

1 cup/130 g all-purpose flour

1½ tbsp brown rice flour

2¼ tsp baking powder

2 cups/260 g coarsely chopped dark chocolate, 60 to 70% cacao

Powdered sugar for topping

1. Position a rack in the center of your oven and preheat to 350°F/ 180°C. Line two 12-cup muffin pans with 16 paper liners, spacing them evenly between the two pans.

2. In the bowl of a stand mixer fitted with the paddle attachment, beat the almond paste, granulated sugar, salt, and cocoa powder on medium speed until the mixture looks and feels sandy. Be sure all the almond paste is broken up into a fine meal with no clumps. Add the butter and beat for 1 to 2 minutes on medium. Incorporate the eggs, two at a time, beating well after each addition. Add the vanilla, then pause mixing. Add both flours, the baking powder, and chopped chocolate. Mix cautiously, on low speed, just until incorporated; then fold by hand to be sure it's properly, but gently, incorporated.

3. Fill the muffin cups with batter, all the way to the top, then bake. If both pans won't fit on the center rack, just bake in batches until the muffins just barely spring back when pressed, 20 to 22 minutes.

4. Allow to cool completely before dusting with powdered sugar.

   These keep well, tightly wrapped, at room temperature, for up to 3 days.

I've always thought of banana muffins as a staple muffin. It's truly good any time of day. Middle of the night after too many drinks? Banana muffin. Afternoon tea? Banana muffin. Grumpy kid? Rushing off to work? Banana muffin.

I make the batter for these muffins on the less-sweet side, since you get a hit of sweetness from the sugared bananas on top. Keep in mind that the darker and riper your bananas are, the sweeter your muffin will be. It's really important to get good color on these before they are done baking, so if only one tray can be on the top rack at a time, be sure to switch the two trays halfway through baking; or bake one tray at a time to make sure each muffin is colorful and beautiful.

At Huckleberry, we serve these with a side of cream cheese.

banana poppy seed muffins

MAKES 16 MUFFINS

½ cup/110 g unsalted butter, cubed, at room temperature

½ cup + 3 tbsp/140 g sugar, plus more for topping

1¼ tsp kosher salt

2 eggs

7 ripe bananas, 5 mashed by hand (not pulverized), and 2 thinly sliced

1 cup/125 g all-purpose flour

1 cup/125 g whole-wheat flour

1 tsp baking powder

1 tsp baking soda

1 tbsp poppy seeds

½ cup/120 ml whole plain yogurt

¾ cup/130 ml buttermilk

2 tsp vanilla extract

1. Position a rack toward the top of your oven and preheat to 375°F/190°C. Line two 12-cup muffin pans with 16 paper liners, spacing them evenly between the two pans.

2. In the bowl of a stand mixer fitted with the paddle attachment, cream the butter, sugar, and salt on medium speed until nice and fluffy, 1 to 2 minutes. Incorporate the eggs, one at a time, beating well after each addition, followed by the mashed bananas.

3. Add both flours, the baking powder, baking soda, poppy seeds, yogurt, buttermilk, and vanilla on low speed. Mix cautiously, just until incorporated.

4. Fill the muffin cups with batter almost all the way to the top. Top each muffin with 3 banana slices and sprinkle with sugar.

5. Bake for 25 to 30 minutes, until the muffins brown and slightly spring back to the touch; don't overbake.

These keep well, tightly wrapped, at room temperature, for up to 3 days.

This is the only muffin we always run at Huckleberry. Whenever we try to swap it out for another, many angry customers cry, "Where's my bran muffin?!" When my younger brother comes to visit from New York, my mom gives him one of these the second he gets off the plane. And sends him back with two on his return trip. The key is toasting the bran to a deep golden color. If you're craving these muffins and don't have any blueberries, substitute 1 cup/185 g chopped, soaked raisins instead, and mix them in right before portioning out the butter. Sometimes I actually prefer them that way. They are also delicious in the wintertime with fresh cranberries in place of the blueberries. These muffins are so incredibly moist they don't need to be served with butter.

blueberry bran muffins

MAKES 14 MUFFINS

½ cup + 2 tbsp/140 g unsalted butter, melted and slightly cooled

¼ cup/55 g brown sugar, plus more for sprinkling

½ tsp kosher salt

1 egg

¼ cup/60 ml maple syrup

¼ cup/60 ml honey

6 tbsp/90 ml canola oil

1 cup/130 g all-purpose flour

1 cup/200 g wheat germ, toasted

1 tsp baking soda

1 cup/240 ml whole plain yogurt

2 cups/300 g fresh blueberries

Granulated sugar for sprinkling

1. Evenly space two racks in your oven and preheat to 350°F/180°C. Line two 12-cup muffin pans with 14 paper liners, spacing them evenly between the two pans.

2. Pour the butter into a large bowl. Add the brown sugar and salt and whisk together by hand. Whisk in the egg, followed by the maple syrup, honey, and canola oil. Add the flour, wheat germ, baking soda, and yogurt, mixing cautiously until just incorporated.

3. Fill the muffin cups with batter almost all the way to the top, then top with the blueberries and sprinkle with a little brown sugar and granulated sugar.

4. Bake for about 20 minutes until the muffins are browned and spring back when touched.

These are best eaten the day they're made.

I make these almost every week for my son's swim class. I can't really ever get him to stay in the water for the whole class, or really even half the class, but at least the muffins never fail to be an insane hit with the kids. These would also be great for a high tea or a Sunday brunch. I love these with raspberries, but you can easily use any berry you prefer. It's very important not to overbake these, so please stay close to your oven when baking them. If you don't have rice flour, feel free to omit it.

vanilla raspberry muffins

MAKES 12 MUFFINS

1¼ cup/160 g all-purpose flour

2 tbsp brown rice flour

1 tsp baking powder

1 tsp baking soda

1 cup/200 g sugar, plus more for sprinkling

½ tsp kosher salt

1 cup + 2 tbsp/255 g unsalted butter, cubed, at room temperature

2 eggs

3 egg yolks

2 tbsp vanilla extract

3 tbsp buttermilk

1½ cups/180 g fresh raspberries

1. Position a rack in the middle of your oven and preheat to 375°F/190°C. Line one 12-cup muffin pan with 12 paper liners.

2. In a stand mixer fitted with the paddle attachment, mix both flours, the baking powder, baking soda, sugar, salt, and butter on low speed until lumpy but starting to come together.

3. With the mixer on low speed, slowly pour in the eggs, egg yolks, vanilla, and buttermilk. Mix until just combined. Scrape the sides of the mixer bowl well, making sure everything is incorporated. Gently fold the berries in by hand, trying hard not to crush them.

4. Fill the muffin cups three-quarters full with batter and sprinkle with sugar. Bake until the muffins just barely spring back to the touch, about 20 minutes.

These keep well, tightly wrapped at room temperature, for up to 2 days.

This muffin tastes how you always wished that hippie muffin at the health food store would taste. I love using whole grains and wholesome ingredients but at the same time I don't want you to feel as if you're settling for a healthful but less tasty alternative. It must still be delicious. The key is a good balance between those nice healthful nutty-tasting grains and enough fat and sweetness to round them out. Once you taste this muffin, you will understand.

apple cinnamon crumble muffins

MAKES 12 MUFFINS

CRUMBLE

½ cup/40 g rolled oats

¼ cup/30 g whole-wheat flour

3 tbsp unsalted butter, at room temperature

2 tbsp brown sugar

1 tbsp honey

1 tbsp millet

1 tbsp cracked wheat, chia seeds, or poppy seeds

1 tbsp flax seeds

¼ tsp kosher salt

MUFFINS

1¼ cups/130 g whole-wheat flour

2 tbsp almond flour

1 tbsp wheat germ, toasted

1 tbsp millet

1 tbsp cracked wheat, chia seeds, or poppy seeds

1 tbsp flax seeds

1 tbsp rolled oats

1½ tsp cinnamon

½ tsp baking powder

½ tsp baking soda

¼ cup/55 g brown sugar

¼ cup/50 g granulated sugar

1 tsp kosher salt

4 tbsp/55 g unsalted butter, melted

⅓ cup/30 ml honey

½ cup/120 ml buttermilk

½ cup + 2 tbsp/150 ml canola oil

1 egg

1 tsp vanilla extract

1 large apple, peeled and grated

1. Position a rack near the top of your oven and preheat to 350°F/180°C. Line one 12-cup muffin pan with 12 paper liners.

2. To make the crumble: Combine the oats, whole-wheat flour, butter, brown sugar, honey, millet, cracked wheat, flax seeds, and salt in a bowl and blend with your fingertips until homogenous. Refrigerate until needed.

3. To make the muffins: Whisk the whole-wheat flour, almond flour, wheat germ, millet, cracked wheat, flax seeds, oats, cinnamon, baking powder, baking soda, brown sugar, granulated sugar, and salt together in a large bowl to remove any lumps. In a small bowl or pitcher, combine the melted butter, honey, buttermilk, canola oil, egg, and vanilla. Whisk to combine.

4. Pour the wet mixture into the dry mixture and whisk together by hand until just combined. Fold in the apples.

5. Fill the muffin cups almost all the way to the top and sprinkle with the crumble. Bake for 20 minutes, until the muffins are browned and spring back slightly when touched.

These keep well, tightly wrapped, at room temperature for up to 2 days.

These muffins just scream *holiday*. If you want to channel your inner Martha, bake these, put them in a tin, and give as a gift. They stay incredibly moist overnight. This recipe can have many different incarnations. They are just as good with apples or cranberries as they are with pears, and honestly sometimes I think they're even better without any fruit, but if you're doing them without pears, substitute ¾ cup/180 ml apple juice for the pear poaching liquid. If you choose to bake them without any cut fruit, just remember to shorten your baking time slightly, as they'll bake quicker without the juices from the fruit. I love serving these with fresh whipped cream and a light dusting of powdered sugar. This batter also bakes beautifully as a teacake.

pear ginger muffins

MAKES 18 MUFFINS

3 medium pears, peeled and chopped

1 pinch sugar

1 pinch kosher salt, plus ¾ tsp

1 pinch ground cinnamon, plus 1 tsp

1¾ cups/220 g all-purpose flour

¼ cup + 1 tsp/60 g brown sugar

1½ tsp baking powder

1½ tsp baking soda

1 tbsp + 1½ tsp ground ginger

¼ tsp ground nutmeg

¼ tsp ground black pepper

⅛ tsp ground cloves

½ cup/120 ml canola oil

¼ cup + 2 tbsp/90 ml molasses

¼ cup + 1 tbsp/75 ml maple syrup

2 eggs

Zest of 1 orange

1. Position a rack in the middle of your oven and preheat to 350°F/180°C. Line two 12-cup muffin pans with 18 paper liners, spacing them evenly between the two pans.

2. Combine the pears, sugar, the pinch of salt, and pinch of cinnamon in a small saucepan. Cover with 2 cups/430 ml water and cook over high heat until soft, about 10 minutes. Strain out the fruit and reserve ¾ cup/180 ml of the cooking liquid. Refrigerate both until cool.

3. Combine the flour, brown sugar, baking powder, baking soda, ginger, nutmeg, pepper, cloves, and the remaining salt and cinnamon in a large bowl; whisk to remove lumps.

4. Combine the reserved pear cooking liquid, canola oil, molasses, maple syrup, eggs, and orange zest in a small bowl; whisk to combine. Pour the wet mixture into the dry mixture and whisk together by hand until smooth. Fold in the cooked pears.

5. As this is an incredibly loose batter, pour it into a large liquid measuring cup, and then pour it into the muffin cups, filling them a little more than three-quarters full. Bake for 15 to 18 minutes, until the muffins just barely spring back to the touch.

These keep beautifully, wrapped tightly, at room temperature, for up to 4 days.

I started out trying to make a brown sugar–peach muffin, and somehow after a lot of trial and error, I ended up with a decadent branny fig–brown sugar muffin. Don't ask. I may have gotten very off track, but I promise you won't be disappointed, because now they are one of my favorite muffins. These would also be great with raspberries, blueberries, sliced bananas, or plums instead of figs, and you can make them gluten-free by substituting our gluten-free flour mix (see page 55) for the wheat germ, whole-wheat, and all-purpose flours. That's how I like to make them at home.

fig–brown sugar muffins

MAKES 12 MUFFINS

1 cup/130 g whole-wheat flour

2 tbsp all-purpose flour

3 tbsp chia seeds or poppy seeds

1 tsp baking soda

1 tsp baking powder

2 tbsp wheat germ

½ cup/120 g cream cheese or yogurt

2 tbsp whole milk

¾ cup/180 ml canola oil

½ cup/100 g brown sugar

¼ cup/60 g granulated sugar

1 tsp kosher salt

4 tbsp/55 g unsalted butter, melted and slightly cooled

1 tbsp vanilla extract

1 egg

6 to 8 ripe figs, sliced into eighths

1. Position a rack near the top of your oven and preheat to 350°F/180°C. Line one 12-cup muffin pan with 12 paper liners.

2. Whisk the whole-wheat flour, all-purpose flour, chia seeds, baking soda, baking powder, and wheat germ in a large bowl to remove lumps. In a small bowl, whisk the cream cheese and milk together until smooth. Add the canola oil, brown sugar, granulated sugar, salt, unsalted butter, vanilla, and egg. Whisk to combine.

3. Pour the wet mixture into the dry mixture and whisk together by hand just until combined. Stir in the figs, allowing them to break up slightly as you incorporate them.

4. Fill the muffin cups about two-thirds full. Bake for 20 to 25 minutes, until the muffins are brown and just barely spring back to the touch. Allow the muffins to cool before removing from the pans.

These keep well, tightly wrapped, at room temperature, for up to 2 days.

As Laurel and I tested recipes like crazy at our homes for this book, our families were definitely the benefactors. Laurel said these muffins immediately grabbed her husband's attention. After a thoughtful bite he said, "I have no feedback." Then he shoved the rest of it in his face and said with a mouthful, "I better get a thank you in that book." Oh, how he sacrificed. And oh yeah, thank you, Ethan.

This batter is incredibly versatile. During the summer we often mix in 2 cups/300 g fresh blueberries or strawberries, omit the lemon zest, and top with a combination of white and brown sugar before baking. During the holidays we sometimes substitute orange zest for the lemon zest and fold in 2 cups/300 g fresh cranberries.

lemon cornmeal muffins with lemon glaze

MAKES 18 MUFFINS

MUFFINS

¾ cup + 1 tbsp/190 g unsalted, cubed butter, at room temperature

¾ cup + 3 tbsp/190 g granulated sugar

1½ tsp kosher salt

Zest of 4 lemons, plus 2 tbsp lemon juice

2 eggs

4½ tbsp/70 ml canola oil

3 tbsp maple syrup

1 tbsp vanilla extract

1¾ cups/215 g all-purpose flour

¾ cup/120 g cornmeal

2¼ tsp baking powder

¾ tsp baking soda

1¾ cup/400 g ricotta

GLAZE

1 cup/120 g powdered sugar

2 tbsp + 1 tsp fresh lemon juice

1 tsp heavy cream

Lemon wheels for garnish (optional)

1. To make the muffins: Position a rack near the top of your oven and preheat to 350°F/180°C. Line two 12-cup muffin pans with 18 paper liners, spacing them out evenly between the two pans.

2. In a stand mixer fitted with the paddle attachment, cream the butter, granulated sugar, salt, and zest on medium speed for 1 to 2 minutes, until the butter looks nice and fluffy. Incorporate the eggs slowly, one at a time, beating well after each addition on medium speed. Be sure to scrape the sides of the bowl well.

3. Slowly pour in the canola oil, maple syrup, lemon juice, and vanilla. Scrape the sides again. Add the flour, cornmeal, baking powder, baking soda, and ricotta. Mix cautiously, just until incorporated. Please don't overmix!

4. Fill the muffin cups three-quarters full. Bake for about 18 minutes, until the muffins just barely spring back to the touch.

5. When you take the muffins out of the oven, begin to make your glaze: Sift the powdered sugar into a medium mixing bowl. Add the lemon juice and whisk until free of lumps. Add the cream and whisk until incorporated.

6. Spread the glaze on each muffin with an offset spatula or butter knife. This is best to do when the muffin is still warm. Garnish each with a lemon wheel, if desired.

These keep beautifully, wrapped tightly, at room temperature, for up to 2 days.

Anyone who knows Huckleberry knows that when corn is in season, I tend to go a little crazy. These muffins are always one of the first things I make. In fact, once you make these muffins you'll have a hard time seeing corn and not wanting to rush off and make them right away; they just scream *summer*. However, do resist the temptation to make them at any point when corn is not in peak season because they won't be nearly as good.

Serve these muffins with soft butter and homemade Strawberry Jam (page 55).

sweet corn muffins

MAKES 16 MUFFINS

½ cup + 2 tbsp/140 g unsalted, cubed butter, at room temperature

¾ cup/150 g sugar, plus more for topping

1½ tsp kosher salt

2 eggs

6 tbsp/80 g canola oil

2 tbsp honey

1 tbsp vanilla extract

1½ cups/135 g all-purpose flour

⅔ cup/90 g cornmeal

2 tsp baking powder

¼ tsp baking soda

1⅓ cups/320 ml whole milk yogurt

2 cups/490 g fresh corn kernels (3 or 4 cobs)

1. Position a rack near the top of your oven and preheat to 350°F/180°C. Line two 12-cup muffin pans with 16 paper liners, spacing them evenly between the two pans.

2. In a stand mixer fitted with the paddle attachment, cream the butter, sugar, and salt on medium speed for 1 to 2 minutes, until the butter looks nice and fluffy. Incorporate the eggs, one at a time, beating well after each addition. Be sure to scrape the sides of the bowl well. With the mixer on low speed, pour in the canola oil, honey, and vanilla, then pause mixing. Add the flour, cornmeal, baking powder, baking soda, yogurt, and corn kernels. That's right, all at the same time. Mix cautiously, just until incorporated. Do not overmix!

3. Fill the muffin cups three-quarters full with batter and sprinkle the tops with a little sugar. Bake until the muffins are nicely browned and spring back slightly to the touch, 25 to 28 minutes.

These keep well, tightly wrapped, at room temperature, for up to 3 days.

These muffins are really forgiving. They're great to eat the day after you bake them, and for that reason they make great gifts. When we hold a special evening event at Huckleberry, I love to bake a bunch of these for people to take home for breakfast the next morning.

If you don't have zucchini, you can easily substitute carrots—or even mix zucchini and carrot. You can play with these by subbing other flours for the white flour, too. In fact, when I make them at home, I often use some whole-wheat flour or our gluten-free flour mix (see page 55) instead of the all-purpose and add 1 tbsp ground flax seeds and 2 tsp chia seeds or poppy seeds.

In my opinion, these are perfect slathered in cream cheese.

zucchini muffins

MAKES 12 MUFFINS

¾ cup/130 g raisins or currants

¾ cup/180 ml canola oil

1 cup + 2 tbsp/230 g sugar, plus more for topping

¾ tsp kosher salt

Zest of 1 orange

3 eggs

1½ tsp vanilla extract

1½ cup/190 g all-purpose flour

1 tsp baking powder

1½ tsp baking soda

1½ tsp cinnamon

1¾ cups + 2 tbsp/260 g unpeeled, grated zucchini

1 cup + 2 tbsp/140 g walnuts, toasted and hand crushed

1. Plump the raisins in 1 cup/240 ml warm water for 10 minutes, then drain and finely chop.

2. Position a rack near the top of your oven and preheat to 350°F/180°C. Line one 12-cup muffin pan with 12 paper liners.

3. In a large bowl, combine the canola oil, sugar, salt, orange zest, eggs, and vanilla and whisk to combine. Add the flour, baking powder, baking soda, and cinnamon and whisk together by hand until lump-free. Fold in the zucchini, walnuts, and raisins.

4. Fill the muffin cups almost all the way to the top and sprinkle with sugar. Bake for 25 to 30 minutes, until the muffins are browned and spring back slightly to the touch.

These keep well, tightly wrapped, at room temperature, for up to 4 days.

Please play with this recipe. Add and subtract to your heart's content. Don't eat meat? Add additional cheese and herbs for super-cheesy herby muffins. No rye flour in the pantry? Substitute another flour, like whole-wheat, buckwheat, or, if you must, more all-purpose flour. Black pepper is not my thing but Laurel is obsessed. She always adds a healthy dose to these. Ham instead of bacon? Do it. Goat cheese? Why not? Like I said, play!

Browning the tops of these before they overbake inside is the key to success. So you may want to bake one muffin pan at a time, right at the top of your oven. Feel free to ride your oven dial and go hotter or cooler to control the browning, but just remember that color is flavor, so you want these pretty dark.

bacon cheddar muffins

MAKES 15 MUFFINS

6 tbsp/85 g unsalted butter, cubed, at room temperature

2 tbsp sugar

1½ tsp kosher salt

3 eggs

¾ cup/100 g all-purpose flour

¾ cup/120 g cornmeal

6 tbsp/40 g rye flour

1½ tbsp baking powder

½ cup + 1 tbsp/135 ml canola oil

3 tbsp + 2 tsp/55 ml maple syrup

1 cup + 2 tbsp/175 ml buttermilk

½ cup/70 g diced Cheddar
(cut into 1-in/2.5-cm cubes), plus
¼ cup/30 g grated Cheddar

6 tbsp/40 g grated Parmesan

11 slices cooked bacon, coarsely chopped, plus 1½ tbsp bacon fat, cooled

¼ cup/10 g fresh chives, parsley, or a combo, finely chopped

Chopped rosemary for garnishing

1. Position a rack near the top of your oven and preheat to 400°F/200°C. Line two 12-cup muffin pans with 15 paper liners, spacing them evenly between the two pans.

2. In a stand mixer fitted with the paddle attachment, cream the butter, sugar, and salt for 1 to 2 minutes until nice and fluffy. Incorporate the eggs slowly, one at a time, beating well after each addition. Add the all-purpose flour, cornmeal, rye flour, and baking powder and mix until incorporated. Add the canola oil, maple syrup, and buttermilk. Scrape the mixer bowl well, making sure everything is well incorporated. Add the diced Cheddar, 4 tbsp/25 g of the Parmesan, the bacon, and chives. Mix just until dispersed, folding by hand to be sure.

3. Fill the muffin cups to the very top.

4. In a small bowl toss the grated Cheddar with the remaining 2 tbsp Parmesan and sprinkle evenly over the muffins. Bake for about 15 minutes, until nicely browned but not overbaked inside. Garnish with chopped rosemary.

These are best eaten the day they're made.

There is nothing I hate more than a gummy pastry. For that reason I don't like most gluten-free pastries out there, and I find it especially challenging to find a delicious gluten-free *and* vegan pastry. But once I realized you don't have to use xanthan gum to make one of those said pastries hold together, I got hooked on the challenge of making this stuff actually taste good. This was the first gluten-free and vegan recipe I made that I really liked. And honestly, sometimes I prefer it to the white flour, butter-heavy devils I usually make.

gluten-free vegan banana chocolate muffins

MAKES 12 MUFFINS

1 cup + 2 tbsp/140 g Huckleberry Gluten-Free Flour Mix (page 55)

6 tbsp/35 g almond flour

2 tsp baking powder

2 tsp baking soda

¾ tsp kosher salt

½ tsp cinnamon

3 tbsp flax seed meal

6 tbsp/90 ml canola oil

7 tbsp/100 ml agave syrup

6 tbsp/90 ml coconut milk

2 tsp vanilla extract

6 ripe bananas; 4 mashed, 2 sliced

3 tbsp walnuts, toasted and ground

1 cup/130 g chopped dark chocolate, 60 to 70% cacao

1. Position a rack near the top of your oven and preheat to 350°F/180°C. Line one 12-cup muffin pan with 12 paper liners.

2. In a large bowl, whisk the flour mix, almond flour, baking powder, baking soda, salt, cinnamon, and flax seed meal to remove any lumps. In a small bowl or pitcher, combine the canola oil, 5 tbsp/75 ml of the agave syrup, the coconut milk, and vanilla. Whisk to combine.

3. Pour the wet mixture into the dry mixture and whisk together by hand just until combined. Fold in the mashed bananas, walnuts, and chocolate.

4. Lightly toss the sliced bananas with the remaining 2 tbsp agave syrup. Fill the muffin cups almost all the way to the top. Top with about 3 banana slices per muffin.

5. Bake for about 25 minutes, until the muffins are browned and spring back slightly to the touch.

These muffins keep very well, tightly wrapped, at room temperature, for up to 3 days.

I find this to be the most satisfying gluten-free recipe we have in the book. Nothing about it makes you miss white flour in any way, shape, or form. This recipe calls for strawberry jam, but most other jams or jellies will work as well, so please use this as a vehicle for whatever fresh jam you've decided to make this month. You can also omit the jam, throw 2 cups/300 g fresh blueberries into the batter, and turn these into fantastic gluten-free blueberry muffins.

gluten-free strawberry jam muffins

MAKES 12 MUFFINS

¾ cup + 2 tbsp/210 ml canola oil

¾ cup + 2 tbsp/175 g granulated sugar

2 tsp kosher salt

Zest of 4 lemons, plus ½ cup/120 g lemon juice

¾ cup + 2 tbsp/210 ml crème fraîche, sour cream, or whole plain yogurt

2 tbsp honey

1 tsp vanilla extract

4 eggs

1¾ cups/220 g Huckleberry Gluten-Free Flour Mix (page 55)

¼ cup/25 g almond flour

2 tsp baking powder

¾ cup/180 g Strawberry Jam (facing page) or other homemade jam

Powdered sugar for dusting

1. Position a rack near the top of your oven and preheat to 350°F/180°C. Line one 12-cup muffin pan with 12 paper liners.

2. In a large bowl, whisk the canola oil, granulated sugar, salt, lemon zest, lemon juice, crème frâiche, honey, and vanilla until combined. Add the eggs and whisk.

3. Add the flour mix, almond flour, and baking powder. Whisk just until combined.

4. Scoop the batter into the prepared muffin pans, filling almost all the way to the top.

5. Bake for about 20 minutes, until almost done, but not completely.

6. Remove from the oven and make a hole in the center with a small spoon, and spoon about 1 tbsp jam into each muffin, mounding it nice and high. Be sure to move quickly, as it's important to get them back in the oven as soon as possible. Return to the oven and bake for another 3 to 5 minutes, until the jam is set and the muffins are browned and spring back slightly to the touch.

7. Allow to cool and dust the edges with powdered sugar, attempting to avoid the jam.

    These keep nicely, wrapped well, at room temperature, for up to 2 days.

Always taste your fruit before baking or cooking with it. If your berries are very sweet, hold back a little sugar. Then taste the jam as it cooks; you can always add sugar back in if needed.

Strawberry jam can tend to be overly sweet, but the acidity of the balsamic cuts that sweetness a little. You can substitute saba (see page 233) or even a splash of red wine for the balsamic if you have an open bottle lying around.

This jam is also a wonderful addition to the Mini Strawberry Galettes (page 133). Toss the fresh strawberries with ¾ cup/180 g jam for a more layered strawberry flavor and then build and bake them as the recipe states.

strawberry jam

MAKES ABOUT ¾ CUP/180 G

4 cups/610 g fresh strawberries, halved
¼ cup/50 g sugar
¼ tsp kosher salt
¼ cup/60 ml water
1 tbsp balsamic vinegar

1. Combine everything in a medium saucepan and simmer over medium heat for about 10 minutes, until strawberries begin to fall apart.

2. Mash with a potato masher, reduce the heat to medium-low, and cook until jammy, about 10 minutes longer. Refrigerate until needed.

This keeps well, refrigerated, for up to 2 weeks.

If you like to bake gluten-free, whip up a big batch of this mix and keep it on hand. It lasts forever. You can use a store-bought gluten-free flour mix if you must, but your pastry will not taste nearly as good. I cannot stress enough what a difference this mix makes in both flavor and texture. If you don't like the graininess of the cornmeal, you can always omit it and use a little more of the oat flour or potato starch.

huckleberry gluten-free flour mix

MAKES 6½ CUPS/815 G

2¾ cups/430 g brown rice flour
1¾ cups/430 g oat flour
1¾ cups/230 g potato starch
½ cup/90 g cornmeal

Combine all the ingredients in a bowl and whisk until thoroughly blended.

This keeps indefinitely at room temperature.

4 A.M.

biscuits and scones

I look around the kitchen. The caffeine is kicking in, everyone's energy is beginning to lift, and the night cleaning crew looks as though they might finally be ready to clear out of our way, which they were supposed to do an hour ago.

Our pastry girl is making possets and starts telling us how her weird blind date last night kept making dirty jokes about how good her "cupcakes" looked after she told him she was a baker. Needless to say, it doesn't seem like a second date will be happening.

One of our morning bakers is not here yet. I just called her for the fourth time, but she's not picking up and I'm about to hurl my phone across the kitchen. It doesn't look as though she's going to show up, and that's going to make our already difficult morning a lot harder. Those are the hazards of staying out past 7 P.M. when you're a baker. You have to remember we have no sun, no trash trucks, and no noisy kids waking us up, so if you hit snooze on your alarm because you're in the middle of a good dream, you can easily sleep through half your shift and we're all screwed.

I will say that some of my bakers, more than others, are prone to such things, but it's never happened to me. I'm just saying.

Anyway, we have an order for twenty-five maple bacon biscuits at 8 A.M. and another at 8:30. Plus the fifty we need for the house. So someone has to jump in and start making them, or we're going down.

One girl yells: "Not it!" Then from all around the kitchen: "Not it!" "Not it!" "Not it!"

Ugh. Fine. Honestly, they're all just trying to stay on top of their work flow. I get it.

It will push me back a little, but I don't care. I love making biscuits. Ever since my mom taught me how to make them at home I've always loved it. She was the first one to show me that food can create space, express love, and slow life down in a way nothing else can. Biscuits are all about the process. It's just a few basic ingredients.

I grab a bowl and start scaling . . .

how to make biscuits and scones

SHAPING BISCUITS

SHAPING SCONES

My favorite flavor combination has always been salty-sweet. I grew up dipping my french fries in my milkshake and eating roast chicken with applesauce and bacon covered in maple syrup. Just writing this makes my mouth water for these salty-sweet combinations, and that's what I tried to create with these biscuits. If you want to make your guests really happy when they walk into your house, have these coming out of the oven. The aroma is amazing.

These have been one of our signature items at Huckleberry since we opened. They are loaded up with bacon and maple syrup, two of the more expensive ingredients in the bakery. However, using good-quality bacon and maple syrup really does make a difference, so don't skimp. Though they're not cheap for us to make, we make them anyway. It's a labor of love.

We like to use a larger biscuit cutter because these biscuits are one of those over-the-top foods that should both look and taste that way. You can always cut them smaller if you like; just remember they'll bake faster.

maple bacon biscuits

MAKES 18 BISCUITS

15 slices thick-cut bacon

6 cups/750 g all-purpose flour

2 tbsp baking powder

1½ tsp baking soda

¼ cup/50 g sugar

2¼ tsp kosher salt

2 cups/450 g cold unsalted butter, cut into ½-in/12-mm cubes

½ cup/120 ml cold maple syrup, plus ¾ cup/180 ml maple syrup for glaze

¾ cup/130 ml cold buttermilk

1 batch Egg Wash (page 74)

Fleur de sel for topping

1. Preheat your oven to 375°F/190°C.

2. Lay the bacon on a sheet pan and bake until golden brown, about 15 minutes. Allow the bacon and bacon fat to cool. Chop the bacon into ½-in/12-mm pieces. Set aside. Reserve 2 tbsp bacon fat; discard the rest.

3. In a very large bowl, combine the flour, baking powder, baking soda, sugar, and salt and toss well. Throw in the cold butter and work it with your fingertips until the pieces are pea- and lima bean–size. Add the ½ cup/120 ml maple syrup, buttermilk, bacon, and reserved bacon fat. Lightly toss to distribute.

4. Immediately dump everything onto a clean surface with more than enough space to work the dough. Using only the heel of your palm, quickly flatten out the dough. Gather the dough back together in a mound and repeat. After two or three repetitions, the dough should begin holding together. Be sure to avoid overworking. You should still see some pea-size bits of butter running through it.

5. Flatten the dough into a 1-in/2.5-cm thickness and cut out the biscuits. Transfer them to an ungreased sheet pan. Very gently push the scraps back together and cut once more. Freeze for at least 2 hours before baking, or for up to 1 month, tightly wrapped.

6. Preheat your oven to 375°F/190°C. Remove the biscuits from the freezer. Space them with plenty of breathing room on two ungreased sheet pans, brush with the egg wash, and sprinkle with fleur de sel. Bake from frozen, until cooked through and starting to brown, about 25 minutes. Pour 2 tsp maple syrup over each biscuit to glaze, and bake 5 minutes longer.

These are best eaten the day they're made.

These are your chicken pot pie biscuits, your "please pass the biscuits" biscuits, your tea sandwich biscuits, your fried chicken biscuits, and, of course, your go-to simple breakfast biscuits with butter and jam.

When I gave this recipe to a friend, she told me she always cuts the scraps into irregular shapes and sprinkles them with cinnamon-sugar, something she said her grandma would always do. Ever since she told me that I always make sure I do that, too.

comfort food biscuits

MAKES THIRTEEN 2-IN/5-CM BISCUITS

3 cups/380 g all-purpose flour

1 tbsp + 2¼ tsp baking powder

1 tbsp sugar, plus more for sprinkling

1 tsp kosher salt

¾ cup/170 g cold unsalted butter, cubed

¾ cup/180 g cold cream cheese

6 tbsp/90 ml cold heavy cream

1 batch Egg Wash (page 74)

Fleur de sel for sprinkling

1. In a very large bowl, combine the flour, baking powder, sugar, and salt and toss well. Throw in the cold butter and work it with your fingertips until the pieces are pea- and lima bean–size. Then do the same with the cream cheese. Add the cream. Lightly toss to distribute.

2. Immediately dump everything onto a clean surface with more than enough space to work the dough. Using only the heel of your palm, quickly flatten out the dough. Gather the dough back together in a mound and repeat. After two or three repetitions, the dough should begin holding together. Be sure to avoid overworking. You should still see some pea-size bits of butter running through it.

3. Flatten the dough to a 1-in/2.5-cm thickness and cut out the biscuits. Transfer them to an ungreased sheet pan. Very gently push the scraps back together and cut once more. Freeze for at least 2 hours before baking, or up to 1 month, tightly wrapped.

4. Preheat your oven to 350°F/180°C. Remove the biscuits from the freezer. Space them with plenty of breathing room on two ungreased sheet pans, brush with the egg wash, and sprinkle with both sugar and fleur de sel. Bake from frozen until cooked through, nicely browned, and easily lifted off the pan, about 30 minutes.

These are best eaten the day they're made.

When I was working on this recipe, my goal was to make something that tasted like a very upscale Cheez-It. I have to say, I'm pretty happy with the results.

These biscuits are amazing for breakfast with Vanilla Apple Butter (page 132) or just on their own. They're also great as mini biscuits served with beer, wine, or cocktails to kick off a party. To do so, either use a smaller scoop or flatten the dough to a ¾-in/2-cm thickness and cut with a small biscuit cutter. If you set out a bowl of these salty cheesy bites, I promise they'll be gone in an instant.

If you can't get your hands on rye flour you can substitute whole-wheat, but I do feel there is a slight tanginess that you get only from the rye.

three-cheese rye biscuits

MAKES 12 TO 15 BISCUITS

1½ cups/160 g rye flour

¾ cup/100 g all-purpose flour

6 tbsp/45 g whole-wheat flour

1 tbsp baking powder

1 tbsp + 1 tsp sugar

1½ tsp kosher salt

½ tsp freshly ground black pepper

⅛ tsp cayenne pepper

¾ cup/170 g cold unsalted butter, cut into ½-in/12-mm cubes

½ cup + 3 tbsp/160 g cold cream cheese

2 cups/160 g grated Cheddar

¾ cup/55 g grated Parmesan

⅓ cup/80 ml cold buttermilk

1 batch Egg Wash (page 74)

Fleur de sel for sprinkling

1. In a very large bowl, combine the rye flour, all-purpose flour, whole-wheat flour, baking powder, sugar, salt, black pepper, and cayenne and toss well.

2. Throw in the cold butter and work it with your fingertips until the pieces are pea- and lima bean–size. Then do the same with the cream cheese. Add the Cheddar, Parmesan, and buttermilk. Lightly toss to distribute.

3. Immediately dump everything onto a clean surface with more than enough space to work the dough. Using only the heel of your palm, quickly flatten out the dough. Gather the dough back together in a mound and repeat. After two or three repetitions, the dough should begin holding together. Be sure to avoid overworking. You should still see some pea-size bits of butter running through it.

4. Form the biscuits by tightly packing the dough into an ice-cream scoop. Place on an ungreased sheet pan. Freeze for at least 2 hours before baking, or up to 1 month, tightly wrapped.

5. Preheat your oven to 375°F/190°C. Remove the biscuits from the freezer. Space them with plenty of breathing room on two ungreased sheet pans, brush with the egg wash, and sprinkle with fleur de sel. Bake from frozen until cooked through, nicely browned, and easily lifted off the pan, about 25 minutes.

These are best eaten the day they're made.

These simple biscuits are great with butter and honey or a big hunk of Cheddar cheese and quince paste. But my husband likes to eat them with a cool glass of rosé while watching a baseball game after Milo goes to sleep. Whichever way you choose to eat these, they should become one of your family staples. They have an amazing texture and a great savory saltiness that I think makes them good for breakfast, great as a biscuit sandwich at lunch, and perfect with Thanksgiving dinner.

herb biscuits

MAKES 12 TO 15 BISCUITS

1¾ cups/220 g all-purpose flour

1 tbsp whole-wheat flour

2 tsp baking powder

1 tsp baking soda

1 tbsp + 1 tsp sugar

1¼ tsp kosher salt

½ tsp freshly ground black pepper

½ cup + 2 tbsp/140 g cold unsalted butter, cubed

⅓ cup/80 ml cold buttermilk

½ cup/40 g grated Cheddar

1 tbsp grated Parmesan

1 tbsp chopped fresh dill

2 tbsp chopped fresh parsley

2 tbsp chopped fresh chives

1 batch Egg Wash (page 74)

Fleur de sel for sprinkling

1. In a very large bowl, combine the all-purpose flour, whole-wheat flour, baking powder, baking soda, sugar, salt, and pepper and toss well.

2. Throw in the cold butter and work it with your fingertips until the pieces are pea- and lima bean–size. Add the buttermilk, cheddar, parmesan, dill, parsley, and chives. Lightly toss to distribute.

3. Immediately dump everything onto a clean surface with more than enough space to work the dough. Using only the heel of your palm, quickly flatten out the dough. Gather the dough back together in a mound and repeat. After two or three repetitions, the dough should begin holding together. Be sure to avoid overworking. You should still see some pea-size bits of butter running through it.

4. Flatten the dough into a 1-in/2.5-cm thickness and cut out the biscuits. Transfer them to an ungreased sheet pan. Very gently push the scraps back together and cut once more. Freeze for at least 2 hours before baking, or up to 1 month, tightly wrapped.

5. Preheat your oven to 375°F/190°C. Remove the biscuits from the freezer. Space them with plenty of breathing room on two ungreased sheet pans, brush with the egg wash, and sprinkle with fleur de sel. Bake from frozen until cooked through, nicely browned, and easily lifted off the pan, about 30 minutes.

These are best eaten the day they're made.

These scones taste traditional in every sense. The problem with most blueberry scones is they have been overmixed—the blueberries get smashed and the result is a very off-putting grayish-blue dough. I avoid this problem by mixing the dough almost completely without the blueberries and then rolling them in, like you would a cinnamon roll, at the very last minute. These steps will leave you with a much cleaner-looking pastry. You can also make great lemon buttermilk scones with this recipe; just omit the blueberries and add the zest of three more lemons. I love to serve these scones with very lightly sweetened Whipped Cream (page 149) or fresh-made jam, honey, or maple syrup.

blueberry buttermilk scones

MAKES 9 OR 10 SCONES

3¼ cups + 2 tbsp/420 g
all-purpose flour

½ cup + 2 tbsp/130 g granulated sugar,
plus more for sprinkling

¼ cup/55 g brown sugar

1 tbsp baking powder

1 tsp baking soda

1¼ tsp kosher salt

1 cup/230 g cold unsalted butter,
cut into ½-in/12-mm cubes

¾ cup/180 ml cold buttermilk

Zest of 1 lemon

1½ cups/225 g fresh blueberries,
frozen on a plate

1 batch Egg Wash (page 74)

1. In a very large bowl, combine the flour, granulated sugar, brown sugar, baking powder, baking soda, and salt. Throw in the butter and work it in with your fingertips until the pieces are pea- and lima bean–size. Add the buttermilk and lemon zest. Lightly toss to distribute.

2. Immediately dump everything onto a clean surface with more than enough space to work the dough. Using only the heel of your palm, quickly flatten out the dough. Gather the dough back together in a mound and repeat. After two or three repetitions, the dough should begin holding together. Be sure to avoid overworking. You should still see some pea-size bits of butter running through it.

3. Pat down the dough to a ¾-in/2-cm thickness, about a 9-by-12-in/ 23-by-30.5-cm slab, and spread the frozen blueberries evenly on top. Roll the long side of the dough, like a jelly roll, into a log with the blueberries enveloped inside. Shape the dough into a 12-in-/30.5-cm-long cylinder. Lightly flatten the top so that it is a little less than ½ in/12 mm thick and cut out nine or ten triangles. Transfer them to an ungreased sheet pan and freeze for at least 2 hours before baking, or up to 1 month, tightly wrapped.

4. Preheat your oven to 350°F/180°C. Remove the scones from the freezer. Space them with plenty of breathing room on two ungreased sheet pans, brush with the egg wash, and sprinkle liberally with granulated sugar. Bake from frozen until cooked through, nicely browned, and easily lifted off the pan, about 25 minutes.

These are best eaten the day they're made.

These are my mother's favorite scones because they're decadent without being overly sweet. When you grind the toasted walnuts, you are almost inevitably going to have leftovers. Refrigerate any extra and throw them into your next batch of pancakes, oatmeal, or just sprinkle on yogurt. When you've owned restaurants long enough, it pains you to throw away something you can use.

I love serving these either plain or with lightly sweetened Whipped Cream (page 149).

walnut jam scones

MAKES FIFTEEN 3-IN/7.5-CM SCONES

1¾ cups + 2 tbsp/240 g all-purpose flour

3 tbsp cornmeal

1 tbsp + 1½ tsp baking powder

4½ tbsp walnuts, toasted and ground

1 tbsp + 1½ tsp sugar,
plus more for topping

¾ tsp kosher salt

1 cup + 1 tbsp/240 g cold unsalted butter, cut into ½-in/12-mm cubes

6 tbsp/90 ml cold buttermilk

1¼ cups/230 g raspberry jam or Raspberry Preserves (page 70)

1 batch Egg Wash (page 74)

1. In a very large bowl, combine the flour, cornmeal, baking powder, walnuts, sugar, and salt and toss well. Throw in the cold butter and work it with your fingertips until the pieces are pea- and lima bean–size. Add the buttermilk. Lightly toss to distribute.

2. Immediately dump everything onto a clean surface with more than enough space to work the dough. Using only the heel of your palm, quickly flatten out the dough. Gather the dough back together in a mound and repeat. After two or three repetitions, the dough should begin holding together. Be sure to avoid overworking. You should still see some pea-size bits of butter running through it.

3. Form the scones by tightly packing 4 to 5 tbsp of dough into an ice-cream scoop, and then transfer to an ungreased sheet pan. Dip a 1-tbsp measure in flour, pressing the back of it into each scone to form a deep well for the jam. Scoop 1 to 2 tbsp of the jam into each well. Freeze for at least 2 hours before baking, or up to 1 month, tightly wrapped.

4. Preheat your oven to 375°F/190°C. Remove the scones from the freezer. Space them with plenty of breathing room on two ungreased sheet pans; brush the outer rims with the egg wash and sprinkle liberally with sugar. Bake from frozen until cooked through, nicely browned, and easily lifted off the pan, about 30 minutes.

These are best the day they're made but keep well, tightly wrapped, at room temperature, for up to 2 days.

This is a great jam to have kicking around your fridge at all times. It's good with just about everything and is very simple to make. Remember, if you plan to use this in the Walnut Jam Scones (page 69), be sure to cool completely before building your scones.

As a family, we do most of our shopping on Wednesday at the farmers' market and by Sunday we have little amounts of assorted berries hanging around the fridge that are just screaming to be used. We often sub those assorted berries for the raspberries in this recipe and it makes a great mixed berry jam.

raspberry preserves

MAKES ABOUT 1½ CUPS/275 G

5 cups/620 g fresh raspberries
½ tsp kosher salt
¾ cup/150 g sugar
⅔ cup/160 ml water

1. Combine everything in a medium stainless-steel pot. Cover and simmer over medium-low heat until the berries fall apart, about 10 minutes.

2. Uncover and cook down until thickened, stirring frequently to avoid burning, about 25 minutes. If you do burn it, sadly, there is no saving it.

3. Refrigerate until needed.

   This keeps well, refrigerated, for up to 2 weeks.

I started developing this scone after spending a month in France with Josh and my family, just before we got married. I became obsessed with having light and delicious whole-wheat scones for Huckleberry. I wanted them to taste as close to graham crackers as I could manage. We've tried to replace these at Huckleberry numerous times with other variations and we always end up with enough angry snarls that we have to bring them back right away.

During the holidays, we love to add the zest of an orange and substitute dried cranberries for the raisins. These are also delicious with currants instead of raisins. Serve them with very lightly sweetened Whipped Cream (page 149).

whole-wheat raisin scones

MAKES 10 SCONES

¾ cup/130 g raisins

1½ cups/190 g all-purpose flour

½ cup/60 g whole-wheat flour

2 tsp baking powder

1½ tsp baking soda

⅓ cup/65 g sugar, plus more for sprinkling

½ tsp kosher salt

½ cup + 2 tbsp/140 g cold, unsalted butter, cut into ½-in/12-mm cubes

⅓ cup/80 ml cold buttermilk

1 batch Egg Wash (page 74)

1. Plump the raisins in 1 cup/240 ml warm water for 10 minutes, then drain and finely chop.

2. In a very large bowl, combine the all-purpose flour, whole-wheat flour, baking powder, baking soda, sugar, and salt and toss well. Throw in the cold butter and work it with your fingertips until the pieces are pea- and lima bean–size. Add the buttermilk and raisins. Lightly toss to distribute.

3. Immediately dump everything onto a clean surface with more than enough space to work the dough. Using only the heel of your palm, quickly flatten out the dough. Gather the dough back together in a mound and repeat. After two or three repetitions, the dough should begin holding together. Be sure to avoid overworking. You should still see some pea-size bits of butter running through it.

4. Shape the dough into a 12-in/30.5-cm-long cylinder. Lightly flatten the top and cut into ten triangles. Transfer to an ungreased sheet pan and freeze for at least 2 hours before baking, or up to 1 month, tightly wrapped.

5. Preheat your oven to 375°F/190°C. Remove the scones from the freezer. Space them with plenty of breathing room on two ungreased sheet pans, brush with the egg wash, and sprinkle liberally with sugar. Bake from frozen until baked through, nicely browned, and easily lifted off the pan, about 25 minutes.

These are best eaten the day they're made.

At the bakery, we mix up big batches of egg wash and run through them like crazy. Using an egg wash is an absolute must in many recipes in this book, but the actual recipe for egg wash itself is pretty flexible. You can always use whole milk if you don't have cream kicking around your fridge. You can always use one whole egg instead of the two yolks. And if you have no eggs, you can use just the cream, but it will be a little less shiny. And, finally, if you don't have any dairy in the house, use the eggs alone. Just make sure to always use the salt.

egg wash

MAKES ABOUT ¼ CUP/60 ML

2 egg yolks
2 tbsp heavy cream
Pinch of kosher salt

Combine the egg yolks, heavy cream, and salt and whisk until homogeneous. Refrigerate until needed.

This keeps, refrigerated, for up to 2 days.

Make these scones for all the poor souls who have been scared away by those horrible leaden dry hunks of dough ruining the rep of this beautiful pastry. These scones taste as if hazelnuts, butter, and chocolate had a baby, and oh what a cute baby it is! They give scones a good name.

I find using ground nuts in scones gives them a fantastically tender and crumbly texture. It's one of my favorite scone tricks, up there with not being afraid to use a lot of butter. I always serve these with very lightly sweetened Whipped Cream (page 149).

chocolate hazelnut scones

MAKES 10 SCONES

1¾ cups + 2 tbsp/40 g all-purpose flour

½ cup/50 g hazelnuts, toasted and ground

1 tbsp + 1½ tsp baking powder

5 tbsp/40 g sugar, plus more for sprinkling

1 tsp kosher salt

1 cup + 2 tbsp/255 g cold unsalted butter, cut into ½-in/12-mm cubes

6 tbsp/90 ml cold buttermilk

1 tsp vanilla extract

1 cup/140 g chopped dark chocolate, 60 to 70% cacao

1 batch Egg Wash (facing page)

1. In a very large bowl, combine the flour, hazelnuts, baking powder, sugar, and salt and toss well. Throw in the cold butter and work it with your fingertips until the pieces are pea- and lima bean–size. Add the buttermilk, vanilla, and chocolate. Lightly toss to distribute.

2. Immediately dump everything onto a clean surface with more than enough space to work the dough. Using only the heel of your palm, quickly flatten out the dough. Gather the dough back together in a mound and repeat. After two or three repetitions, the dough should begin holding together. Be sure to avoid overworking. You should still see some pea-size bits of butter running through it.

3. Form the scones by tightly packing the dough into an ice-cream scoop; and then transfer to an ungreased sheet pan. Freeze for at least 2 hours before baking, or up to 1 month, tightly wrapped.

4. Preheat your oven to 350°F/180°C. Remove the scones from the freezer. Space them with plenty of breathing room on two ungreased sheet pans, brush with the egg wash, and sprinkle liberally with sugar. Bake from frozen until cooked through, nicely browned, and easily lifted off the pan, about 30 minutes.

These are best eaten the day they're made.

4:30 A.M.

rustic cakes
and teacakes

Four-thirty is the morning's sweet spot. We're awake. We're flowing. We're hitting our stride and we own the kitchen. There's no front-of-house staff; there's no customer feedback. We have no awareness that the egg delivery will be late, the bacon will burn, the meat soup will be mislabeled veggie, and a server will spill a tub of jam all over the walk-in floor literally 5 minutes after he clocked in.

I turn around and look at my morning girls and get lost in a temporary moment of pride. These girls are good and it's not easy to find good morning bakers. A lot of people come through my kitchen and ask for jobs. Some have spent a small fortune on culinary school; some are fresh off the street with no experience but just want to learn. I generally prefer the latter. Regardless of their background or enthusiasm, most of them don't work out. They start with good intentions, but eventually the early mornings, the repetition, or the reality that this is real manual labor gets to them and they leave to pursue something else.

I'd say three out of every four who start at Huckleberry don't last longer than a couple of months. But the ones who do are tough and I love them for it. They have what you would call "hops" in basketball, or as an old chef friend of mine used to put it, "They can dance." It's not that they're good in the club (although many of my girls with a day off the next day are pretty good at that, too). It's that they eventually can get into the rhythm, and, just like a good dancer, they know when to move quick, when to slow down, and when to give the floor to someone else. These qualities are essential when you're part of a team that's creating hundreds of pastries and desserts each morning, all the while not letting quality drop for a second.

Often a new baker will see one of my cake recipes and look like a deer in headlights. Most of my recipes at Huckleberry don't have step-by-step instructions, they're just a list of ingredients and then a vague, if at all, description of what to combine with what. The good bakers aren't afraid to ask questions, so they don't just learn the recipe, they learn our style of baking. They begin to realize that if they know what they are trying to create—whether it's a scone, quick bread, or a more complicated cake—they just need a list of ingredients and they will know immediately which mixing method to choose. Eventually, all my morning girls can translate any recipe they see into exactly what it should be, and I am indebted to them for it.

These moments when I see them all working together seamlessly are what makes it all worthwhile. But I can't absorb them for too long, I've got to get this blueberry cornmeal cake in the oven.

how to line cake pans

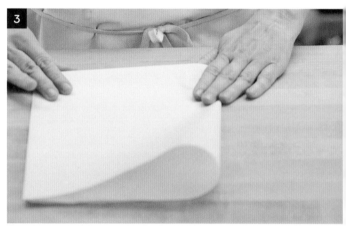

This is our signature cake at Huckleberry. I actually made this cake with vanilla-corn ice cream for Josh when I was trying out for the pastry chef position at Rustic Canyon. This recipe was a favorite then and still is after all these years.

You can really play with the fruit on this cake. Instead of blueberries, try fresh huckleberries or thinly sliced strawberries sprinkled with brown sugar instead of white. Or, during the holidays, add the zest of one orange and top with fresh cranberries and both brown and white sugar. And, while I'm giving you all my secrets, these are also killer as muffins.

blueberry cornmeal cake

MAKES ONE 10-IN/25-CM CAKE

¾ cup + 1½ tbsp/195 g unsalted butter, cubed, at room temperature

¾ cup + 3 tbsp/190 g sugar, plus 2 tbsp

1½ tsp kosher salt

2 eggs

4½ tbsp canola oil

3 tbsp maple syrup

1 tbsp vanilla extract

1½ cups/200 g all-purpose flour

¾ cup/120 g cornmeal

2¼ tsp baking powder

¾ tsp baking soda

1 cup + 2 tbsp/270 ml whole plain yogurt

½ cup + 1 tbsp/130 g ricotta

1 cup/150 g fresh blueberries

1. Position a rack in the middle of your oven and preheat to 350°F/180°C. Line and grease a 10-in/25-cm round cake pan (see page 78).

2. In a stand mixer fitted with the paddle attachment, cream the butter, ¾ cup + 3 tbsp/190 g sugar, and salt on medium-high speed, until light and fluffy, about 2 minutes. Incorporate the eggs, one at a time, beating well after each addition. Be sure to scrape the sides of the bowl well.

3. With the mixer on low speed, pour in the canola oil, maple syrup, and vanilla. Pause mixing and add the flour, cornmeal, baking powder, baking soda, yogurt, and ricotta. Mix cautiously, just until incorporated. Do not overmix!

4. Scoop the batter into the prepared pan, top with the blueberries, and sprinkle with the remaining sugar. Bake for 1 hour and 10 minutes, or until a cake tester comes out clean. Do not overbake! Allow to cool for about 15 minutes in the pan.

5. Place a flat plate on top of the cake and pan. Carefully invert the cake onto the plate by flipping both upside down. Then lift the pan off the cake. Gently pull the parchment from every nook and cranny of the cake, being careful not to break the cake. Rest your serving plate on the bottom of the cake and turn the cake right-side up onto the plate.

This cake is best served the day it's made but keeps, tightly wrapped, at room temperature, for up to 2 days.

This is one of my go-to winter breakfast cakes, when there is almost no fruit to cook with and I'm getting a little tired of lemon by itself. This cake is buttery, but the richness is cut by its strong lemon flavor and the nuttiness of the toasted pistachios. It is very important to toast your pistachios to a golden brown to get that rich flavor. Another integral part of this recipe is not chopping the nuts for the topping too finely: if I could ask you to cut each nut in half and not sound like a total jerk I would, because the larger pieces on top of the cake make it look rustic and beautiful.

This cake can easily be made gluten-free by decreasing the butter to 1½ cups/ 330 g and subbing 1 cup plus 2 tbsp/140 g gluten-free flour mix (see page 55) for the all-purpose flour. You can serve this cake with lightly sweetened Whipped Cream (page 149) or not; it can completely stand on its own.

lemon pistachio cake

MAKES ONE 10-IN/25-CM CAKE

CAKE

1¾ cups + 2 tbsp/430 g unsalted butter, cubed, at room temperature

2½ cups/450 g sugar

2½ tsp kosher salt

Zest of 3 lemons

1 tsp vanilla extract

8 eggs

2 cups/200 g toasted, ground pistachios

2 cups/200 g almond meal

¾ cup/100 g all-purpose flour

2 tsp baking powder

GLAZE

½ cup/100 g toasted chopped pistachios

½ cup/100 g sugar

½ cup/100 g freshly squeezed lemon juice

1. To make the cake: Position a rack in the middle of your oven and preheat to 350°F/180°C. Line and grease a 10-in/25-cm round cake pan (see page 78).

2. In a stand mixer fitted with the paddle attachment, cream the butter, sugar, salt, and lemon zest on medium-high speed, until light and fluffy, about 2 minutes. Incorporate the vanilla and eggs one at a time, beating well after each addition. Be sure to scrape the sides of the bowl well. Pause mixing and add the pistachios, almond meal, flour, and baking powder on low speed. Mix cautiously, just until incorporated.

3. Scoop the batter into the prepared pan. Bake for 1 hour and 5 minutes, or until a cake tester comes out clean. Do not overbake! Allow to cool for about 15 minutes in the pan.

4. While the cake is cooling, make the glaze: Simmer the pistachios, sugar, and lemon juice together until the sugar is completely dissolved and the pistachios are nicely coated, about 2 minutes. Set aside.

5. Place a flat plate on top of the cake and pan. Carefully invert the cake onto the plate by flipping both upside down. Then lift the pan off the cake. Gently pull the parchment from every nook and cranny of the cake, being careful not to break the cake. Rest your serving plate on the bottom of the cake and turn the cake right-side up onto the plate.

6. While the cake is still warm, immediately spoon the glaze and nuts all over the top.

This cake is best served the day it's made but keeps, tightly wrapped, at room temperature, for up to 3 days.

This cake is one of the most beautiful cakes we serve at Huckleberry, but it is not a cake that flies off the shelves. Honestly, it's just not for everyone, but if you love the earthy taste of buckwheat, as I do, this buttery cake will be a favorite.

If buckwheat isn't your thing, remove it from this recipe and substitute different kinds of flours, like whole-wheat, rye, spelt, quinoa, oat, etc. In terms of swapping out the fruit, I don't say this often, but I think apples work best with this cake, and other fruits don't quite cut the buckwheat the same way.

apple buckwheat cake
MAKES ONE 10-IN/25-CM CAKE

CAKE

1 cup/225 g unsalted butter, cubed, at room temperature

1⅔ cups/340 g sugar, plus 2 tbsp

2 tsp kosher salt

1 tbsp vanilla extract

6 eggs

3 or 4 apples; 1 peeled and grated, and 2 or 3 peeled and sliced ⅛ in/3 mm thick, cores reserved

1½ cups/150 g almond flour

¾ cup/100 g buckwheat flour

⅔ cup/75 g all-purpose flour

⅓ cup/55 g cornmeal

2 tsp baking powder

GLAZE

½ cup/100 g sugar

½ cup/120 ml water

Pinch of kosher salt

1 vanilla bean, scraped (optional)

Apple cores (reserved from making the cake)

1. To make the cake: Position a rack in the middle of your oven and preheat to 350°F/180°C. Line and grease a 10-in/25-cm round cake pan (see page 78).

2. In a stand mixer fitted with the paddle attachment, cream the butter, 1⅔ cups/340 g sugar, and salt on medium-high speed, until light and fluffy, about 2 minutes. Incorporate the vanilla and eggs, one at a time, scraping the sides of the bowl well between each addition. Add the grated apple and mix. Then add the almond flour, buckwheat flour, all-purpose flour, cornmeal, and baking powder. Mix cautiously, just until incorporated. Do not overmix!

3. Scoop the batter into the prepared pan, top with the sliced apples, arranging them in pretty concentric circles, and sprinkle with the remaining sugar. Bake for 1 hour and 15 minutes, or until a cake tester comes out clean. Do not overbake! Allow to cool for about 15 minutes in the pan.

4. Meanwhile, make the glaze: Simmer the sugar, water, salt, vanilla bean seeds and pod (if using), and apple cores together in a saucepan until the sugar is completely dissolved, about 2 minutes. Set aside to infuse.

5. Place a flat plate on top of the cake and pan. Carefully invert the cake onto the plate by flipping both upside down. Then lift the pan off the cake. Gently pull the parchment from every nook and cranny of the cake, being careful not to break the cake. Rest your serving plate on the bottom of the cake and turn the cake right-side up onto the plate.

6. While the cake is still warm, brush the glaze all over the top and sides and garnish with the nonedible vanilla pod.

This cake is best served the day it's made but keeps well, tightly wrapped, at room temperature, for up to 2 days.

This cake is a real testament to our whatever-vessel-suits-your-fancy theory. Dump this batter into a cake pan, teacake pan, muffin tin, or a Bundt pan and it will bake up beautifully and be a big hit.

I rarely include the nuts at home, but we always do at Huckleberry. If you are allergic to nuts, omit the almond flour and toasted walnuts and increase the whole-wheat flour to 1 cup/125 g.

chocolate banana walnut cake

MAKES ONE 10-IN/25-CM CAKE

½ cup/110 g unsalted butter, cubed, at room temperature

½ cup/100 g sugar, plus 2 tbsp

1 tsp kosher salt

2 eggs

1 cup/130 g all-purpose flour

¾ cup/90 g whole-wheat flour

¼ cup/30 g almond flour

1½ tsp baking powder

1½ tsp baking soda

1 cup/240 ml whole plain yogurt

2 tsp vanilla extract

5 very ripe bananas, mashed; plus 3 bananas, sliced

¾ cup/130 g chopped dark chocolate, 60 to 70% cacao

½ cup/60 g walnuts, chopped and toasted

1. Position a rack in the middle of your oven and preheat to 350°F/180°C. Line and grease a 10-in/25-cm round cake pan or springform pan (see page 78).

2. In a stand mixer fitted with the paddle attachment, cream the butter, ½ cup/100 g sugar, and salt on medium-high speed until light and fluffy, about 2 minutes. Incorporate the eggs, one at a time, beating well after each addition. Be sure to scrape the sides of bowl well. Pause mixing and add the all-purpose flour, whole-wheat flour, almond flour, baking powder, baking soda, yogurt, vanilla, mashed bananas, chocolate, and walnuts. Mix cautiously, just until incorporated. Do not overmix!

3. Scoop the batter into the prepared pan, top with the sliced bananas, and sprinkle with the remaining sugar. Bake for 1 hour and 5 minutes, or until a cake tester comes out clean. Do not overbake! Allow to cool for about 15 minutes in the pan.

4. Place a flat plate on top of the cake and pan. Carefully invert the cake onto the plate by flipping both upside down. Then lift the pan off the cake. Gently pull the parchment from every nook and cranny of the cake, being careful not to break the cake. Rest your serving plate on the bottom of the cake and turn the cake right-side up onto the plate.

This is best served the day it's made but keeps well, tightly wrapped, at room temperature, for up to 3 days.

At first, I have to admit, I didn't buy the whole no-gluten thing and found it pretty annoying. But when I started to meet people who truly are gluten intolerant, I began to embrace gluten-free baking. Now I'm having a lot of fun with it. The reality is, I'm in this business to make people smile, and baking things for people who struggle to find pastries they can enjoy gives me a special satisfaction.

My one caveat with this recipe is that the lack of gluten causes the chocolate to sink. But that never bothered anyone, trust me. I often serve this with lightly sweetened Whipped Cream (page 149), but it is also great on its own.

gluten-free chocolate hazelnut cake

MAKES ONE 10-IN/25-CM CAKE

1 cup + 2 tbsp/255 g unsalted butter, cubed, at room temperature

1½ cups/300 g sugar, plus 2 tbsp

2½ tsp kosher salt

Zest of 1 orange

1 tbsp vanilla extract

6 eggs

1½ cups/110 g hazelnuts, toasted, cooled and ground

1½ cups/140 g almond flour

¾ cup + 1 tbsp/105 g Huckleberry Gluten-Free Flour Mix (page 55)

2 tsp baking powder

1½ cups/250 g chopped dark chocolate, 60 to 70% cacao

1. Position a rack in the middle of your oven and preheat to 350°F/180°C. Line and grease a 10-in/25-cm round cake pan (see page 78).

2. In a stand mixer fitted with the paddle attachment, cream the butter, 1½ cups/300 g sugar, salt, and orange zest on medium-high speed until light and fluffy, about 2 minutes. Incorporate the vanilla and eggs, one at a time, beating well after each addition. Be sure to scrape the sides of the bowl well. Pause mixing and add the hazelnuts, almond flour, gluten-free flour mix, baking powder, and chopped chocolate. Mix cautiously, just until incorporated.

3. Scoop the batter into the prepared pan and sprinkle with the remaining sugar. Bake for about 1 hour, or until a cake tester comes out clean. Do not overbake! Allow to cool for about 15 minutes in the pan.

4. Place a flat plate on top of the cake and pan. Carefully invert the cake onto the plate by flipping both upside down. Then lift the pan off the cake. Gently pull the parchment from every nook and cranny of the cake, being careful not to break the cake. Rest your serving plate on the bottom of the cake and turn the cake right-side up onto the plate.

This is best served the day it's made but keeps well, tightly wrapped, at room temperature, for up to 2 days.

The more I bake, the more I find myself playing with different grains; not for health reasons but for their wonderful depth of flavor. I added the rye flour to this recipe at the last minute because of its nutty sourness, and the toasted wheat germ for its sweet roundness. This cake is a perfect teatime treat; it's buttery, earthy, and not overly sweet. When putting this cake together, be sure to have a few pieces of pear poke through the crumble so they brown, making the cake more flavorful and giving it a beautiful rustic look.

Because pears have a short season I sometimes make this cake with blueberries, raspberries, cranberries, apricots, peaches, or figs.

pear whole-wheat crumb cake

MAKES ONE 10-IN/25-CM CAKE

TOPPING

½ cup/110 g unsalted butter, at room temperature

½ cup + 2 tbsp/55 g almond flour

¼ cup + 2 tbsp/20 g rolled oats

¼ cup/50 g granulated sugar

¼ cup/30 g whole-wheat flour

3 tbsp all-purpose flour

2 tbsp wheat germ, toasted

2 tbsp brown sugar

¼ tsp kosher salt

¼ cup/20 g sliced almonds

CAKE

¾ cup/170 g unsalted butter, cubed, at room temperature

1 cup/200 g granulated sugar

2 tbsp brown sugar

¾ tsp kosher salt

1 tbsp vanilla extract

2 eggs

1¼ cups/160 g all-purpose flour

¾ cup/55 g wheat germ, toasted

¼ cup/25 g almond flour

3 tbsp rye flour

2 tsp baking powder

½ tsp baking soda

1 cup/240 ml whole plain yogurt

Zest of 1 orange, fruit reserved

3 pears, peeled and thickly sliced

1. To make the topping: In a bowl, combine the butter, almond flour, oats, granulated sugar, whole-wheat flour, all-purpose flour, wheat germ, brown sugar, salt, and sliced almonds and blend with your fingertips until homogenous. Refrigerate until needed.

2. To make the cake: Position a rack in the middle of your oven and preheat to 350°F/180°C. Line and grease a 10-in/25-cm round cake pan or springform pan (see page 78).

3. In a stand mixer fitted with the paddle attachment, cream the butter, granulated sugar, brown sugar, and salt on medium-high speed, until light and fluffy, about 2 minutes. Incorporate the vanilla and eggs, one at a time, beating well after each addition. Be sure to scrape the sides of the bowl well. Pause mixing and add the all-purpose flour, wheat germ, almond flour, rye flour, baking powder, baking soda, yogurt, and orange zest. Mix cautiously, just until incorporated. Do not overmix!

4. Scoop the batter into the prepared pan and cover evenly with the pears. Top with the crumble, allowing a little fruit to poke through. Bake for 1 hour and 15 minutes, or until a cake tester comes out clean. Do not overbake! Allow to cool for about 15 minutes in the pan; then squeeze the orange over the entire cake.

5. Place a flat plate on top of the cake and pan. Carefully invert the cake onto the plate by flipping both upside down. Then lift the pan off the cake. Gently pull the parchment from every nook and cranny of the cake, being careful not to break the cake. Rest your serving plate on the bottom of the cake and turn the cake right-side up onto the plate.

This is best served the day it's made but keeps, tightly wrapped, at room temperature, for up to 2 days.

This cake is as traditional as it gets, comfort food at its best. You can mix and assemble it the day before and refrigerate the completely assembled unbaked cake overnight. In the morning, just pull your cake out of the refrigerator and put it directly into your preheated oven. But if you do this, remember, it will take a little longer because it's going in cold, so use a cake tester to be sure it's done.

The batter is incredibly versatile. This is a recipe to play with and cater to your own family. Be creative: add fruit, cinnamon, chocolate chips. The possibilities are endless.

old-fashioned coffee cake

MAKES ONE 10-IN/25-CM CAKE

CRUMBLE

5½ tbsp/80 g unsalted butter, at room temperature

½ cup/65 g all-purpose flour

½ cup/45 g almond meal

4½ tbsp/55 g sugar

½ tsp kosher salt

STREUSEL

1 cup/130 g walnuts, toasted

3 tbsp sugar

½ tsp cinnamon

CAKE

1½ cups/340 g unsalted butter, cubed, at room temperature

1¾ cups + 2 tbsp/380 g sugar

1½ tsp kosher salt

1 tbsp + 1 tsp vanilla extract

3 eggs

2½ cups/310 g all-purpose flour

½ cup/45 g almond flour

1 tbsp baking powder

½ tsp baking soda

1½ cups/350 ml sour cream

1. To make the crumble: In a bowl, combine the butter, all-purpose flour, almond meal, sugar, and salt and rub together between your fingertips until everything is moistened, but a few little bits of butter remain. Refrigerate until needed.

2. To make the streusel: In a food processor, combine the walnuts, sugar, and cinnamon and pulse until the walnuts are ground but not becoming a paste. Set aside.

3. To make the cake: Position a rack in the middle of your oven and preheat to 350°F/180°C. Line and grease a 10-in/25-cm round cake pan or springform pan (see page 78).

4. In a stand mixer fitted with the paddle attachment, cream the butter, sugar, and salt on medium-high speed until light and fluffy, about 2 minutes. Incorporate the vanilla and eggs, one at a time, beating well after each addition. Be sure to scrape the sides of the bowl well. Pause mixing and add the all-purpose flour, almond flour, baking powder, baking soda, and sour cream. Mix cautiously, just until incorporated. Do not overmix!

5. Scoop half of the batter into the prepared pan and smooth it with damp fingertips or a small offset spatula. Sprinkle evenly with the streusel. Top with the rest of the batter, coaxing it into covering the streusel layer. Top with the crumble. (At this point, the assembled cake can be refrigerated for up to 2 days.) Bake for 1 hour and 10 minutes, or until a cake tester comes out clean (a little longer if coming from the refrigerator). Allow to cool for about 15 minutes in the pan.

6. Place a flat plate on top of the cake and pan. Carefully invert the cake onto the plate by flipping both upside down. Then lift the pan off the cake. Gently pull the parchment from every nook and cranny of the cake, being careful not to break the cake. Rest your serving plate on the bottom of the cake and turn the cake right-side up onto the plate.

This is best served the day it's made but keeps well, tightly wrapped, at room temperature, for up to 3 days.

The first persimmons usually make their appearance around Halloween, right when I'm starting to feel festive and craving wintery spices, and this is always the first thing I make. When I ran this at Rustic Canyon, I called it a steamed cake, even though it really wasn't; because of its soft, gooey texture, I didn't know how else to describe it. It's important to use ridiculously soft Hachiya persimmons for this cake. The harder Fuyu persimmons will just not work. If for some reason you find yourself staring at the wrong persimmons, make a different cake and use those Fuyus in a salad. Top this cake with a dusting of powdered sugar once it's cooled.

persimmon spice cake

MAKES ONE 10-IN/25-CM CAKE

½ cup/80 g raisins

5 to 6 very ripe Hachiya persimmons

1 lemon, zested and juiced

1 tbsp vanilla extract

2 tsp baking soda

½ cup/110 g unsalted butter, cubed, at room temperature

1 cup/220 g brown sugar

¾ tsp kosher salt

1 egg

1½ cups/190 g all-purpose flour

2 tsp baking powder

1 tsp cinnamon

¼ tsp nutmeg

¼ tsp ginger

¼ tsp cloves

1 cup/120 g walnuts, toasted and chopped

½ cup/75 g coarsely chopped dates

2 tbsp granulated sugar

1. Position a rack in the middle of your oven and preheat to 350°F/180°C. Line and grease a 10-in/25-cm round cake pan (see page 78). Plump the raisins in 1 cup/240 ml warm water for 10 minutes, then drain and finely chop.

2. Remove the stems from the persimmons and put in a food processor or blender with half of the lemon juice. (Discard the remaining juice.) Purée until smooth. Strain the purée, using a wooden spoon to help work it through the mesh; it will take some elbow grease. Discard the skins and set aside 1½ cups/360 g of purée.

3. Add the vanilla and baking soda to the purée and whisk to combine. It may foam and thicken. Set aside.

4. In a stand mixer fitted with the paddle attachment, cream the butter, brown sugar, salt, and lemon zest on medium-high speed, until light and fluffy, about 2 minutes. Incorporate the egg and then the purée mixture. Be sure to scrape the sides of the bowl well. Pause mixing and add the flour, baking powder, cinnamon, nutmeg, ginger, and cloves. Mix cautiously, just until incorporated. Do not overmix! Fold in the walnuts, raisins, and dates by hand.

5. Scoop the batter into the prepared pan and sprinkle with the granulated sugar. Bake for 45 minutes, or until a cake tester comes out clean. Do not overbake! Allow to cool for about 15 minutes in the pan.

6. Place a flat plate on top of the cake and pan. Carefully invert the cake onto the plate by flipping both upside down. Then lift the pan off the cake. Gently pull the parchment from every nook and cranny of the cake, being careful not to break the cake. Rest your serving plate on the bottom of the cake and turn the cake right-side up onto the plate.

This keeps beautifully, tightly wrapped, at room temperature, for up to 3 days.

This cake is delicious by itself, with a cup of tea or served with strawberry jam (see page 55) and whipped cream (see page 149). If you have any leftover pear poaching liquid (see page 44), quince poaching liquid (see page 138), or lemon glaze (see page 46), it can be fun to use that instead of the maple syrup. Feel free to play with different fruit in this teacake, too, but lean toward the less juicy, like blackberries, grapes, figs, and cranberries, just to name a few.

apricot–vanilla bean pound cake

MAKES ONE 9-BY-5-IN/23-BY-12-CM LOAF

1 vanilla bean

1 cup + 2 tbsp/230 g sugar

1½ cups/190 g all-purpose flour

¾ tsp baking powder

¾ tsp kosher salt

1 cup + 2 tbsp/255 g unsalted butter, cubed, at room temperature

2 eggs

3 egg yolks

½ cup/120 g ricotta

2 tsp vanilla extract

10 ripe apricots, halved

⅓ cup/80 ml maple syrup

1. Position a rack in the middle of your oven and preheat to 350°F/ 180°C. Grease a 9-by-5 in/23-by-12-cm loaf pan. Split the vanilla bean lengthwise and scrape out the seeds.

2. In a stand mixer fitted with the paddle attachment, combine the vanilla bean seeds and sugar. Mix on low speed until the sugar is infused with the vanilla, about 5 minutes. Add the flour, baking powder, and salt to the bowl and mix slowly to combine. Add the butter and mix until still lumpy but starting to come together. Incorporate the eggs, egg yolks, ricotta, and vanilla and mix until fairly smooth. With the mixer off, fold in the apricots by hand.

3. Scoop half the batter into the prepared pan. Bake for 60 to 65 min- utes, until the cake springs back slightly to the touch, but it still looks a little wet right at the center. Do not overbake! Allow to cool for about 15 minutes in the pan.

4. Place a flat plate on top of the cake and pan. Carefully invert the cake onto the plate by flipping both upside down. Then lift the pan off the cake. Rest your serving plate on the bottom of the cake and turn the cake right-side up onto the plate.

5. In a small saucepan, warm the maple syrup and brush it on all sides of the cake while the cake is still warm.

This is best served the day it's made but keeps, tightly wrapped, at room temperature, for up to 3 days.

I love this, my son loves this, my husband loves this, and you will love this. There is something so fun and naughty about eating chocolate for breakfast, and I for one think it should be done more often. Even though this teacake is rich in chocolate it is not overly sweet and the coffee gives it a slightly more grown-up flavor, but not so grown-up that the little ones won't love it.

Add ½ cup/60 g chopped, toasted walnuts if you're in the mood. These are also great made into muffins. Serve plain or with lightly sweetened Whipped Cream (page 149) on the side.

chocolate chocolate teacake

MAKES ONE 9-BY-5-IN/23-BY-12-CM LOAF

¾ cup/100 g pastry flour

6 tbsp/45 g all-purpose flour

6 tbsp/30 g unsweetened cocoa powder

1 tsp baking powder

¾ tsp baking soda

½ cup/120 ml strong brewed coffee, cooled

½ cup/120 ml buttermilk

1 tsp vanilla extract

1¾ cups/300 g coarsely chopped dark chocolate, 60 to 70% cacao

½ cup + 2 tbsp/140 g unsalted butter, cubed, at room temperature

1 cup + 2 tbsp/225 g sugar

½ tsp kosher salt

3 eggs

Powdered sugar for topping (optional)

1. Position a rack in the middle of your oven and preheat to 350°F/180°C. Grease a 9-by-5-in/23-by-12-cm loaf pan.

2. Sift together the pastry flour, all-purpose flour, cocoa powder, baking powder, and baking soda. Set aside.

3. Combine the coffee, buttermilk, and vanilla. Set aside. Melt ¾ cup/130 g of the chocolate gently over a double boiler or in a small bowl set over a small saucepan of simmering water. Remove the pan from the heat, but leave the chocolate over the double boiler to keep warm while you mix the cake.

4. In a stand mixer fitted with the paddle attachment, cream the butter, sugar, and salt on medium-high speed until light and fluffy, about 2 minutes. Incorporate the eggs, one at a time, beating well after each addition. Be sure to scrape the sides of the bowl well. Pause mixing and add the flour mixture. Mix just until incorporated. With the mixer on low speed, pour in the coffee mixture. Fold in both the melted and chopped chocolate.

5. Pour the batter into the prepared pan and bake for 55 minutes, or until a cake tester comes out clean. Do not overbake! Allow to cool completely.

6. Place a flat plate on top of the cake and pan. Carefully invert the cake onto the plate by flipping both upside down. Then lift the pan off the cake. Rest your serving plate on the bottom of the cake and turn the cake right-side up onto the plate. Once cooled, top with powdered sugar, if desired.

This keeps beautifully, tightly wrapped, at room temperature, for up to 4 days.

This cake is the quintessential teatime treat. It is slightly dense and extremely moist. When I make this at home, I like to make it gluten-free by subbing our gluten-free flour mix (see page 55) for the all-purpose and pastry flours. Gluten-free or not, it's imperative to use the lemon kumquat glaze—otherwise it doesn't have the punch that every lemon lover needs.

lemon kumquat poppy teacake

MAKES ONE 9-BY-5-IN/23-BY-12-CM LOAF

1 cup + 2 tbsp/255 g unsalted butter, at room temperature

1 cup/200 g sugar, plus 3 tbsp

¾ tsp kosher salt

Zest of 8 kumquats, fruit reserved

Zest and juice of 3 lemons

Zest of 1 tangerine

2 eggs, plus 2 egg yolks

1¼ cups/160 g all-purpose flour

¼ cup/35 g pastry flour

1½ tsp baking powder

1 tbsp + 1 tsp poppy seeds

2 tbsp buttermilk

1 tbsp vanilla extract

1. Position a rack in the middle of your oven and preheat to 350°F/180°C. Grease a 9-by-5-in/23-by-12-cm loaf pan.

2. In a stand mixer fitted with the paddle attachment, cream the butter, 1 cup/200 g sugar, salt, and kumquat, lemon, and tangerine zests on medium-high speed until light and fluffy, about 2 minutes.

3. Incorporate the eggs and egg yolks slowly, one at a time, beating well after each addition. Be sure to scrape the sides of the bowl well. Pause mixing and add the all-purpose flour, pastry flour, baking powder, poppy seeds, buttermilk, and vanilla. Mix cautiously, just until incorporated. Do not overmix!

4. Scoop the batter into the prepared pan. Bake for 1 hour, or until the cake springs back when touched and a cake tester comes out clean. Do not overbake!

5. Meanwhile, combine the lemon juice, 3 tbsp sugar, and reserved kumquats in a blender. Blend to a coarse purée. In a small saucepan, simmer the kumquat purée until the sugar dissolves completely, about 2 minutes. Set aside and allow to infuse while the cake bakes.

6. Quickly remove the cake from the pan, strain the glaze, and brush it on all sides of the cake while the cake is still warm.

This is best served the day it's made but keeps, tightly wrapped, at room temperature, for up to 3 days.

This is a spiced-up version of the cake we all grew up with. I love to serve it with cream cheese on the side, but it is also incredible topped with a fluffy layer of cream cheese frosting. When I plan to frost the cake, I often bake it in a 10-by-2-in/25-by-5-cm springform or cake pan and, when cool, top it with the frosting. To make the frosting, simply take 2 cups/450 g room-temperature cream cheese, ½ cup/45 g sifted powdered sugar, and 2 tsp vanilla and mix in a stand mixer fitted with the paddle attachment until fluffy and smooth. After frosting, top with extra chopped toasted walnuts and a little sprinkle of cinnamon. It's perfect for a birthday brunch.

carrot apple teacake

MAKES ONE 9-BY-5-IN/23-BY-12-CM LOAF

¾ cup/130 g raisins

¾ cup/180 ml canola oil

1 cup + 2 tbsp/230 g sugar,
plus more for topping

1¼ tsp kosher salt

Zest of 1 orange

3 egg whites

1 tbsp vanilla extract

1 cup + 2 tbsp/140 g all-purpose flour

¼ cup + 2 tbsp/45 g whole-wheat flour

1½ tsp wheat germ or ground flax seeds

¾ tsp baking powder

1½ tsp baking soda

2 tsp cinnamon

½ tsp nutmeg

1½ cups/180 g shredded, unpeeled carrots

¾ cup/80 g grated, peeled apple

1¼ cups/150 g chopped walnuts, toasted

1. Preheat your oven to 350°F/180°C. Grease a 9-by-5-in/23-by-12-cm loaf pan. Plump the raisins in 1 cup/240 ml warm water for 10 minutes, then strain and finely chop.

2. Dump everything into a big bowl and stir together. No, really. Throw it all into a bowl and mix it all up together. That's it. Sometimes I even like to use my hands.

3. Pour the batter into the prepared pan and sprinkle with sugar. Bake for 50 minutes, or until a cake tester comes out clean. Do not overbake! Allow to cool for about 15 minutes in the pan.

4. Place a flat plate on top of the cake and pan. Carefully invert the cake onto the plate by flipping both upside down. Then lift the pan off the cake. Rest your serving plate on the bottom of the cake and turn the cake right-side up onto the plate.

This keeps beautifully, tightly wrapped, at room temperature, for up to 4 days.

5:30 A.M.

breads and other things that rise

"Mom" is the most important member of our bread team, and I'm not just saying this because we're a female-run kitchen. When I say "mom," I'm not talking about my mom, or myself, or any matriarch who works for us. I'm talking about our bread starter, a.k.a. "the mother." The mother needs to be fed twice a day (*every day!*) in order to be the foundation for many of the breads we produce at Huckleberry.

I turn to Melissa, our enthusiastic new bread girl, and ask the question I ask every morning at this time: "Did you feed the mother yet?" She's slow to respond, so I brace myself because I have a sense that I know the answer. "No, I'm sorry, I forgot," she says earnestly and apologetically. "I'm doing a bunch of things right now: making flatbread, pulling brioche out of the oven, and mixing the croissant dough. I'm sorry I missed it." I roll my eyes with a high level of annoyance and not much sympathy, even though I know she's working hard and there's a lot to manage on that station. "This is not really something that you can *forget!*" I say with as much diplomacy as I can muster, which is not very much. "If you feed the mother too late, it can dramatically affect how our bread tastes and feels, and if you're really late, the bread could be way too sour or worse, you could kill the mother and it can take weeks to get the bread looking and tasting right again!"

Now keep in mind, I don't believe all the voodoo magic crap you hear from other bakeries about how the flavor of their mother resulted from making it on the night of a full moon, or that it was brought over from France in a suitcase, or that their weird

hippie friend blessed it with a combination of sage, lavender, and honeysuckle. A mother is good because you start it correctly and feed it correctly and care for it properly; but like anything good, it takes time to build, and right now the new girl is in serious danger of letting all that hard work go to waste!

Between you and me, I feel the same way about bagels, pizza, and sourdough bread. I believe you can achieve great quality in all these things without flying your water in from New York, your flour from Italy, or moving your bakery to San Francisco. The best thing about bread is that it's about process. We start with a few simple good-quality ingredients, and then it's all about how it's treated and how committed you are to getting it exactly as you want it. People say it takes a lot of patience to make bread, but it really just takes a willingness to mess up a lot and keep trying in order to get the ingredients to do what you want them to do. But I don't have time to explain all this in this moment to Melissa, because poor Mom is wasting away. "Aaagh," I say trying my best to be patient. "Just feed the poor girl, please!"

Now that my biscuits are cooling down in the freezer, I turn my energy to baking the English muffins. Luckily I turned my griddle on more than an hour ago, so I can jump right in.

We have these English muffins at Huckleberry every day. Occasionally, we make a larger batch and set some dough aside to mix with something like chocolate chips, cinnamon and raisins, dried blueberries and flax seeds, roasted jalapeños and Cheddar, Gruyère and bacon, and so many other combinations. Feel free to play with these and figure out the kind of English muffins your family loves. If you do choose to mix in ingredients, do it in the last minute of mixing your dough. Also, please always split English muffins by hand, do not slice them in half, so you can see and enjoy all those nooks and crannies. And if you've gone through the trouble of making these, I highly recommend making Green Eggs and Ham (page 223) for your family, too.

english muffins

MAKES ABOUT 12 MUFFINS

3 cups/710 ml buttermilk

2 tbsp active dry yeast

3 tbsp unsalted butter, at room temperature

3 tbsp honey

6 cups/820 g bread flour

¼ cup/50 g sugar

4½ tsp kosher salt

1 cup/160 g cornmeal

1. Warm 1½ cups/355 ml of the buttermilk in a small saucepan, but do not boil. Place the remaining 1½ cups/355 ml cold buttermilk in the bowl of a stand mixer with the yeast and whisk by hand to combine. Add the warm buttermilk to the cold buttermilk mixture and whisk to blend. Add the butter, honey, bread flour, sugar, and salt and mix on low speed with the dough hook attachment for about 1 minute, until the dough comes together. Increase the speed to medium-high and work the dough for about 2 minutes, until smooth.

2. Transfer the dough to a greased bowl, cover with plastic wrap, and refrigerate for 1 hour.

3. Sprinkle ½ cup/80 g of the cornmeal on a clean work surface and dump the dough out onto it. Sprinkle another ¼ cup/40 g of the cornmeal on top of the dough and flatten it into a disk with a 1-in/2.5-cm thickness.

4. Sprinkle the last ¼ cup/40 g of the cornmeal onto a sheet pan. With a 3-in/7.5-cm round cutter, cut the English muffins from the dough. Cut them as closely as possible, minimizing the amount of scraps, as you cannot combine and reroll this dough.

5. Arrange the English muffins, 1 in/2.5 cm apart, on the sheet pan. Allow the dough to rise for 1 hour at room temperature. Or refrigerate overnight and allow to rise for 1 hour in the morning.

6. As the English muffins near readiness, preheat your oven to 350°F/ 180°C. When the oven is hot, heat an ungreased griddle or large cast-iron pan over medium-high heat.

7. Drop the English muffins onto the griddle and cook for about 1 minute on each side, until golden brown.

8. Return the English muffins to the sheet pan and immediately bake for 8 to 10 minutes, until they feel light when lifted from the pan. If working in batches, bake each batch as it comes off the griddle.

These keep, tightly wrapped, at room temperature, for up to 3 days; or frozen, for up to 1 month.

Good brioche is all about good ingredients. It's a fair amount of butter and egg, so they must be really good European-style butter and organic farm eggs with big yellow yolks. When I set out to create this recipe, I wanted to create a bread that felt like pure decadence and comfort. I wanted it to taste like soft buttered toast without needing to be slathered in butter at all.

brioche

MAKES ONE LOAF

3 tbsp whole milk

2 tbsp active dry yeast

1¾ cups/215 g all-purpose flour

1¾ cups/215 g bread flour

¼ cup + 1 tsp/55 g sugar

1½ tsp kosher salt

5 eggs, beaten

1 cup/220 g unsalted butter, very soft

1 batch Egg Wash (page 74)

DAY ONE

1. Slightly warm the milk and pour into the bowl of a stand mixer fitted with the dough hook. Add the yeast and whisk by hand to combine. Add the all-purpose flour, bread flour, sugar, salt, and eggs. Mix on low speed until the dough comes together, 1 to 2 minutes.

2. Increase the mixer speed to medium-high and work the dough for 6 minutes. Pause about every minute to push the dough back down into the bowl and off the hook.

3. Reduce the mixer speed to low and slowly add the butter, a little at a time, over the course of 2 minutes. Pause halfway through to scrape down the bowl and hook. When the butter begins to blend in, increase the mixer speed to medium-high to fully incorporate the butter and bring the dough back together, 4 to 6 minutes longer.

4. Transfer the dough to a greased sheet pan, cover with plastic wrap, and refrigerate for at least 1 hour.

5. Divide the dough into two equal balls, about 11 oz/315 g each. Transfer to a greased sheet pan, wrap in plastic, and refrigerate overnight.

DAY TWO

6. Grease a 5-by-9-in/12-by-23-cm loaf pan. Work with one dough ball at a time. First flatten into a disc, then lift an edge and press it into the center. Work your way around the circumference, pressing every edge to the center until you have a ball. Flip the ball over so the pleated side is down and the smooth side is up. Cup the dough in your palm and massage the seam side of the dough firmly against the work surface in a circular motion, allowing the friction to seal the seams. Set aside and cover with plastic wrap or a slightly damp kitchen towel while you shape the next ball.

7. Place the balls into the loaf pan, cover loosely with plastic, and allow to rise in a warm place until more than doubled in size, about 3½ hours.

8. As the dough nears readiness, preheat your oven to 350°F/180°C. Carefully brush the dough with the egg wash, making sure the egg doesn't pool around the edges. Bake until golden, about 35 minutes. Allow to cool for about 10 minutes in the pan, then transfer to a cooling rack.

This is best the day it is made but keeps, tightly wrapped, at room temperature, for up to 3 days; or frozen, for up to 1 month.

This bread is sweet enough that you know you're having a pastry but not so sweet that you can't eat an entire loaf without noticing. This would be soooo good in the Monte Cristo (page 239). It would take that salty sweet sandwich to the next level and it makes an amazing French toast. You can also fold toasted sliced almonds in with the blueberries.

One of my happiest moments while writing this book, was taking this bread out of the oven on a Sunday afternoon and sitting around our dining room table with a few friends ripping it apart while it was piping hot. Everyone enjoyed it so much that by the time I thought of getting a knife it was all gone—and that is, hands down, the best way to serve it. Don't slice it, just drop it in the middle of your table and have people rip it apart right from the oven. That's love.

fresh blueberry brioche

MAKES 1 LOAF

1½ cups/225 g fresh blueberries

2 tbsp whole milk

1 tbsp active dry yeast

1 cup + 2 tbsp/140 g all-purpose flour

1 cup + 2 tbsp/140 g bread flour

6½ tbsp/80 g sugar,
plus more for sprinkling

1 tsp kosher salt

3 eggs

1 egg yolk

½ cup + 2 tbsp/140 g unsalted butter,
very soft

1 batch Egg Wash (page 74)

DAY ONE

1. Place the fresh blueberries on a plate and freeze in a single layer. Do not use frozen blueberries, as they are too watery.

2. Slightly warm the milk and pour into the bowl of a stand mixer fitted with the dough hook attachment. Add the yeast and whisk by hand to combine. Add the all-purpose flour, bread flour, 2½ tbsp of the sugar, the salt, eggs, and egg yolk to the bowl. Mix on low speed until the dough comes together, 1 to 2 minutes.

3. Increase the mixer speed to medium-low and work the dough for 6 minutes. Pause every minute to push the dough back down into the bowl and off the hook until it pulls off the sides and looks like a strong bread dough.

4. Reduce the mixer speed to low and slowly add the butter, a little at a time, over the course of 2 minutes. After 1 minute, pause to scrape down the bowl and hook. When the butter begins to blend in, increase the mixer speed to medium-high to fully incorporate the butter and bring the dough back together, 5 to 6 minutes longer.

5. Dump the dough onto a lightly floured work surface and press into a 16-by-10-in/40-by-25-cm rectangle. It does not need to be exact. Position the dough vertically, with a short side nearest you; distribute the blueberries and 2 tbsp of the sugar along the top edge and gently roll down, toward you, into a log.

6. Place the log on a greased sheet pan, wrap in plastic, and refrigerate for at least 1 hour, or preferably overnight.

CONTINUED

7. Grease a 9-by-5-in/23-by-12-cm loaf pan. Reshape the dough one last time by pressing it into an approximate 12-by-6-in/30.5-by-15-cm rectangle and cover with the remaining 2 tbsp of sugar. With the dough positioned vertically, roll down toward you, tightly this time.

8. Place into the greased loaf pan, loosely wrap in plastic, and allow to rise in a warm place until more than doubled in size, about 3 hours.

9. As the brioche nears readiness, preheat your oven to 350°F/180°C. Carefully brush the dough with the egg wash, making sure the egg doesn't pool around the edges. Liberally sprinkle with sugar. Bake until golden, 40 to 45 minutes. Allow to cool for about 15 minutes in the pan. Then transfer to a cooling rack.

This keeps, wrapped well, at room temperature, for up to 3 days, but who are we kidding, it will be lucky to survive 3 minutes out of the oven.

Bagels are definitely one of my comfort foods. I was raised to think that it was not a family gathering unless there were bagels and cream cheese. It always makes me laugh to see that Milo is being raised exactly the same way. He can't walk into his grandmother's house and not get a bagel slathered in cream cheese shoved into his hands before he can say hello. I hesitated for a long while to make bagels because I know how crazy people can get about them, but once we decided to open our pizzeria, Milo & Olive, and knowing that pizza can cause more debate than any other food I know, I thought, screw it, I might as well make bagels, too. So I set out to make bagels and pizza the same way I have always baked; I made them the way I liked them, with my whole heart, and never once read a review.

These bagels are great topped with poppy seeds, sesame seeds, fleur de sel, or anything else, but make sure the toppings are waiting on a plate beside the water when you boil them. As you take the bagels out of the water, dip them into the toppings just before they go into the oven. You'll need to move quickly, so setup is key.

A super-cheesy bagel is another great variation. Just add 1 cup/85 g grated Gruyère, ½ cup/30 g grated Parmesan, 1 cup/85 g grated sharp Cheddar, 2 tsp mustard powder, ¼ tsp cayenne, and an additional 1 tsp salt when you are mixing your bagel dough. I love topping these with grated Cheddar cheese before baking.

Whatever kind of bagel you decide to make, just remember to plan ahead. You must make the poolish the day before you want to make bagels. It is key to the bagel's flavor and texture.

Serve with cream cheese, butter, homemade jam, or your own cured salmon (see page 118).

milo & olive bagels

MAKES 12 BAGELS

POOLISH

¾ cup/180 ml cool water

1 cup/140 g bread flour

¼ tsp active dry yeast

DOUGH

1 cup + 2 tbsp/270 ml cool water

¼ cup/60 ml light beer

1¼ tsp active dry yeast

3 tbsp honey

1 batch poolish (mixed 1 day ahead)

4 cups/550 g bread flour

¾ cup + 1½ tbsp/100 g whole-wheat flour

1 tbsp kosher salt

2 tbsp baking soda

DAY ONE

1. To make the poolish: In a medium bowl, combine the cool water, bread flour, and yeast and stir with a spoon until incorporated. Cover with plastic wrap. Allow to sit at room temperature overnight. In the morning you should find it bubbly and almost doubled in volume.

DAY TWO

2. To make the dough: In the bowl of a stand mixer fitted with the dough hook attachment, whisk the water, beer, and yeast by hand. Add the honey, poolish, bread flour, whole-wheat flour, and salt. Mix on low speed for about 2 minutes, until it comes together in a tight ball. You may need to pause and push the dough down into the bowl while mixing.

3. Increase the mixer speed to medium and work the dough for 3 to 4 minutes. This is a dry dough, so your mixer might get wobbly. Just hold the mixer down and keep at it.

CONTINUED

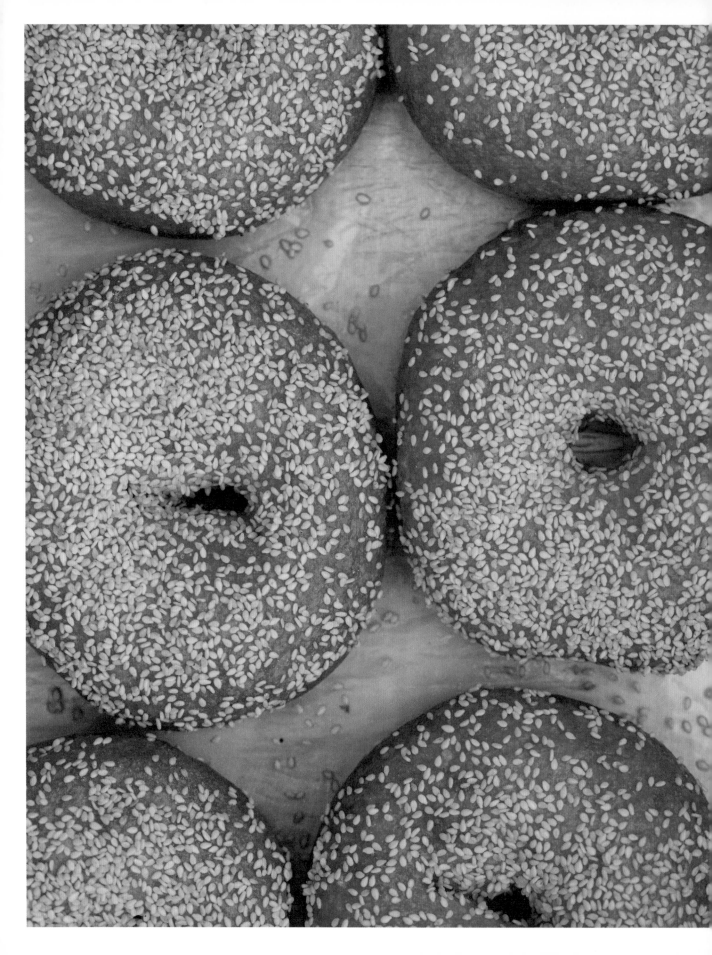

4. Dump the dough onto a clean work surface and knead a little to form a smooth ball. Place in a greased mixing bowl, wrap well with plastic, and allow to rest at room temperature for 1 hour.

5. Drop the dough onto a clean, unfloured surface. Roll it into a log 12 in/30.5 cm long and cut into twelve even 1-in/2.5-cm pieces. Each will weigh about 4 oz/110 g, but feel free to eyeball the size.

6. Shape the bagels by working with one dough ball at a time. First flatten into a disc, then lift an edge and press it into the center. Work your way around the circumference, pressing every edge to the center until you have a ball.

7. Flip the ball over so the pleated side is down and the smooth side is up. Cup the dough in your palm and massage the seam side of the dough firmly against the work surface in a circular motion, allowing the friction to seal the seams. Set aside and cover with plastic wrap or a slightly damp kitchen towel while you shape the rest.

8. Next make the holes by puncturing the centers of the dough balls with your finger and gently expanding the hole until it's about ¾ in/ 2 cm wide.

9. Place the bagels onto two well-greased sheet pans, cover with plastic wrap, and let rise in a warm place until soft, sticky, and slightly puffed, 1 to 1½ hours. (Or, if you would like to make them the next day, allow them to rise for just 20 minutes, refrigerate overnight, and allow to rise the rest of the way in the morning, 1 to 1½ hours.)

10. When you're ready to cook, bring 4 qt/3.8 L water and the baking soda to a boil. Preheat your oven to 425°F/220°C and grease a sheet pan.

11. Gently lift each bagel off the sheet pan with two hands and lower carefully into the boiling water in batches of three or four. Boil, covered, for 2 minutes. Using a slotted spoon, flip and boil, covered, for 2 minutes longer. Be sure your bagels are floating. If your bagel sinks and remains at the bottom of the pot for longer than 45 seconds, it hasn't risen enough. Allow the bagels to continue to rise at room temperature, then try again later.

12. Once boiled, place the bagels on the prepared pan and immediately bake until golden brown, 15 to 20 minutes. Then transfer to a cooling rack.

These are best the day they're made but keep, tightly wrapped, at room temperature, up to 3 days; or frozen, for up to 1 month.

Raisins give these bagels a rustic, homemade look. If you like your bagels a little bit sweeter, after boiling but before baking, dust the tops with cinnamon-sugar using 1 cup/200 g sugar and 2 tsp ground cinnamon. For blueberry bagels, omit the cinnamon and substitute dried blueberries for the raisins.

Remember to plan ahead when making bagels. You must make the poolish the day before you want to make bagels. It is key to the bagel's flavor and texture.

Serve with cream cheese and butter!

cinnamon raisin bagels

MAKES 12 BAGELS

POOLISH

¾ cup/180 ml cool water

1 cup/140 g bread flour

¼ tsp active dry yeast

DOUGH

1½ cups/240 g raisins

1 cup + 6 tbsp/330 ml cool water

1¼ tsp active dry yeast

6 tbsp/130 g honey

1 batch poolish (mixed 1 day ahead)

4 cups/550 g bread flour

¾ cup + 1½ tbsp/100 g whole-wheat flour

1 tbsp cinnamon

1 tbsp kosher salt

1 tbsp baking soda

DAY ONE

1. To make the poolish: In a medium bowl, combine the cool water, bread flour, and yeast and stir with a spoon until incorporated. Cover with plastic wrap. Allow to sit at room temperature overnight. In the morning you should find it bubbly and almost doubled in volume.

DAY TWO

2. Plump the raisins in 3 cups/720 ml warm water for 10 minutes, then strain and finely chop.

3. To make the dough: In the bowl of a stand mixer fitted with the dough hook attachment, whisk the cool water and yeast by hand. Add the honey, poolish, bread flour, whole-wheat flour, cinnamon, and salt. Mix on low speed for about 2 minutes, until it comes together in a tight ball. You may need to pause and push the dough down into the bowl while mixing.

4. Increase the mixer speed to medium and work the dough for 3 to 4 minutes. This is a dry dough, so your mixer might get shaky. Just hold the mixer down and keep at it. At the last minute, add the raisins to the dough and mix until they are distributed.

5. Dump the dough onto a clean work surface and knead a little to form a smooth ball. Place in a greased mixing bowl, wrap well with plastic, and allow to rest at room temperature for 1 hour.

6. Drop the dough onto a clean, unfloured surface. Roll it into a log 12 in/30.5 cm long and cut into twelve even 1-in/2.5-cm pieces. Each will weigh about 4 oz/110 g, but feel free to eyeball the size.

7. Shape the bagels by working with one dough ball at a time. First flatten into a disc, then lift an edge and press it into the center. Work your way around the circumference, pressing every edge to the center until you have a ball.

8. Flip the ball over so the pleated side is down and the smooth side is up. Cup the dough in your palm and massage the seam side of the dough firmly against the work surface in a circular motion, allowing the friction to seal the seams. Set aside and cover with plastic wrap or a slightly damp kitchen towel while you shape the rest.

9. Next make the holes by puncturing the centers of the dough balls with your finger and gently expanding the hole until it's about ¾ in/2 cm wide.

10. Place the bagels onto two well-greased sheet pans, cover with plastic wrap, and let rise in a warm place until soft, sticky, and slightly puffed, 1 to 1½ hours. (Or, if you would like to make them the next day, allow them to rise for just 20 minutes, refrigerate overnight, and allow to rise the rest of the way in the morning.)

11. When you're ready to cook, bring 4 qt/3.5 L water and the baking soda to a boil. Preheat your oven to 425°F/220°C and grease a sheet pan.

12. Gently lift each bagel off the sheet pan with two hands and lower carefully into the boiling water in batches of three or four. Boil, covered, for 2 minutes. Using a slotted spoon, flip and boil, covered, for 2 minutes longer. Be sure your bagels are floating. If your bagel sinks and remains at the bottom of the pot for longer than 45 seconds, it hasn't risen enough. Allow the bagels to continue to rise at room temperature, then try again later.

13. Once boiled, place the bagels on the prepared pan and immediately bake until golden brown, 15 to 20 minutes. Then transfer to a cooling rack.

These are best the day they're made but keep, tightly wrapped, at room temperature, for up to 3 days; or frozen, for up to 1 month.

I am a sucker for all things multigrain. So it's a given that these are the bagels that I make at home if I'm going to take the time to make bagels. The honey in this recipe is the perfect balance to all the grains. I occasionally like to dip these in caraway seeds and sprinkle them with fleur de sel after boiling, just before I bake them. The caraway tastes delicious and works really well with the rest of the ingredients.

Remember to always plan ahead when making bagels. You must make the poolish the day before you want to make bagels. It is key to the bagel's flavor and texture. Serve with cream cheese, butter, homemade jam, or your own cured salmon (see page 118).

honey multigrain bagels

MAKES 12 BAGELS

POOLISH

¾ cup/180 ml cool water

¾ cup/100 g bread flour

¼ cup/25 g rye flour

¼ tsp active dry yeast

DOUGH

1¼ cups/300 ml cool water

1 tsp active dry yeast

6 tbsp/130 g honey

1 batch poolish (mixed 1 day ahead)

2⅓ cups/320 g bread flour

¾ cup/75 g rye flour

1¼ cups/150 g whole-wheat flour

¾ cup/120 g cornmeal

¼ cup/50 g wheat germ, toasted

1 tbsp + 1 tsp kosher salt

2½ tbsp flax seeds

3 tbsp chia seeds or poppy seeds

2 tbsp baking soda

DAY ONE

1. To make the poolish: In a medium bowl, combine the cool water, bread flour, rye flour, and yeast and stir with a spoon until incorporated. Cover with plastic wrap. Allow to sit at room temperature overnight. In the morning you should find it bubbly and almost doubled in volume.

DAY TWO

2. To make the dough: In the bowl of a stand mixer fitted with the dough hook attachment, whisk the cool water and yeast by hand. Add the honey, poolish, bread flour, rye flour, whole-wheat flour, cornmeal, wheat germ, salt, flax seeds, and chia seeds. Mix on low speed for about 2 minutes, until it comes together in a tight ball. You may need to pause and push the dough down into the bowl while mixing.

3. Increase the mixer speed to medium and work the dough for 3 to 4 minutes. This is a dry dough, so your mixer might get a little shaky. Just hold the mixer down and keep at it.

4. Dump the dough onto a clean work surface and knead a little to form a smooth ball. Place in a greased mixing bowl, wrap well with plastic, and allow to rest at room temperature for 1 hour.

5. Drop the dough onto a clean, unfloured surface. Roll it into a log 12 in/30.5 cm long and cut into twelve even 1-in/2.5-cm pieces. Each will weigh about 4 oz/110 g, but feel free to eyeball the size.

6. Shape the bagels by working with one dough ball at a time. First flatten into a disc, then lift an edge and press it into the center. Work your way around the circumference, pressing every edge to the center until you have a ball.

7. Flip the ball over so the pleated side is down and the smooth side is up. Cup the dough in your palm and massage the seam side of the dough firmly against the work surface in a circular motion, allowing the friction to seal the seams. Set aside and cover with plastic wrap or a slightly damp kitchen towel while you shape the rest.

8. Next make the holes by puncturing the centers of the dough balls with your finger and gently expanding the hole until it's about ¾ in/2 cm wide.

9. Place the bagels onto two well-greased sheet pans, cover with plastic wrap, and let rise in a warm place until soft, sticky, and slightly puffed, 1 to 1½ hours. (Or, if you would like to make them the next day, allow them to rise for just 20 minutes, refrigerate overnight, and allow to rise the rest of the way in the morning, 1 to 2½ hours.)

10. When ready to cook, bring 4 qt/3.5 L water and the baking soda to a boil. Preheat your oven to 425°F/220°C and grease a sheet pan.

11. Gently lift each bagel off the sheet pan with two hands and lower carefully into boiling water in batches of three or four. Boil, covered, for 2 minutes. Using a slotted spoon, flip and boil, covered, for 2 minutes longer. Be sure your bagels are floating. If your bagel sinks and remains at the bottom of the pot for longer than 45 seconds, it hasn't risen enough. Allow the bagels to continue to rise at room temperature, then try again later.

12. Once boiled, place the bagels on the prepared pan and immediately bake until golden brown, 15 to 20 minutes. Then transfer to a cooling rack.

These are best the day they're made but keep, tightly wrapped, at room temperature, up to 3 days; or frozen, for up to 1 month.

This is all about simplicity, so you must use the best salmon and serve it with the most delicious tomatoes, a great finishing salt, and anything else that is fresh and wonderful at your farmers' market, such as thinly sliced radishes or fennel. And of course the very best bagels. If you're going to cure your own salmon, you may as well make your own bagels, too. Just call in sick Friday and do it.

   This is another recipe that has a lot of room for play. You can change up the zest (just don't omit) and the spices or herbs, but be sure to keep the salt and sugar the same.

cured salmon platter

SERVES 8 TO 10

Zest of 1 lemon

Zest of 1 orange

Zest of 1 lime

1 tbsp fennel seeds

1 tbsp coriander seeds

2 tbsp whole black peppercorns

1 cup/230 g kosher salt

6 tbsp/75 g sugar

1 tbsp chopped fresh dill

2 lb/1 kg best-quality fresh salmon, not frozen or previously frozen

FIXIN'S

4 ripe tomatoes, sliced

1 cucumber, thinly sliced

1 red onion, thinly sliced, or 1 cup pickled red onion

⅓ cup/50 g capers in brine, drained

4 lemons, quartered

2 cups/450 g cream cheese

¼ cup/15 g tarragon and/or parsley

Bagels or toast for serving

1. Toss together by hand the lemon, orange, and lime zests; fennel seeds; coriander seeds; peppercorns; salt; sugar; and dill.

2. Spread out a 24-in/61-cm sheet of plastic wrap. Place half of the cure in the center and shape it into an even bed, about the size of the salmon. Lay the salmon on top of the cure and spread the remaining cure on top, coating the sides well. Wrap the salmon tightly in the plastic and wrap again with two more sheets of plastic. You do not want any leakage.

3. Transfer the salmon to a plate. Place another plate on top and weigh it down with a few cans of beer or cans of tomatoes. It's important to weigh it down evenly. Allow it to cure, refrigerated, for 48 hours.

4. Once cured, the salmon should be much firmer and darker in color. Discard the plastic and wash the salmon thoroughly to remove the salt. Pat dry. Refrigerate, tightly wrapped, until serving.

5. To serve, slice as thinly as humanly possible on an angle, perpendicular to the grain. Arrange the sliced salmon on a plate. Create another plate with generous piles of all your fixin's, and serve with bagels.

This keeps well, tightly wrapped, refrigerated, for up to 2 weeks.

flaky dough and its many uses

The savory cooks enter the kitchen and now the battle for space begins. Norberto, a wonderful cook, father, and all-around human being who's been with me since the day we opened, comes in and his normally calm demeanor is rattled because someone has moved his pans—and boy does he hate it when anything is not in the place he left it. Ismael walks in next with his signature Dodgers hat and immediately begins asking the girls about when he can get his sheet pans of bacon in the oven so that he can be ready for service right at 8 A.M. Selvin, our killer dishwasher, is clearing the monster crash pit of dishes that have been left for him all the while checking in orders from our vendors, and I'm in the middle trying to time the bake-off while also trying to get everyone to work together and not kill one another before we even open.

This is our prime time, opening will be here before we know it, and we're beginning to move frantically when we hear a pounding at the front door. I ask Selvin, in my broken kitchen Spanish, to take the delivery, but it's not one of our regular vendors, it's P.Y. Pudwill of Pudwill Berry Farms in Nipomo, and she's irritated because I asked her to specially deliver her berries to our door on the way to the Santa Monica Farmers' Market and now she's been standing outside on her busy morning waiting for someone to answer.

"Sorry, P.Y.," I say as I run up to give her a hug and she gives me that half-smirking frown of hers. "The music was so loud, and we're running around . . ."

I yell to Laurel to pull some mixed berry crostatas out of the oven and put them in a box for P.Y. so she can see where her amazing berries are going, and hopefully she'll deliver again next week. P.Y. and two of her guys lug in fifteen flats and she looks over at me and says, "Ugh, so you need the same on Wednesday?" I smile, "Thank you, I'm so sorry. I promise next time I will turn the music down and hear you!" Next week the music will be loud again because that's what keeps us up and P.Y. will be annoyed, but she'll keep delivering because she knows how much I love her and her berries and she can see that they are ending up in the right place.

We give P.Y. and her team the box of warm crostatas and she gives me a big smile and a maternal squeeze. I bring in the berries and Laurel shows me a couple of crostatas that lost their shape while baking. We smile at each other and she pulls the misshapen ones aside and puts them on a plate. Breakfast for me and my girls after we get everything baked off and the front set up.

We use this incredibly versatile dough at Huckleberry for an insane number of different things. It's that versatile. We use it for our Thanksgiving pies, crostatas, quiches, chicken potpies, anything really.

When you settle in to make flaky dough, just commit to making three batches. You'll get into a rhythm and your food processor is going to get dirty anyway. All the recipes in this chapter are a cinch if you have the dough ready, and this batch of dough fits all the recipes in this book. It will keep in your freezer for up to 1 month. Just be sure to double-wrap tightly in plastic.

You can absolutely make this dough by hand, but it's a bit faster in a food processor. You'll find that our dough has less water and more butter than most. Big surprise. It may feel as though it's not nearly enough water, but don't add more; with faith, a little patience, and some elbow grease it will come together.

everyday flaky dough

MAKES 1 BATCH

2 cups/250 g all-purpose flour

¼ cup/50 g sugar

½ tsp baking powder

¾ tsp kosher salt

1 cup/220 g cold unsalted butter, cubed

¼ cup/60 ml water

1. To mix with a food processor, pulse the flour, sugar, baking powder, and salt once to blend. Add the butter to the work bowl and pulse about three times until pea-size pieces form. Pour the water over the flour mixture and pulse another three times until the dough is only just starting to come together.

   To mix by hand, combine the flour, sugar, baking powder, and salt in a very large bowl. Stir to blend. Add the butter, working it between your fingertips until the pieces are pea- and lima bean–size. Add the water and lightly toss to distribute.

2. The dough should be shaggy, dry, and clumpy. Dump it onto a clean work surface to bring the dough together by hand. (Do not flour the counter, as you do not want to add any more flour to the dough.)

3. Begin by firmly pressing the entire surface of the dough with the heel of your palm. Toss and squeeze the dough to redistribute the wet and dry patches. Repeat, pressing thoroughly again with the heel of your palm, and continue pressing, tossing, and squeezing until the dough begins to hold together. But be sure not to overwork the dough! It should stay together but you should still see pea-size bits of butter running through.

4. Press the dough into a disc ¾ in/2 cm thick, wrap tightly in plastic, and refrigerate for at least 1 hour, or freeze for up to 1 month.

5. When you're ready to use the dough, if refrigerated for longer than 1 hour, allow the dough to warm up at room temperature for a few minutes. If frozen, thaw in the refrigerator overnight before shaping. The dough should feel cold to the touch but malleable. Never allow the dough to become too soft or warm. Chill as needed while working.

If you find yourself with oozingly sweet, overripe fruit on your countertop, make something with this dough. The earthy, whole-wheat flour will balance the sweetness of the fruit. If you want to experiment with different flours, try a little rye, buckwheat, or oat flour for all or a portion of the whole-wheat flour.

whole-wheat flaky dough

MAKES 1 BATCH

1 cup/130 g whole-wheat flour

¾ cup/100 g all-purpose flour

2 tbsp + 2 tsp sugar

1 tsp baking powder

1 tsp kosher salt

1 tsp brown sugar

1 cup/220 g cold unsalted butter, cubed

¼ cup/60 ml ice water

1. To mix with a food processor, pulse the whole-wheat flour, all-purpose flour, sugar, baking powder, salt, and brown sugar once to blend. Add the butter to the work bowl and pulse about three times until pea-size pieces form. Pour the water over the flour mixture and pulse another three times until the dough is only just starting to come together.

   To mix by hand, combine the whole-wheat flour, all-purpose flour, sugar, baking powder, salt, and brown sugar in a very large bowl. Stir to blend. Add the butter, working it between your fingertips until the pieces are pea- and lima bean–size. Add the water and lightly toss to distribute.

2. The dough should be shaggy, dry, and clumpy. Dump it onto a clean work surface to bring the dough together by hand. (Do not flour the counter, as you do not want to add any more flour to the dough.)

3. Begin by firmly pressing the entire surface of the dough with the heel of your palm. Toss and squeeze the dough to redistribute the wet and dry patches. Repeat, pressing thoroughly again with the heel of your palm, and continue pressing, tossing, and squeezing until the dough begins to hold together. But be sure not to overwork the dough! It should stay together but you should still see pea-size bits of butter running through it.

4. Press the dough into a disc ¾ in/2 cm thick, wrap tightly in plastic, and refrigerate for at least 1 hour, or freeze for up to 1 month.

5. When you're ready to use the dough, if refrigerated for longer than 1 hour, allow the dough to warm up at room temperature for a few minutes. If frozen, thaw in the refrigerator overnight before shaping. The dough should feel cold to the touch but malleable. Never allow the dough to become too soft or warm. Chill as needed while working.

This is a recipe you should play with. Throw a bunch of finely chopped herbs into it, switch up the cheeses, or add chile flakes, cayenne, or black pepper. But whatever you do, don't skimp on the fatty cheesiness.

This dough works well for any savory thing, from crostatas to quiches, or it might even be awesome for an apple pie. If you have leftover dough, you can make delicious little cocktail crackers. Just cut with a small cookie cutter, brush with Egg Wash (page 74), and sprinkle with additional cheese, fleur de sel, and black pepper and bake at 350°F/180°C until golden.

savory flaky dough

MAKES 1 BATCH

1½ cups/200 g all-purpose flour

⅓ cup/35 g rye flour

¼ cup/30 g whole-wheat flour

3 tbsp sugar

1 tbsp cornmeal

1 tsp baking powder

1 tsp kosher salt

2 tbsp grated Parmesan

2 tbsp grated Gruyère

1 cup/220 g cold unsalted butter, cubed

2 tbsp crème fraîche

¼ cup/60 ml ice water

1. To mix with a food processor, pulse the all-purpose flour, rye flour, whole-wheat flour, sugar, cornmeal, baking powder, salt, Parmesan, and Gruyère once to blend. Add the butter and crème fraîche to the work bowl and pulse about three times until pea-size pieces form. Pour the water over the flour mixture and pulse another three times until the dough is only just starting to come together.

   To mix by hand, combine the all-purpose flour, rye flour, whole-wheat flour, sugar, cornmeal, baking powder, salt, Parmesan, and Gruyère in a very large bowl. Stir to blend. Add the butter and crème fraîche, working it between your fingertips until the pieces are pea- and lima bean–size. Add the water and lightly toss to distribute.

2. The dough should be shaggy, dry, and clumpy. Dump it onto a clean work surface to bring the dough together by hand. (Do not flour the counter, as you do not want to add any more flour to the dough.)

3. Begin by firmly pressing the entire surface of the dough with the heel of your palm. Toss and squeeze the dough to redistribute the wet and dry patches. Repeat, pressing thoroughly again with the heel of your palm, and continue pressing, tossing, and squeezing until it begins to hold together. But be sure not to overwork the dough! It should stay together but you should still see pea-size bits of butter running through it.

4. Press the dough into a disc ¾ in/2 cm thick, wrap tightly in plastic, and refrigerate for at least 1 hour, or freeze for up to 1 month.

5. When you're ready to use the dough, if refrigerated for longer than 1 hour, allow the dough to warm up at room temperature for a few minutes. If frozen, thaw in the refrigerator overnight before shaping. The dough should feel cold to the touch but malleable. Never allow the dough to become too soft or warm. Chill as needed while working.

This quiche is the quintessential summer brunch food. The rich corn filling tastes almost like creamed corn, and the colors are beautiful together. Be sure to let the spinach and tomatoes poke up through the filling to give it height and excitement.

This would be delicious served with a large salad and some thinly sliced salami or roasted sausages.

corn, spinach, and cherry tomato quiche

SERVES 8 TO 10

1 batch Everyday Flaky Dough (page 122)

4 tbsp/60 ml extra-virgin olive oil

1¼ cups/190 g fresh corn kernels (from 2 cobs)

4 sprigs fresh thyme

1½ tsp kosher salt

1 garlic clove

2 cups/360 g whole cherry tomatoes

1 pinch chile flakes

3 large eggs

¾ cup + 2 tbsp/210 ml crème fraiche

¾ cup + 2 tbsp/210 ml heavy cream

¾ tsp freshly ground black pepper

½ cup/15 g spinach leaves

2 to 3 tbsp grated Gruyere or Parmesan

1. Allow the flaky dough to soften at room temperature for 10 to 20 minutes, depending on the temperature of your house, before rolling. The dough should be cold but malleable.

2. On a lightly floured surface, roll out the dough to a 15-in/38-cm square.Gently transfer the dough to a greased tart pan, allowing the edges to drape over the sides. Gently press the dough into the pan without stretching it. Get it into the bottom corners, against the sides, and into every crevice. Then, trim any excess dough by raking it off with the back of a butter knife. Gently press your fingertips into the sides of the pan in order to push the dough slightly above the pan's edges by about ¼ in/6 mm. (This will make up for. the inevitable shrinking when the shell bakes.)

3. Freeze for at least 1 hour, or up to 1 month, tightly wrapped.

4. Preheat your oven to 350°F/180°C.

5. Line the inside of the frozen shell with parchment paper and fill with pie weights. Bake from frozen for about 35 minutes, until the outer rim is starting to brown. Then, carefully remove the parchment and pie weights, return the shell to the oven, and continue baking until the whole shell is a nicely browned, 15 to 20 minutes longer. Let it get a little darker than you think it should!

6. Meanwhile, heat 2 tbsp of the olive oil in a medium sauté pan over medium-high heat. Add the corn, 2 sprigs thyme, and ¼ tsp salt and sauté for 1 to 2 minutes. Remove the thyme stems, transfer the mixture to a plate, and set aside.

7. In the same pan, add the remaining 2 tbsp olive oil, then sauté the garlic for about 1 minute, until it is very aromatic. Add the cherry tomatoes, remaining sprigs of thyme, ½ tsp salt, and the chile flakes. Raise the heat to high and cook, covered, for 3 minutes, until the tomatoes burst. Remove the lid and continue cooking to thicken for another 3 to 4 minutes. Don't stir too often because you don't want the tomatoes to break down into a sauce. Remove the thyme, transfer the tomatoes to a plate, and set aside.

8. When your shell has finished baking, increase the oven temperature to 450°F/230°C.

9. Whisk the eggs, crème fraiche, cream, remaining ¾ tsp salt, and the pepper together in a medium bowl.

10. Sprinkle the cooked corn evenly all over the bottom of the cooked shell (still in its pan). Top with the cooked tomatoes, then the raw spinach. Re-whisk the egg mixture to make sure it hasn't settled and pour it over the top. Do not allow it to spill over the edges. Top with the grated Gruyère. Allow some of the vegetables to poke out the top for a beautiful, rustic appearance.

11. Bake for about 25 minutes, or until still soft, yet set and golden brown. Serve warm or at room temperature.

This keeps well, refrigerated, for up to 3 days.

These are beautifully simple ripe summer peaches on squares of whole-wheat flaky dough. They're wonderful to throw together if you're tight on time. Great for breakfast with Whipped Cream (page 149) or for dessert hot out of the oven with vanilla ice cream. Apricots work just as well as peaches if you prefer. Another twist is to top these with a whole-wheat oat crumble (see page 152) before they go into the oven.

peach squares

MAKES 10 TO 12 SQUARES

1 batch Whole-Wheat Flaky Dough (page 124)

5 or 6 ripe peaches, halved, skin on

¼ cup/50 g granulated sugar, plus more for sprinkling

¼ cup/55 g brown sugar

6 tbsp/85 g unsalted butter, melted

¼ tsp kosher salt

1 batch Egg Wash (page 74)

1. Allow the flaky dough to soften at room temperature for 10 to 20 minutes, depending on the temperature of your house, before rolling. The dough should be cold but malleable.

2. On a lightly floured surface, roll the dough to a 14-in/35.5-cm square, and about an even ⅛ in/3 mm thick. Trim the edges to make them even and slice nine 4-in/10-cm squares (that's three squares down and three across). Transfer them, evenly spaced, to two greased sheet pans. Press any scraps together and re-roll. You should get at least one more square. If you're feeling especially efficient, you might get another three.

3. In a bowl, toss the halved peaches, granulated sugar, brown sugar, melted butter, and salt until well coated.

4. Brush each square with egg wash and place a peach half, cut-side up, on each square. Sprinkle any exposed dough with a little granulated sugar and freeze for 25 minutes.

5. Preheat your oven to 350°F/180°C. Bake from frozen until a deep golden brown, about 35 minutes. Don't be afraid of good color. Trust us: Deep golden brown is what you want! Transfer to a cooling rack to keep crisp.

These are best the day they're made but keep, tightly wrapped, at room temperature for up to 2 days.

This is the closest we come to making a toaster pastry at Huckleberry, but don't try to drop these in a toaster. The dough is super-flaky and it will shatter. You can always add more or less cinnamon or a whole mess of pie spices to the filling if you're in that sort of a mood.

apple cinnamon hand pies

SERVES 10 TO 12

1 batch Whole-Wheat Flaky Dough (page 124)

1 batch Egg Wash (page 74)

1 batch Vanilla Apple Butter (page 132) with 1 cinnamon stick added during cooking; cooled completely

⅓ cup/65 g sugar

1 tsp ground cinnamon

1. Allow the flaky dough to soften at room temperature for 10 to 20 minutes, depending on the temperature of your house, before rolling. The dough should be cold but malleable.

2. On a lightly floured surface, roll the dough to a 14-in/35.5-cm square, and about an even ⅛ in/3 mm thick. Trim the edges to make them even and slice nine 4-in/10-cm squares (that's three squares down and three across). Transfer them, evenly spaced, to two greased sheet pans. Press any scraps together and re-roll. You should get at least one more square. If you're feeling especially efficient, you might get another three.

3. Brush the squares with egg wash and spoon 3 tbsp apple butter, two-thirds of the way down the center of each square. Fold the dough in half over the filling. Lightly press a fork into the edges to seal, but do not puncture the dough. A little apple butter might ooze out, but that's okay. With a very sharp knife, slice a ½-in/12-mm X into the top of each square. Be sure to cut all the way through the top layer, but not through the bottom. Freeze completely for about 1 hour, or up to 1 month, tightly wrapped.

4. Preheat your oven to 350°F/180°C. Stir together the sugar and cinnamon in a small bowl. Brush each pie with egg wash and sprinkle liberally with cinnamon-sugar. Bake from frozen for 35 to 40 minutes, or until deeply browned. Transfer to a cooling rack to keep crisp.

These are best the day they're made but keep, tightly wrapped, at room temperature, for up to 2 days.

This is a great base recipe that can be adapted in many ways. Try swapping out a cinnamon stick for the vanilla, or add ½ tsp ground cinnamon, ¼ tsp ginger, ¼ tsp nutmeg, and ¼ tsp cloves. It also works well with pears or peeled quince in place of the apples.

vanilla apple butter

MAKES 1½ CUPS/480 G

8 apples, anything but Fuji
2 cups/480 ml water
6 tbsp/75 g sugar
½ tsp kosher salt
1 vanilla bean
Juice of 1 lemon

1. Preheat your oven to 350°F/180°C. Peel, core, and cut the apples into eighths.

2. Combine the apples, water, sugar, salt, vanilla bean, and lemon juice in an ovenproof sauté pan and cook over medium-high heat, covered, until the apples are very soft, about 15 minutes.

3. Transfer the apple mixture to a food processor or a blender and process until very smooth. Pour the mixture back into the same pan and bake, stirring every 10 minutes or so to prevent the bottom from burning, until it browns and thickens, about 1 hour. Refrigerate until needed.

Keeps well, refrigerated, for up to 2 weeks.

We recently made these galettes in front of a small audience at our local farmers' market. A few weeks later, a tiny elderly woman approached us in the bakery with a berry-stained copy of the recipe in hand. She peppered us with questions about the process and told us all about the way hers turned out at home. The very last thing she asked us was where to buy mini strawberries. Which made us giggle for days. Just to be clear, the galettes are mini, not the berries.

If for some reason your berries are not as sweet as you would like, you can always add a bit more sugar. Color is important here; these galettes are so simple that the color becomes an ingredient. Bake until the dough is a deep brown and the flavor will really pop.

mini strawberry galettes

SERVES 10 TO 12

1 batch Everyday Flaky Dough (page 122)

4 tbsp/55 g unsalted butter

3 cups/460 g halved strawberries

2 tbsp brown sugar

2 tbsp granulated sugar, plus more for sprinkling

¼ tsp kosher salt

1 batch Egg Wash (page 74)

Powdered sugar for dusting (optional)

1. Allow the flaky dough to soften at room temperature for 10 to 20 minutes, depending on the temperature of your house, before rolling. The dough should be cold but malleable.

2. Melt the butter and toss with the strawberries. Set aside.

3. In a separate bowl combine the brown sugar, granulated sugar, and salt. Set aside.

4. On a lightly floured surface, roll the dough to a 14-in/35.5-cm square, and about an even ⅛ in/3 mm thick. Trim the edges to make them even and slice into nine 4-in/10-cm squares (that's three squares down and three across). Transfer them, evenly spaced, to two greased sheet pans. Press any scraps together and re-roll. You should get at least one more square. If you're feeling especially efficient, you might get another three.

5. Toss the sugar mixture with the strawberry mixture. Evenly pile the strawberry filling into the center of each square, leaving a 1-in/2.5-cm border all around. Lightly brush the border with egg wash. Fold the border over the filling like a picture frame. Press the corners to seal. Freeze for at least 20 minutes, or up to 1 month, tightly wrapped.

6. Preheat your oven to 375°F/190°C. When ready to bake, brush the crust with egg wash, sprinkle with sugar, and bake from frozen until *deep* golden brown, 30 to 35 minutes. Transfer to a cooling rack to keep crisp. Dust with powdered sugar if you're so moved.

These are best the day they're made but keep, tightly wrapped, at room temperature, for up to 2 days.

This tart is also really delicious with blood oranges, Meyer lemon, or any citrus you find at your farmers' market. When I'm not in the mood for grapefruit, I particularly like it with Cara Cara oranges, because they have the sweetness of an orange and the wonderful acidity of a grapefruit. If you have a nut allergy, feel free to omit the almonds; they are totally not necessary, but their crispy fattiness cuts through the sweet-and-sourness of the tart beautifully.

grapefruit galette

SERVES 8 TO 10

6 grapefruits

1 batch Everyday Flaky Dough (page 122)

1 batch Pastry Cream (page 148)

5 tbsp/75 g sugar

1 pinch kosher salt

1 batch Egg Wash (page 74)

2 tbsp sliced almonds, toasted (optional)

1. First, segment the grapefruits with a paring knife. Trim the skin and pith away from the fruit inside by cutting off the top and bottom until the fruit is exposed. Then follow the curve of the fruit, shaving off all the white pith, leaving just the fruit behind. Now, carefully hold the fruit in your palm and cut along the natural lines between the segments to remove the membrane from the flesh. Set the segments aside.

2. Meanwhile, allow the flaky dough to soften at room temperature for 10 to 20 minutes, depending on the temperature of your house, before rolling. The dough should be cold but malleable.

3. Grease a sheet pan. On a lightly floured surface, roll the dough to a 13-by-15 in/33-by-38 cm rectangle, about an even ⅓ in/3 mm thick. Trim the edges to make them even and transfer to the prepared pan.

4. Spread the pastry cream on the dough, leaving a 3-in/7.5-cm border. Arrange the grapefruit over the pastry cream in even rows of slightly overlapping slices. Sprinkle the fruit with 3 tbsp of the sugar and the salt.

5. Brush the exposed dough with egg wash and fold it over the filling, pressing the corners to seal. The dough should only partially cover the filling and you should have a nice rectangular galette. Brush the crust with egg wash and sprinkle with the remaining 2 tbsp sugar. Freeze for 25 minutes, or up to 1 month, tightly wrapped.

6. Preheat your oven to 375°F/190°C. Bake from frozen until the crust is very, very dark brown and the grapefruit is beginning to burn slightly in a few spots, about 1 hour. Allow to cool on the sheet pan. Sprinkle with the almonds, if desired, and transfer to a serving platter or slice and serve right from the pan at room temperature.

This is best the day it's made but keeps, tightly wrapped, refrigerated, for up to 2 days.

This is one of my favorite things in this chapter because I love the subtle sweet flavor of poached quince mixed with the sour saltiness of the goat cheese. It's one of those perfect sweet and savory pastries.

Consider saving the quince poaching liquid for a red wine punch: Mix with a very light but fruity red wine like a Bourgogne Rouge, add orange slices and 6 cinnamon sticks, then refrigerate for 3 hours. Serve by topping each glass with a little Prosecco. Or you can always mix little spoonfuls of poaching liquid into plain yogurt or your afternoon tea. It's also amazing used as a glaze on muffins and cakes.

quince and goat cheese galette

SERVES 8

10 cups/2.4 L water

4 cups/800 g sugar, plus more for sprinkling

1 vanilla bean, split and scraped

1 pinch salt

4 quince, peeled

1 batch Everyday Flaky Dough (page 122)

1 cup/220 g goat cheese

2 tbsp crème fraîche

1 batch Egg Wash (page 74)

2 tbsp unsalted butter

1. Bring the water, sugar, vanilla bean, and salt to a simmer in a pot over high heat, whisking until the sugar dissolves. Reduce the heat to low, add the quince, cover, and simmer until the quince are fork-tender but not falling apart, about 50 minutes. Refrigerate until cooled completely.

2. Meanwhile, allow the flaky dough to soften at room temperature for 10 to 20 minutes, depending on the temperature of your house, before rolling. The dough should be cold but malleable.

3. In a small bowl, stir together the goat cheese and crème fraîche. Set aside.

4. Core and slice the quince into slices ¼ in/6 mm thick. Set aside. Reserve the poaching liquid.

5. On a lightly floured surface, roll the dough to a 13-by-15 in/ 33-by-38 cm rectangle about an even ⅛ in/3 mm thick. Trim the edges to make them even and transfer to a baking sheet.

6. Spread the goat cheese mixture in the center of the dough, leaving a 3-in/7.5-cm border all around the edge.

7. With a paper towel, lightly dry the quince and position the quince over the goat cheese mixture in even rows of overlapping slices. Brush the exposed dough with egg wash and fold it over the filling, pressing the corners to seal. The dough should only partially cover the filling and you should have a nice rectangular galette. Brush the top of the dough with egg wash and sprinkle with sugar. Dot the exposed quince with the butter. Freeze for 25 minutes, or up to 1 month, tightly wrapped.

8. Preheat your oven to 375°F/190°C. Bake from frozen for about 1 hour, or until deep golden brown. Don't be afraid of good color. Trust us. Immediately brush the dough and the exposed fruit with the quince poaching liquid. Allow to cool on the sheet pan before transferring to a serving platter. Serve at room temperature.

This is best the day it's made but keeps, tightly wrapped, at room temperature, for up to 1 day.

I think there is nothing more satisfying and beautiful than a savory galette. It's delicious with a sunny-side-up egg on the side, it's good with sausage instead of bacon, and it's great with sautéed fresh corn inside during the summer months.

Be sure to bake this to a very deep, dark brown, which allows the crust and filling to become incredibly caramelized and flavorful.

onion, potato, and bacon galette

SERVES 8

6 slices thick-cut bacon

3 cups/455 g medium diced fingerling potatoes

6 tbsp/90 ml extra-virgin olive oil

1 tsp chopped fresh rosemary

2½ tsp kosher salt

4 yellow onions, sliced

1 tsp chopped fresh thyme

1 bay leaf

¼ tsp freshly ground black pepper

1 batch Savory Flaky Dough (page 125)

¼ cup/60 ml crème fraîche

1 batch Egg Wash (page 74)

Sugar for sprinkling

Fleur de sel for sprinkling

2 to 3 tbsp grated Parmesan or Gruyère

1. Preheat your oven to 425°F/220°C.

2. Spread the bacon on a sheet pan and roast for 10 minutes. When cooled, chop the bacon and set aside in a medium bowl.

3. Toss the potatoes with 4 tbsp/60 ml of the olive oil, the rosemary, and 2 tsp of the salt. Spread out on a sheet pan and roast until browned, about 35 minutes.

4. Meanwhile, in a large sauté pan, combine the onions, thyme, bay leaf, the remaining 2 tbsp olive oil, the remaining ½ tsp salt, and the black pepper and cook over medium-high heat for about 10 minutes or until the onions are very deeply browned but not mushy. Stir often to avoid burning.

5. Combine the sautéed onions and chopped bacon with the potatoes. Toss together and refrigerate until cooled completely.

6. Meanwhile, allow the flaky dough to soften at room temperature for 10 to 20 minutes, depending on the temperature of your house, before rolling. The dough should be cold but malleable.

7. On a lightly floured surface, roll the dough to a 13-by-15 in/ 33-by-38 cm rectangle, about an even ⅛ in/3 mm thick. Trim the edges to make them even and transfer to a greased sheet pan.

8. Spread the crème fraîche on the dough, leaving a 2½-in/6-cm border around the edge. Evenly distribute the bacon, potato, and onion mixture on top of the crème fraîche. Brush the exposed 2½-in/6-cm border of dough with egg wash and fold it over the filling, pressing to seal the corners.

9. Now brush the top of the dough with egg wash and sprinkle with a little sugar and a little fleur de sel. Then sprinkle the entire pastry with the grated Parmesan. Freeze for at least 20 minutes, or up to 1 month, tightly wrapped.

10. Preheat your oven to 425°F/220°C. Bake from frozen until the crust and cheese are golden brown, about 45 minutes. Serve warm or at room temperature.

This is best the day it's made but keeps, tightly wrapped, in the refrigerator, for up to 1 day.

Don't be jealous, but in California we have good cherry tomatoes until just before Thanksgiving. There's a sweet spot around late September when summery produce, like tomatoes, and fall produce, like leeks, overlap. And during this time I love making this crostata. It's a wonderful combination of salty-sweet. Just be sure to cook the filling down so it's nice and thick and not a big watery mess, which will cause the crostata to fall apart.

tomato leek cornmeal crostata

SERVES 8

CRUST

1½ cups/200 g all-purpose flour

½ cup/80 g cornmeal

¼ cup/100 g sugar

½ tsp baking powder

¾ tsp kosher salt

1 cup/220 g cold unsalted butter, cubed

¼ cup/60 ml ice water

FILLING

4 tbsp/60 ml extra-virgin olive oil

2 cups/455 g large chopped leeks, white and green parts only

1 bay leaf

1 tsp kosher salt

1 pinch freshly ground black pepper

1 garlic clove

4 cups/720 g cherry tomatoes

2 or 3 sprigs fresh thyme

1 pinch chile flakes

1 batch Egg Wash (page 74)
Fleur de sel for sprinkling

1. To make the crust: To mix with a food processor, pulse the flour, cornmeal, sugar, baking powder, and salt once to blend. Add the butter to the work bowl and pulse about three times until pea-size pieces form. Pour the water over the flour mixture and pulse another three times until the dough is only just starting to come together.

   To mix by hand, combine the flour, cornmeal, sugar, baking powder, and salt in a very large bowl. Stir to blend. Add the butter, working it between your fingertips until the pieces are pea- and lima bean-size. Add the water and lightly toss to distribute.

2. The dough should be shaggy, dry, and clumpy. Dump it onto a clean work surface to bring the dough together by hand. (Do not flour the counter, as you do not want to add any more flour to the dough.)

3. Begin by firmly pressing the entire surface of the dough with the heel of your palm. Toss and squeeze the dough to redistribute the wet and dry patches. Repeat, pressing thoroughly again with the heel of your palm, and continue pressing, tossing, and squeezing until it begins to hold together. But be sure not to overwork the dough! It should stay together but you should still see pea-size bits of butter running through it.

4. Press the dough into a disc ¾ in/2 cm thick, wrap tightly in plastic, and refrigerate for at least 30 minutes, or freeze for up to 1 month. If frozen, thaw in the refrigerator overnight before using.

5. Meanwhile, to make the filling: Heat 2 tbsp of the olive oil in a medium sauté pan over high heat. Add the leeks, bay leaf, ½ tsp of the salt, and the black pepper and cook, covered, for 2 minutes, stirring occasionally. Uncover, lower the heat to medium, and continue cooking, stirring occasionally, for 2 to 3 minutes longer, until the leeks are nice and soft with a little bit of color. Transfer to a bowl and set aside.

6. In the same pan, sauté the garlic in the remaining 2 tbsp olive oil for about 1 minute until it is very aromatic. Then add the cherry tomatoes, thyme sprigs, remaining ½ tsp salt, and chile flakes. Sauté over high heat for 3 minutes, covered, until the tomatoes burst. Remove the lid and allow the tomatoes to cook down and thicken for 3 to 4 minutes longer.

7. Add the cooked leeks to the tomatoes and continue cooking until thickened, 1 to 2 minutes. Don't stir too often; you don't want the tomatoes to break down into a sauce, you want them whole. Transfer to a plate, remove the thyme, and refrigerate until cooled completely.

8. When the filling has cooled, shape the dough. Be prepared to work quickly with this dough, as it becomes especially impossible to shape if it gets too warm. Have all your tools and components at your fingertips before you take the dough out of the freezer.

9. On a lightly floured surface, roll the dough to a 15-in/38-cm square. Quickly, but carefully, transfer the dough to a greased springform pan, allowing the edges to drape over the sides.

10. Evenly spread the filling in the center of the dough and fold the edges of the crust over the filling. Brush the top of the crust with egg wash and sprinkle with fleur de sel. Freeze for 25 minutes, or for up to 1 month tightly wrapped.

11. Preheat your oven to 375°F/190°C. Bake from semi-frozen for 1 hour, or until the filling bubbles and the crust is a deep golden brown. Don't be afraid of good color. Trust us.

12. Allow the crostata to cool for about 15 minutes before releasing the springform pan. Run a knife around the edges to ensure it doesn't stick. Gently release the pan. If you feel any resistance, stop, close the clamp, and run the knife around the edge again. Remove the ring, but leave the base underneath. Serve warm or at room temperature.

This is best the day it's made but keeps, well wrapped, at room temperature, for up to 1 day.

The colors on this tart are so deep, rich, and beautiful. Sometimes to make those colors pop even more I sprinkle it with powdered sugar or toasted sliced almonds. The contrast is breathtaking.

Plums seem to kick around the farmers' market long after the other stone fruit has vanished. But if you're using those less sweet, late-season plums, you may need to add a bit more sugar to this recipe.

A fun twist is to substitute seedless grapes for half of the plums, but be sure to keep the grapes whole or the filling may get too watery. Or if you want it a little more sophisticated, substitute goat cheese for the pastry cream and use all grapes and no plums. And if you're not feeling the multigrain dough or you have a flaky dough packet stashed in your freezer, that always works, too.

Serve warm or at room temperature with Whipped Cream (page 149).

plum multigrain crostata

SERVES 6 TO 8

CRUST

¾ cup/100 g all-purpose flour

¾ cup/100 g whole-wheat flour

¼ cup/25 g rye flour

1 tbsp flax seed meal

1 tbsp cornmeal

¼ cup/50 g granulated sugar

1 tsp baking powder

1 tsp kosher salt

1 cup/220 g cold unsalted butter, cubed

¼ cup/60 ml ice water

FILLING

4 tbsp/55 g unsalted butter

¼ cup/50 g granulated sugar

¼ tsp kosher salt

8 or 9 small to medium ripe plums, cut into eighths

1 batch Pastry Cream (page 148) or ½ cup/120 ml crème fraîche

1 batch Egg Wash (page 74)

Granulated sugar for sprinkling

Powdered sugar for dusting (optional)

1. To make the crust: To mix with a food processor, combine the all-purpose flour, whole-wheat flour, rye flour, flax seed meal, cornmeal, granulated sugar, baking powder, and salt and pulse once to blend. Add the butter to the work bowl and pulse about three times until pea-size pieces form. Pour the water over the flour mixture and pulse another three times until the dough is only just starting to come together.

   To mix by hand, combine the all-purpose flour, whole-wheat flour, rye flour, flax seed meal, cornmeal, granulated sugar, baking powder, and salt in a very large bowl. Stir to blend. Add the butter, working between your fingertips until the pieces are pea- and lima bean–size. Add the water. Lightly toss to distribute.

2. The dough should be shaggy, dry, and clumpy. Dump it onto a clean work surface to bring the dough together by hand. (Do not flour the counter, as you do not want to add any more flour to the dough.)

3. Begin by firmly pressing the entire surface of the dough with the heel of your palm. Toss and squeeze the dough to redistribute the wet and dry patches. Repeat, pressing thoroughly again with the heel of your palm, and continue pressing, tossing, and squeezing until it begins to hold together. But be sure not to overwork the dough! It should stay together but you should still see pea-size bits of butter running through it.

4. Press the dough into a disc ¾ in/2 cm thick, wrap tightly in plastic, and refrigerate for at least 30 minutes, or freeze for up to 1 month. If frozen, thaw in the refrigerator overnight before using.

5. Meanwhile, to make the filling: Add the butter, granulated sugar, and salt to a large sauté pan. Cook over medium-high heat until the mixture turns a deep dark brown. Stir occasionally so it browns evenly, but not so often that it takes forever to color.

6. Add the plums and stir once to coat. Cook for 90 seconds without stirring. Then stir once and let it sit for another 90 seconds untouched. Repeat one last time, then slide the plums onto a plate. Refrigerate until cooled completely.

7. When the plums are cool, start to shape the dough. If the dough feels hard, allow it to warm up at room temperature for a few minutes before working. It should still feel cold to the touch but malleable. Never allow the dough to become too soft or warm. Chill as needed while working.

8. On a lightly floured surface, roll the dough to a 14-in/35.5-cm square. Trim the edges; the final dough should be about a 13-in/33-cm square.

9. Gently transfer the dough to a greased springform pan, allowing the edges to drape over the sides. Spread the pastry cream on the bottom, then evenly spread the plum filling on top. Brush the overhanging dough with egg wash and fold over the filling. Then brush the top of the crust with egg wash and sprinkle with granulated sugar. Freeze for 20 to 25 minutes, or up to 1 month tightly wrapped.

10. Preheat your oven to 350°F/180°C. Bake from semi-frozen for 50 minutes, or until the filling bubbles and the crust is a deep golden brown. Don't be afraid of good color. Trust us.

11. Allow the crostata to cool for about 15 minutes before releasing the springform. Run a knife around the edges to ensure it doesn't stick. Gently release the pan. If you feel any resistance, stop, close the clamp, and run the knife around the edge again. Remove the collar, but leave the base underneath. Cool before dusting with powdered sugar, if desired, and serving.

This is best the day it's made but keeps, wrapped well, at room temperature, for up to 2 days.

This composed tart has a beautiful, traditional French look, especially if you take the time to arrange your apricots in neat circles. If you miss apricot's short season, the only other fruit that really works in this tart is figs. Most other fruits are just too watery. Another delicious variation is to make this tart with a cinnamon pastry cream. All you have to do is steep two cinnamon sticks in the cream-milk mixture while you make the pastry cream. It will add a lot of depth of flavor to this simple tart.

vanilla apricot tart

SERVES 8 TO 10

1 batch Everyday Flaky Dough (page 122)

1 batch Pastry Cream (page 148)

8 ripe apricots, pitted and halved

2 tbsp granulated sugar

2 tbsp brown sugar

¼ tsp kosher salt

2 tbsp unsalted butter, melted

¼ cup/30 g toasted sliced almonds

1. Allow the flaky dough to soften at room temperature for 10 to 20 minutes, depending on the temperature of your house, before rolling. The dough should be cold but malleable.

2. On a lightly floured surface, roll out the dough to a 15-in/38-cm square. Gently transfer the dough into a greased 11- or 12-in/28- or 30.5-cm tart pan. Gently press the dough into the pan without stretching it. Get it into the bottom edges, against the sides, and into every crevice. Then, trim any excess dough by raking it off with the back of a butter knife. Gently press your fingertips into the sides of the pan in order to push the dough slightly above the pan's edges by about ¼ in/6 mm. (This will make up for the inevitable shrinking when the shell is baked.)

3. Freeze the dough for at least 1 hour, or up to 1 month, tightly wrapped.

4. Preheat your oven to 350°F/180°C.

5. Line the inside of the frozen shell with parchment paper and fill with pie weights. Bake from frozen for about 35 minutes, until the outer rim is starting to brown. Then, carefully remove the parchment and weights, return the shell to the oven, and continue baking until the whole shell is nicely browned, 15 to 20 minutes longer. Let it get a little darker than you think it should!

6. When the shell has cooled, spread the pastry cream evenly over the bottom.

7. Toss the halved apricots, granulated sugar, brown sugar, salt, and melted butter together in a bowl. Then arrange the apricots, cut-side up, on the pastry cream.

8. Bake for 1 hour and 25 minutes, until the pastry cream looks set and the fruit is browned. Allow to cool to room temperature. Sprinkle with the toasted almonds before cutting and serving.

This is best served the day it's made.

This is a great base recipe that you can use for many things. We often play with this recipe by making flavored pastry creams or steeping different things in the cream, such as a couple of cinnamon sticks, toasted nuts, citrus zest, or coffee grounds. It makes a slightly larger batch than some of the recipes require, so be sure to wrap any leftovers and use it within a few days in another recipe, or just have it for dessert with fresh ripe fruit.

pastry cream

MAKES ABOUT 3 CUPS/740 G

3 tbsp unsalted butter

2 tsp vanilla extract, or 1 vanilla bean, split and scraped

¾ cup/180 ml whole milk

¾ cup/180 ml heavy cream

1 pinch kosher salt

1½ tbsp cornstarch

5 tbsp/60 g sugar

1 egg

1 egg yolk

1. Before you begin, put the butter in a medium bowl and set up a mesh strainer over it. If you are using vanilla extract instead of a vanilla bean, add that to the bowl as well.

2. In a medium saucepan, heat the milk, cream, salt, and vanilla bean (if using) over medium heat.

3. Meanwhile, in another bowl, whisk together the cornstarch, sugar, and egg and egg yolk and keep nearby.

4. When the cream mixture boils, reduce the heat to low. To make sure you don't cook the egg mixture, add only ¼ cup/60 ml of the hot cream mixture to the egg mixture and immediately whisk it in. Repeat twice more, so the egg mixture is gradually warmed by the cream mixture.

5. Pour the warmed egg mixture into the remaining cream mixture in the saucepan and whisk to combine. Increase the heat to medium and whisk constantly until it begins to thicken, 1 to 2 minutes.

6. When the mixture is the texture of pudding, remove the pan from the heat and immediately strain the pastry cream into the bowl with the butter.

7. Whisk the butter into the pastry cream until completely incorporated. Immediately cover with plastic wrap, pressing the plastic directly onto the surface of the pastry cream in order to prevent a skin from forming. Refrigerate until cool.

This keeps well, tightly wrapped, refrigerated, for up to 4 days.

I like whipped cream with almost every pastry in this book. I always put out a bowl with any brunch spread; it just makes everything better. We like the addition of crème fraîche to make the flavor of this whipped cream a little more complex. If you don't have crème fraîche just use all cream and it will still work perfectly. You can also use honey or maple syrup instead of sugar or add a ½ tsp cinnamon for a cinnamon whipped cream.

whipped cream

MAKES ABOUT 2 CUPS/240 G

1 cup/240 ml heavy cream
2 tbsp crème fraîche
1 tbsp sugar

Combine the cream, crème fraîche, and sugar in a medium bowl or in the bowl of a stand mixer with the whisk attachment. Whip by hand or on medium speed until fluffy and smooth. Be careful not to overwhip. Take it slow as you get close and do not let it get textured or curdled looking. Serve immediately or refrigerate for a few hours and lightly re-whip before serving if it loses its structure.

It's best used the day it's made but can be gently whipped back to life after 1 day.

7 A.M.

baked in a dish

The servers saunter in, tired, chatting each other up, moving at a snail's pace. This is the busiest time for the bakery with less than an hour to get everything out of the ovens and looking presentable out front. A young, enthusiastic, but slightly confused server meanders his way around the kitchen looking for the juicer. He clearly doesn't realize that we've been here for almost four hours already and are not in any way just waking up. "Get out of my way," Laurel screams. "We have hot sheet pans in our hands and mixing bowls going at full speed and you're sauntering through the kitchen like you're at a garden party." One of my bakers chimes in, "And say 'behind,' damn it, you're going to get burned or worse you're going to get me burned!" I chime in with my usual line, "Burn 'em; they'll learn." Immediately Joel, our GM, peeks his head around the corner and, of course, I'm the one who gets busted. "Zoe, you said you would stop saying that, it's a liability and it's also rude!" Joel's generally right and I feel like a teenager who's just been scolded. "Fine, but they can at least say 'behind' or move a little quicker!" I retort. Joel has been our general manager at Huckleberry from the day we opened our doors. We have fought and cried and made up with one another way more times than I can possibly count. Josh and I hired him because he was honestly everything that we are not: organized, detail oriented, a lover of rules and handbooks and writing memos. He loves Velcro-ing things wherever he can and can text faster than any human alive. He is also sweet and funny and constantly questions Josh and me, which makes our restaurant better each day.

The servers scurry, seeing that they have disturbed the lions. The guys on the line are really getting antsy to take over the ovens and roast the twenty sheet pans of bacon they have piled up waiting to go in. They start to harass me. I apologize that the cobblers are not done yet. I'm not risking having them taste like bacon, so they will have to wait. And honestly, my heart goes out to them; Huckleberry is one of the few kitchens where pastry doesn't take a back seat to savory. In most restaurant kitchens, pastry chefs and bakers fall pretty far down on the totem pole. They are given the least amount of space to work in, are the last to be able to use shared equipment, and are the first to get cut if labor costs get too high. If you see panna cotta, bread pudding, or crème brûlée on a menu, you know they either never had a pastry chef or she just got fired. But hopefully she will soon be hired by me.

I promise them just a few more minutes. This cobbler is taking a year and a day to bake!

My mom always talked to me about living one's life like an artist and turning your daily tasks into works of art, living your art form as life. I've kept those words in my heart, and to me there is no better installation than the scent of apples and cinnamon filling the air. It instantly makes your house feel like a home.

Any given week during apple season, there are ten to twelve wonderful varieties of apples available at our farmers' market and they are almost all amazing for baking. The only ones to avoid are Fuji. They're just too sweet to bake.

As different apples have different bake times, use the time mentioned in this recipe not as law but as a guideline. Stick with the one variety you love the most so they cook evenly, and give them a poke before you pull them from the oven to make sure the fruit is nice and soft.

Scoop directly from the casserole dish and serve with Whipped Cream (page 149) or plain Greek yogurt and maple syrup.

baked apples with oat crumble

SERVES 10 TO 12

CRUMBLE

¾ cup/170 g unsalted butter, cubed, at room temperature

½ tsp cinnamon

1 tsp vanilla extract

1 cup/120 g whole-wheat flour

2¼ cups/115 g rolled oats

1 tsp kosher salt

2 tbsp honey

½ cup + 2 tbsp/140 g brown sugar

6 apples, peeled, halved, and cored

4 tbsp/55 g unsalted butter, melted

3 tbsp granulated sugar

2 tbsp brown sugar

¼ tsp kosher salt

½ tsp cinnamon

1¾ cups/410 ml apple juice

1. Preheat your oven to 375°F/190°C.

2. To make the crumble: Combine the butter, cinnamon, vanilla, whole-wheat flour, oats, salt, honey, and brown sugar in a bowl and blend with your fingertips until homogenous. Refrigerate until needed.

3. In a medium bowl, toss the apples with the butter, granulated sugar, brown sugar, salt, and cinnamon.

4. Pour the apple juice into a 9½-by-13½-in/24-by-34-cm baking dish, then fit the apples in snugly, cut-side up. Cover with foil.

5. Bake until the apples are soft, about 1 hour. As different varieties have different bake times, be sure to give them a poke to see if they're ready.

6. Remove the foil and top the apples with the crumble. Increase the oven temperature to 425°F/220°C and bake until the topping is nice and brown, about 20 minutes longer. Serve warm or at room temperature.

This keeps, refrigerated, for up to 3 days.

This is an incredibly simple, beautiful, and delicious dish. When topping the peaches with the crumble, it's important to pile the crumble only into the center cavity of each peach, so it's easy to plate them individually. When serving them, use a spatula to carefully remove each peach from the baking dish, so each person has a beautiful peach half on their plate. Set out bowls of yogurt or lightly sweetened Whipped Cream (page 149) at breakfast, or serve with vanilla ice cream after dinner. Feel free to use whatever nut you have in your pantry for the crumble, but I definitely prefer it with walnuts.

roasted peaches with nut crumble

SERVES 12

CRUMBLE

1 cup/50 g rolled oats

½ cup/50 g almond flour

½ cup/110 g brown sugar

½ cup/60 g chopped walnuts, lightly toasted

6 tbsp/85 g unsalted butter

3 tbsp maple syrup

½ tsp kosher salt

6 ripe yellow peaches, halved, pits discarded

2 tbsp unsalted butter, melted

1 tbsp brown sugar

1 tbsp granulated sugar

pinch kosher salt

1. Preheat your oven to 375°F/190°C.

2. To make the crumble: Combine the oats, almond flour, brown sugar, walnuts, butter, maple syrup, and salt in a bowl and blend with your fingertips until homogenous. Refrigerate until needed.

3. In a medium bowl, toss the peach halves, melted butter, brown sugar, granulated sugar, and salt.

4. Arrange the peaches, cut-side up, in a 9½-by-13½-in/24-by-34-cm baking dish. Fill each cavity with 2 to 3 tbsp of the crumble, keeping the outer edges of the peaches visible.

5. Bake until the topping is browned and the peaches are tender, about 50 minutes. Serve warm or at room temperature.

This keeps well, refrigerated, for up to 2 days. Reheat in a 350°F/180°C oven as needed, or just nibble on them cold.

This recipe calls for a lot of berries and it's best to use fresh ones, so please try not to curse me when you see how much it costs to make. The best thing to do is to make it at the height of summer when the berries are at their best, and cheapest. If you remember ahead of time, go to your local berry farmers at the farmers' market and ask them to bring you seconds the next week at a cheaper price.

Use whatever berries you like best and also remember it's important to get a good deep brown on the biscuits for depth of flavor and to give the fruit enough time to bake.

This cobbler should be juicy and messy in the best possible way. Set it out with a big spoon and a stack of coffee mugs for guests to scoop it into. Serve with lightly sweetened Whipped Cream (page 149).

mixed berry cobbler

SERVES 10 TO 12

BISCUIT TOPPING

6 tbsp/45 g whole-wheat flour

1½ cups/200 g all-purpose flour

7 tbsp/40 g ground nuts or toasted oats

1 tbsp + 1½ tsp baking powder

¼ cup/50 g granulated sugar

1¼ tsp kosher salt

1 cup + 2 tbsp/255 g cold unsalted butter, cubed

7 tbsp/110 ml cold buttermilk

FILLING

10 cups/1.4 kg mixed berries, such as blueberries, blackberries, raspberries, and strawberries

Zest of ½ lemon

1 tbsp brown sugar

⅓ cup/65 g granulated sugar

½ tsp kosher salt

1 tbsp cornstarch

½ cup/120 ml water

1 batch Egg Wash (page 74)

Granulated sugar for sprinkling

1. To make the biscuit topping: Combine the whole-wheat flour, all-purpose flour, nuts, baking powder, granulated sugar, and salt in a very large bowl, stirring to blend. Toss the butter with the flour mixture. Work the butter between your fingertips until the pieces are pea- and lima bean–size. Add buttermilk and lightly toss to distribute.

2. Dump the dough onto a clean work surface. Begin by firmly pressing the entire surface of the dough with the heel of your palm. Toss and squeeze the dough to redistribute the wet and dry patches. Repeat, pressing thoroughly again with the heel of your palm, and continue pressing, tossing, and squeezing until the dough begins to hold together. But be sure not to overwork the dough! It should stay together but you should still see pea-size bits of butter running through it.

3. Press the dough into a 7½-by-12½-in/19-by-32-cm rectangle about ½ in/12 mm thick. Slice the dough into fifteen 2½-in/6-cm squares (that's five across and three down). Transfer to an ungreased sheet pan and freeze for at least 1 hour, or up to 1 month tightly wrapped.

4. When you're ready to bake, preheat the oven to 350°F/180°C.

5. To make the filling: Toss together the berries, lemon zest, brown sugar, granulated sugar, salt, cornstarch, and water. Pour the filling into a 9½-by-13½-in/24-by-34-cm baking dish.

6. Brush the frozen biscuits with egg wash, sprinkle with granulated sugar, and position on top of the filling, five across and three down. Bake until the filling bubbles and the biscuits are a deep golden brown, about 1 hour. Serve warm or at room temperature.

This is best eaten the day it's made but keeps, refrigerated, for up to 2 days, and is great to eat cold right from the fridge.

This is one of my favorite breakfasts to make during the summer. It won't look or feel like a traditional deep-dish cobbler, because it's made in a skillet and there isn't an overabundance of tomatoes; think of it more as a shallow-dish cobbler. It's meant to be served family-style, and there's nothing more fun and beautiful than sitting around a table drinking coffee, all eating from the same warm skillet. I keep a bunch of these biscuits ready to bake in my freezer, so throwing this together at the last minute is easy. This cobbler is really just as much about the biscuits as it is about the tomatoes. Depending on my mood and my crowd, I'll add more or less goat cheese.

cherry tomato–goat cheese cobbler

SERVES 4

BISCUIT TOPPING

3 tbsp whole-wheat flour

¾ cup/100 g all-purpose flour

3½ tbsp cornmeal

2¼ tsp baking powder

1½ tbsp sugar

½ tsp kosher salt

½ cup + 1 tbsp/130 g cold unsalted butter, cubed

3½ tbsp cold buttermilk

FILLING

5 cups/900 g cherry tomatoes

2 tbsp extra-virgin olive oil

4 sprigs fresh thyme

1 tsp kosher salt

1 batch Egg Wash (page 74)

4 to 6 tbsp/55 to 85 g goat cheese

1. To make the biscuit topping: Combine the whole-wheat flour, all-purpose flour, cornmeal, baking powder, sugar, and salt in a very large bowl. Stir to blend. Toss the butter with the flour mixture. Work the butter between your fingertips until the pieces are pea- and lima bean–size. Add the buttermilk and lightly toss to distribute.

2. Dump the dough onto a clean work surface. Begin by firmly pressing the entire surface of the dough with the heel of your palm. Toss and squeeze the dough to redistribute the wet and dry patches. Repeat, pressing thoroughly again with the heel of your palm, and continue pressing, tossing, and squeezing until it begins to hold together. But be sure not to overwork the dough! It should stay together but you should still see pea-size bits of butter running through it.

3. Press the dough into a disc ¾ in/2 cm thick. Cut the dough into nine biscuits. Transfer to an ungreased sheet pan and freeze for 1 to 2 hours. Preheat your oven to 350°F/180°C.

4. To make the filling: Combine the cherry tomatoes, olive oil, 2 sprigs of the thyme, and the salt in an ovenproof sauté pan. Cover and cook over high heat until the tomatoes begin to soften, 2 to 3 minutes. Uncover and continue cooking until all the tomatoes burst slightly.

5. Brush the frozen biscuits with egg wash and arrange them, 1 in/ 2.5 cm apart, on top of the tomato mixture in the skillet. Bake for 25 minutes. Remove briefly and quickly dollop the goat cheese between the biscuits over any exposed tomato. Return to the oven, increasing the temperature to 475°F/240°C, and continue baking until the top is nicely browned, about 10 minutes longer. Serve warm or at room temperature, topped with the remaining thyme.

This is best eaten the day it's made.

This crisp can be completely assembled the day before and thrown right into the oven the next morning. I love recipes like this, especially when you're trying to prepare a big brunch in 2 hours. Please only make this at the peak of summer, when the nectarines are ripe and soft and the blueberries are full of flavor. Also, don't let the crumble completely blanket the fruit. I always like it when little bits of fruit peek through and are allowed to brown during baking. This adds to the crumble's flavor and makes it look beautifully rustic.

Serve with Whipped Cream (page 149) for brunch or with vanilla ice cream for dessert.

blueberry nectarine crisp

SERVES 8 TO 10

TOPPING

1 cup/130 g all-purpose flour

½ cup + 3 tbsp/160 g unsalted butter, cubed, at room temperature

1 cup/95 g almond flour

½ cup + 1 tbsp/110 g granulated sugar

1 tsp kosher salt

FILLING

11 ripe nectarines, sliced into eighths

3 cups/450 g fresh blueberries

2 tsp cornstarch

3 tbsp granulated sugar

3 tbsp brown sugar

¼ tsp kosher salt

1. Preheat your oven to 350°F/180°C.

2. To make the topping: Combine the all-purpose flour, butter, almond flour, granulated sugar, and salt in a bowl and blend with your fingertips until homogenous. Refrigerate until needed.

3. To make the filling: Toss the nectarines and blueberries with the cornstarch, granulated sugar, brown sugar, and salt.

4. Pour the filling into a 9½-by-13½-in/24-by-34-cm baking dish and sprinkle with the topping, allowing bits of fruit to peek through.

5. Bake until the filling bubbles and the topping is deeply browned, about 1 hour. Serve warm or at room temperature.

This keeps, refrigerated, for 2 to 3 days.

This is our whole-wheat shortbread with tons of fruit on top and a whole lot of crumble, my idea of pure heaven. These would also be great with cranberries, sautéed apples, sautéed peaches, or sour cherries. But blackberries and blueberries are our traditional combination.

The best way to enjoy these is simply with a tall glass of milk. Or, if you want to take it to the next level, spike your milk. I can't imagine a better cure for a sleepless night.

It's key to slice the bars the moment they emerge from the oven. If you let them cool at all, they'll be too crumbly and you'll end up with a big ol' mess instead of beautiful, clean-looking squares.

black and blue oat bars

MAKES 16 BARS

CRUST

1 cup + 2 tbsp/255 g unsalted butter, cubed, at room temperature

⅓ cup/65 g granulated sugar

½ tsp kosher salt

1⅓ cups/170 g all-purpose flour

¾ cup/95 g whole-wheat flour

⅔ cup/85 g cornstarch

CRUMBLE

1 cup + 2 tbsp/55 g rolled oats

½ cup/60 g whole-wheat flour

6 tbsp/85 g unsalted butter, cubed, at room temperature

5 tbsp/70 g brown sugar

1 tbsp honey

½ tsp kosher salt

FILLING

5 cups/750 g blackberries and blueberries

1 tbsp cornstarch

½ cup + 2 tbsp/130 g granulated sugar

1 tbsp water

¼ tsp kosher salt

1. Grease an 8-in/20-cm square baking pan.

2. To make the crust: Cream the butter, granulated sugar, and salt in a stand mixer fitted with the paddle attachment until fluffy, 1 to 2 minutes. Add the all-purpose flour, whole-wheat flour, and cornstarch. Mix cautiously, just until combined.

3. Press the dough into the prepared pan, distributing it evenly. Refrigerate for at least 30 minutes. Preheat your oven to 350°F/180°C.

4. Meanwhile, to make the crumble: Combine the oats, whole-wheat flour, butter, brown sugar, honey, and salt in a bowl and blend with your fingertips until homogenous. Set aside in the refrigerator until needed.

5. Bake the crust until golden, about 35 minutes.

6. When the crust nears readiness, make the filling: Toss together the berries, cornstarch, granulated sugar, water, and salt to combine.

7. Remove the crust from the oven and, immediately, while hot, fill it with the berry mixture and top with the crumble. Return it to the oven to continue baking until the filling bubbles and the crumble is deeply browned, about 1 hour longer.

8. While it's hot, quickly slice into squares. I like to cut sixteen squares, which is four by four, but you can go with any size or shape you like— just as long as you cut them right away. Allow to cool completely before removing the squares from the pan. The best way is to run a knife through the original cuts a second time, then pry the squares out with a small spatula. Once you snag the first one, it gets easier.

These keep beautifully, tightly wrapped, at room temperature, for up to 3 days.

In terms of squash, you can always use butternut or whatever looks gorgeous at your farmers' market. I chose kabocha squash for this recipe, honestly, because it was what looked most beautiful at the market the day I first made it. If you don't eat meat, feel free to omit the sausage—but I will say the saltiness of the sausage next to the sweetness of the squash is the thing that makes this dish feel breakfasty to me. If you choose to omit the meat, you may want to use a little more salt in the breadcrumbs so you still get that salty-sweet taste.

Serve big generous scoops with runny sunny-side-up eggs.

kabocha squash and sausage brown betty

SERVES 10 TO 12

3 tbsp unsalted butter

3 kabocha squash, halved and seeded

2 tbsp brown sugar

2 tsp kosher salt

1 tbsp extra-virgin olive oil

1 garlic clove

6 cups/130 g chopped kale

½ cup/120 ml heavy cream

TOPPING

½ cup/110 g unsalted butter

24 fresh sage leaves

8 oz/110 g raw breakfast sausage, casings removed

2 cups/215 g breadcrumbs

2 tsp brown sugar

1½ tsp kosher salt

1. Preheat your oven to 375°F/190°C.

2. Drop ½ tbsp butter inside each squash half and sprinkle each with 1 tsp brown sugar and ¼ tsp salt. Tightly wrap in foil and roast until very soft, about 2 hours.

3. Meanwhile, in a large sauté pan, heat the olive oil and garlic until fragrant and browned. Add the kale and remaining ½ tsp salt and sauté until wilted. Set aside.

4. To make the topping: In the same pan, melt the butter over high heat. And the sage and sausage. Brown the meat while breaking it up into fine crumbles. Remove from the heat and add the breadcrumbs, brown sugar, and salt to the pan. Toss together and set aside.

5. When the squash has cooled, scoop out the flesh. You should have 8 to 10 cups/1 to 1.4 kg. If you have much more, reserve it for another use. Blend the squash with the cream in a food processor on medium-high until very smooth.

6. Combine the squash purée with the kale, folding until everything is well distributed. Spread the squash mixture into a 9½-by-13½-in/ 25-by-34-cm casserole dish, top with the sausage crumble, and bake until heated through, about 30 minutes. Serve warm.

This keeps well, refrigerated, for up to 3 days. Reheat in a 350°F/180°C oven until heated through.

Once you've started baking from this book, you will begin to understand my love of salty and sweet. This recipe is the epitome of salty-sweet. Whenever I make this pudding I always try to make a double batch. I serve one fresh from the oven and refrigerate the second without the topping. The next morning, I cut 1-in/2.5-cm slices, sear them in a hot sauté pan with butter, and serve them for breakfast with maple syrup. It tastes like the best French toast you have ever had. Also, if you don't like nuts, just don't put them on top, it's no big deal.

This pudding should be served scooped straight from the pan either on its own or with lightly sweetened Whipped Cream (page 149).

maple bacon bread pudding

SERVES 8 TO 10

12 slices thick-cut bacon

9 eggs

6 tbsp/85 g sugar

½ cup/120 ml crème fraîche

1 vanilla bean, split and scraped, pod reserved

1 cup/240 ml whole milk

1 cup/240 ml heavy cream

½ tsp kosher salt

⅔ cup/160 ml maple syrup

1 loaf Brioche (page 105), or any bread going stale in your pantry

½ cup/55 g chopped pecans, toasted (optional)

1. Preheat your oven to 375°F/190°C.

2. Spread the bacon on a sheet pan and bake until nice and brown, about 15 minutes.

3. Meanwhile, make a custard by whisking the eggs, sugar, crème fraîche, and vanilla bean seeds together. Add the milk, cream, salt, and 7 tbsp/100 ml of the maple syrup. Whisk until combined and set aside.

4. Remove the crust from the brioche and cut into slices 1 in/2.5 cm thick. Set aside. Chop the bacon into ¼-in/6-mm pieces. Sprinkle about one-third of the bacon into the bottom of a 5-by-9-in/12-by-23-cm loaf pan. Arrange a few slices of brioche on top, completely covering the pan in one even layer. Continue to alternate layers of bacon and bread until all the ingredients have been used. You should have about three layers. Top with the vanilla bean pod as a nonedible garnish.

5. Re-whisk the custard to make sure it's combined and slowly pour it over the bread layers, allowing it to soak in and completely cover the top. Reserve any excess custard and add later, after the bread has had time to absorb the liquid. You should eventually use all the custard.

6. Wrap in plastic and refrigerate for at least 1 hour, or overnight.

7. Preheat your oven to 325°F/165°C. Bake, uncovered, for 1 hour and 10 minutes, or until the custard is cooked through and the top is nice and brown.

8. Warm the remaining ¼ cup/60 ml maple syrup and toasted pecans in a small sauté pan and pour over the top of the bread pudding when you're read to serve. Serve the pudding warm or at room temperature.

This keeps well, tightly wrapped, refrigerated, for up to 4 days.

This is a great side dish for a summer brunch. You can serve it alongside the Brussels Sprouts and Bacon Frittata (page 171), a big green salad, and Roasted Peaches with Nut Crumble (page 154) for a beautiful meal that will make your guests really happy. When I make this bread pudding, I bake the cornbread the day before so it gets a little dried out and can really soak up the custard. You can put this together the night before you intend to serve it, so all you have to do in the morning is bake it. The key to this recipe is using fresh sweet corn and finishing it with fleur de sel and savory leaves.

cornbread pudding

SERVES 10 TO 12

1 batch Fresh Corn Cornbread, fresh corn omitted, sugar reduced by 3 tbsp (page 167)

1 onion, chopped

2 tbsp unsalted butter

1 tbsp chopped fresh savory, plus ¼ cup/20 g whole, fresh savory leaves

1 tbsp chopped fresh thyme

¾ tsp kosher salt

1 tsp freshly ground black pepper

3½ cups/560 g fresh corn kernels (about 3 cobs)

10 eggs

4 cups/950 ml heavy cream

6 tbsp/20 g chopped fresh chives

¼ cup/50 g sugar

2 cups/200 g grated Cheddar

½ cup/50 g grated Parmesan

1 tsp fleur de sel

1. Preheat your oven to 375°F/190°C.

2. Cut the cornbread into 1½-in/4-cm cubes and arrange in a single layer on one or two sheet pans. Toast until browned and crisp, about 20 minutes.

3. Meanwhile, in a medium sauté pan, combine the onion, butter, chopped savory and thyme, ¼ tsp of the salt, and ¼ tsp of the pepper. Sauté over medium heat until softened but not browned. Add the corn to the pan and sauté, stirring often, until tender, about 2 minutes. Set the onion mixture aside.

4. In a large bowl, whisk together the eggs, cream, chives, sugar, the remaining ½ tsp salt, and remaining ¾ tsp pepper and set aside.

5. Combine the cornbread with the onion mixture in the casserole dish, pour the custard over everything, and top with Cheddar and Parmesan.

6. Bake until the custard sets and the top browns, about 40 minutes.

7. Top with whole fresh savory leaves and fleur de sel. Serve warm or at room temperature.

This keeps well, refrigerated, for up to 3 days.

This is your old-fashioned cornbread made insanely moist and delicious. It is the opposite of dry, and can really stand on its own without needing to be slathered with butter.

This recipe is wildly versatile. Use fresh corn if you can; if it's not in season, you don't need it. For a fun jalapeño Cheddar version, increase the salt to 2 tsp, omit the honey, add ½ cup/120 g grated Cheddar, 2 jalapeños, finely chopped, and 2 tbsp chopped parsley. Take it any direction you please. The honey glaze is optional; if you go in a more savory direction, I would omit it.

If you are making this cornbread for use in our Cornbread Pudding (page 164), omit the fresh corn and reduce the sugar to 6 tbsp/60 g.

fresh corn cornbread

MAKES SIXTEEN 2-IN/5-CM SQUARES

6 tbsp/85 g unsalted butter

½ cup + 1 tbsp/110 g sugar

1¾ tsp kosher salt

4 eggs

1 cup/160 g cornmeal

¾ cup + 2 tbsp/100 g all-purpose flour

¼ cup/30 g whole-wheat flour

1 tbsp + 1 tsp baking powder

½ cup/120 ml whole milk

1 cup/240 ml buttermilk

¾ cup/180 ml canola oil

2 tbsp honey, plus ¼ cup/85 g for glazing (optional)

1½ cups/365 g fresh corn kernels (about 2 cobs; optional)

1. Preheat your oven to 350°F/180°C and grease an 8-by-8-in/ 20-by-20 cm pan.

2. In a stand mixer fitted with the paddle attachment, cream the butter, sugar, and salt on medium-high speed until light and fluffy, about 2 minutes. Incorporate the eggs, one at a time, beating well after each addition. Be sure to scrape the sides of the bowl well. Pause mixing and add the cornmeal, all-purpose flour, whole-wheat flour, and baking powder.

3. With the mixer on low speed, pour in the milk, buttermilk, canola oil, and 2 tbsp honey and mix. This is a very loose batter. Small lumps of butter are no problem, but avoid any lumps of flour. If you see them, mix a little longer or work them out with your fingers.

4. Fold in the corn, if in season; if not, omit.

5. Pour the batter into the prepared pan and bake for 45 to 50 minutes, or until a cake tester comes out clean. Do not overbake!

6. If you are choosing to glaze, slightly warm the ¼ cup/85 g honey in a small saucepan and lightly brush the top of the warm cake.

This is best served the day it's made but keeps, wrapped well, at room temperature, for up to 2 days.

A *strata* is a fancy name for a savory bread pudding. Bread puddings are a great way to turn old bread and a bunch of scraps you have lying around your kitchen into something rich and satisfying. It was hard for me to decide what vegetables to use in this recipe, as there really are a million options. A few of my other favorite combinations are cherry tomatoes, caramelized onions, and corn; ham and cheese; or butternut squash, kale, and caramelized onions. Also feel free to substitute any old bread you have for the multigrain bread.

This should be scooped directly from the casserole dish onto the serving plate. Because it's a heavier entrée, it's best served with a salad.

zucchini, spring onion, and sun-dried tomato strata

SERVES 10 TO 12

4 tbsp/60 ml extra-virgin olive oil

4 garlic cloves

6 cups/550 g sliced zucchini, cut into ½-in/12-mm coins

2¾ tsp kosher salt

4 sprigs fresh thyme

2 pinches chile flakes

5 cups/240 g sliced spring onions, cut into ½-inch/12-mm rounds

8 eggs

½ cup/120 ml crème fraîche

1 tsp sugar

1 cup/240 ml heavy cream

1 cup/240 ml whole milk

½ tsp freshly ground black pepper

1 loaf multigrain bread or large multigrain baguette

Two 7-oz/200-g jars sun-dried tomatoes in oil, drained and sliced

1¼ cups/125 g freshly grated Parmesan

1 batch Béchamel (page 243)

1. Preheat your oven to 325°F/165°C.

2. Heat 2 tbsp of the olive oil and 2 garlic cloves in a large sauté pan over high heat until fragrant. Add the zucchini, ½ tsp of the salt, 2 sprigs of the thyme, and a pinch of chile flakes and sauté until golden brown. Discard the thyme and set the zucchini aside in a very large bowl.

3. In the same pan, heat the remaining 2 tbsp olive oil and remaining garlic over high heat until fragrant. Add the spring onions, ½ tsp salt, the remaining thyme sprigs, and a pinch chile flakes and sauté until golden brown. Discard the thyme and set the spring onions aside in the bowl with the zucchini.

4. Whisk the eggs, crème fraîche, sugar, the remaining 1¾ tsp salt, the cream, milk, and pepper together in a large bowl. Set aside.

5. Slice the bread into 1-in/2.5-cm cubes, leaving the crust on, and drop into the bowl with the vegetable mixture. Add the sundried tomatoes and ½ cup/50 g of the Parmesan.

6. Pour the béchamel over the bread mixture, tossing everything to combine. Transfer to a 9½-by-13½-in/24-by-34-cm casserole dish and pour the egg mixture over it, making sure everything is well saturated.

7. Bake until cooked through, about 1 hour. Peek into the center with a small paring knife to check for doneness; if the eggs are still liquidy, bake for a bit longer. Remove from the oven and quickly top with the remaining ¾ cup/75 g Parmesan. Set your oven to broil and bake until the cheese is browned and bubbling, 5 to 10 minutes longer. Watch like a hawk so it doesn't burn! Serve warm or at room temperature.

This keeps, refrigerated, for up to 3 days. Reheat in a 350°F/180°C oven until heated through.

The first time I had romanesco in a frittata was at my brother-in-law Gabe's house. I was running around after Milo while everyone else sat down to a civilized meal when suddenly my husband shoved a bite into my mouth, and then into Milo's, and we all enjoyed five seconds of calm yum, before Milo went back to trying to run into the street.

Romanesco looks and tastes basically like a mixture of cauliflower and broccoli. When cooked, it takes on a sweet buttery taste. If you can't find it, just substitute cauliflower. Gabe added goat cheese to his, which was wonderful, so feel free to do that, too.

Serve with an arugula salad tossed with torn basil, breadcrumbs, and balsamic vinegar. Any leftover frittata makes a great sandwich the next day, on fresh bread, with aioli and tomato.

mushroom and romanesco frittata

SERVES 6

FILLING

4 cups/370 g sliced mushrooms, lightly rinsed

2 tbsp extra-virgin olive oil

2 tbsp unsalted butter

1 tsp kosher salt

2 tsp chopped fresh thyme

2 pinches chile flakes

2 cups/320 g thinly sliced yellow onions

Freshly ground black pepper

2 cups/140 g chopped romanesco or cauliflower

CUSTARD

10 eggs

2 tbsp crème fraîche

2 tbsp grated Parmesan

1 tbsp chopped fresh chives

½ tsp kosher salt

¼ tsp freshly ground black pepper

¼ cup/30 g grated Gruyère

1. Preheat your oven to 475°F/240°C.

2. To make the filling: In a 10-in/25-cm cast-iron or other ovenproof skillet, sauté the mushrooms in 1 tbsp of the olive oil and 1 tbsp of the butter with ½ tsp of the salt, the thyme, and a pinch of chile flakes and cook over high heat, covered, for about 4 minutes. Lower the heat to medium-high and add the onions, the remaining 1 tbsp olive oil, remaining 1 tbsp butter, and ¼ tsp salt. Season with black pepper and a pinch of chile flakes and cook, covered, for 2 to 3 minutes. Uncover and cook about 15 minutes longer, until the onions are soft and light golden.

3. Add the romanesco and remaining ¼ tsp salt. Continue to cook over medium heat, stirring frequently to avoid burning, until the romanesco is soft, 15 to 20 minutes.

4. Meanwhile, make the custard. In a mixing bowl, whisk together the eggs, crème fraîche, Parmesan, chives, salt, and pepper.

5. When the vegetables are ready, pour the custard into the pan and stir, lightly scrambling the eggs, over medium-high heat. When the eggs are about 30 percent set, sprinkle with the Gruyère and transfer to the oven for 8 to 10 minutes, until the frittata is cooked through and browned on top. If the frittata doesn't show signs of browning, place it under the broiler for 2 minutes, but watch it like a hawk!

6. Immediately transfer the frittata to a plate by running a spatula around the edges and underneath to free it from the pan. Serve hot or at room temperature.

This keeps well, refrigerated, for up to 3 days.

There are so many great obvious food combinations—peas and carrots, peanut butter and jelly, tomatoes and mozzarella, and, of course, Brussels sprouts and bacon. Why fight it if it just works.

Frittatas are just as good at room temperature as they are hot out of the oven; if you are entertaining, this is an ideal thing to make early so you can attend to other tasks once your guests have arrived.

I love to serve this frittata with an arugula salad tossed with sliced dates, olive oil, lemon juice, salt and pepper, and hand-torn crispy breadcrumbs. And Butter and Herb Potatoes (page 172).

brussels sprouts and bacon frittata

SERVES 6

FILLING

8 slices thick-cut bacon, chopped

1 tbsp extra-virgin olive oil

1 tbsp unsalted butter

1 onion, chopped

1 tsp kosher salt

2 sprigs fresh thyme

2 cups/180 g Brussels sprouts, thinly sliced, plus 1 cup/35 g Brussels sprouts leaves

½ tsp freshly ground black pepper

CUSTARD

10 eggs

2 tbsp crème fraîche

2 tbsp grated Parmesan

1 tbsp chopped fresh parsley

2 tbsp unsalted butter

3 tbsp grated Gruyère

1. Preheat your oven to 475°F/240°C.

2. To make the filling: In a large sauté pan over medium-high heat, sauté the bacon in 2 tsp of the olive oil and the butter, until browned. Add the onion, ½ tsp of the salt, and the thyme and sauté until soft, about 10 minutes. Add the sliced Brussels sprouts and sauté for about 5 minutes longer, until soft. Transfer the vegetable mixture to a bowl and set aside.

3. Toss the Brussels sprouts leaves in the remaining 1 tsp olive oil, remaining ½ tsp salt, and the pepper. Set aside.

4. To make the custard: In a mixing bowl, whisk together the eggs, crème fraîche, Parmesan, and parsley. Set aside.

5. In a 10-in/25-cm cast-iron or other ovenproof sauté pan, melt the 2 tbsp butter over medium-high heat. Pour the custard into the pan and stir, lightly scrambling the eggs. Slowly add the vegetable mixture to the custard and continue scrambling. When the eggs are about 30 percent set, sprinkle with the Brussels sprouts leaves, top with the Gruyère, and transfer to the oven for 8 to 10 minutes, until the frittata is cooked through and browned on top. If the frittata doesn't show signs of browning, place under the broiler for 2 minutes, but watch it like a hawk!

6. Immediately transfer the frittata to a plate by running a spatula around the edges and underneath to free it from the pan. Serve hot or at room temperature.

This keeps well, refrigerated, for up to 3 days.

We are blessed to be just a few blocks from the Santa Monica Farmers' Market. Every week we get the most wonderful potatoes from Weiser Farms, which may very well be the best potatoes in the world. The quality of your potatoes does really make a difference, so try to get your hands on the best you can find. If you can't find fingerlings, you can use Yukon golds, Red Bliss, or White Rose. Anything but russets, as the texture just doesn't work.

You'll find our cooking technique here to be a little odd. I've found that the way to get the crispiest, most flavorful potatoes is to remove them from the oven, cool them slightly, then flash-crisp them in a hot oven just before serving. You'll see.

And if you happen to have any duck fat kicking around, I cannot stress enough how awesome these potatoes are if you use it instead of butter! They're also really delicious liberally sprinkled with freshly grated Parmesan before their last trip through the oven.

Of course, serve them alongside any of the frittatas, but they're just as good at the center of a meal with over-easy eggs on top and Spicy Tomato Jam (page 211) on the side.

And remember, potatoes roasted this way are best the day they're made. Any leftovers can be put to good use in a frittata, strata, soup, and savory crostatas.

butter and herb potatoes

SERVES 3 OR 4

2½ tbsp unsalted butter

1 tbsp extra-virgin olive oil

2½ lb/1.2 kg fingerling potatoes, cut into ¼-in/6-mm slices

2 tbsp chopped fresh thyme

2 tbsp chopped fresh rosemary

1 tsp kosher salt

Freshly ground black pepper

½ cup/7 g fresh parsley leaves

1 lemon, quartered

Fleur de sel for sprinkling

1. Preheat your oven to 425°F/220°C.

2. Toss the butter, olive oil, potatoes, thyme, rosemary, and salt in a large bowl. Season with pepper.

3. Arrange in a single layer on a sheet pan and roast until soft but not quite browned, about 25 minutes. Flip the potatoes with a spatula and increase the oven temperature to 475°F/240°C. Return the potatoes to the oven to finish browning, about 10 minutes longer. Set aside and allow to cool for at least 10 minutes, or up to 3 hours. Either way, do not refrigerate; hold at room temperature.

4. After 10 minutes, or whenever you're ready to serve them, return the potatoes to a 475°F/240°C oven for 8 to 10 minutes longer, until crisped to perfection. Toss with the parsley, mound on a serving dish, tuck lemon wedges on the side, and sprinkle with fleur de sel.

These are best eaten the day they're made.

7:30 A.M.

fried stuff

Alexis is about to fry cinnamon-sugar doughnuts, but she wants to see what happens if she throws a raw croissant in the fryer. When she does, it immediately puffs up, bigger and rounder, browner and crisper than the ones in the oven in a fraction of the time. She thinks it's genius. She gives me a look that says "Why haven't you thought of this?" I just shake my head.

She tastes it and her face quickly goes from an excited smile to a look of horror. It's the most disgusting thing she's ever eaten. It tastes of butter and frying oil, and it's oozing grease from its still-raw insides. It wasn't exactly the "cronut" she'd expected.

There comes a time in every cook's life when they get obsessed with the fryer. It comes from boredom, fatigue, or the simple understanding that fried things are good and generally sell really well. So far, this is what I've learned: Do not attempt to fry croissants (real croissants with the right amount of butter don't fry well, as opposed to their leaner "cronut" counterparts), cake batters (to my surprise this is not the way to make a cake doughnut), biscuits, or strawberries.

They do not work. There are certain things that the fryer turns into works of art, and other things that it makes into toxic waste.

Play time is over. I have an order for thirty doughnuts that has to be ready in 20 minutes and I need Alexis to finish them, get them boxed up, and go take her break. Everything in the front display is coming together. We have bacon in the oven, brisket heating on the stove, brioche doughnuts going into the fryer, and I'm starting to load croissants in the oven. We are in our baking home stretch, until the damn fryer breaks.

Laurel and I immediately start brainstorming. Do we call Brian who usually gets the job done, but has to spend 45 minutes in the kitchen eating croissants and flirting with Laurel before he even starts, or Sam who promises he'll be there in 30 minutes and often doesn't show up until the next day? Both sound too depressing and are not going to help me get this order out on time. "Screw it," I tell Alexis. I put a big pot on the stove and fill it with oil. "Let's fry them in there. The people need their doughnuts—and I'll deal with this problem later."

My father loves cinnamon-sugar doughnuts and for that reason we have them every day at Huckleberry. My son, on the other hand, hates cinnamon-sugar doughnuts (I'm pretty sure it's because he swallowed a fair amount of sand in the park one day and the texture feels the same to him), so for that reason we always have another doughnut option as well. On the following pages you'll find a few of our favorite glazes. (If glazing, allow the doughnuts to cool while making the glaze.) These donuts are made with our brioche dough. You'll need to make the dough 1 day ahead, and remember, it's very important to get your butter to a true room temperature, so please think ahead!

cinnamon-sugar doughnuts

MAKES 10 DOUGHNUTS AND 16 DOUGHNUT HOLES

1 batch Brioche dough (see page 105)
2 cups/400 g sugar
1 tbsp cinnamon
¼ tsp kosher salt
Canola oil for frying

1. Remove the dough from the refrigerator and dump it onto a clean, liberally floured work surface. Sprinkle more flour on top of the dough. Flatten the dough by hand or by rolling it to a thickness of 1½ to 1¾ in/4 to 4.5 cm.

2. Using a 3-in-/7.5-cm-round cutter, cut 10 rounds and transfer them to a greased sheet pan, spacing them 1½ in/4 cm apart. Using a ½-in/12-mm round cutter, cut a small hole in each round and place them on the pan as well. Use the leftover dough to cut more holes and place them on the sheet pan, too.

   (With the remaining scraps, you can wrap, refrigerate, and re-roll more doughnuts after 1 hour more of chilling; shape them into a small ball and bake a tiny loaf of brioche, or wrap and freeze for another day.)

3. Loosely cover the dough with plastic wrap and allow to rise at room temperature, or refrigerate overnight and allow to rise in the morning, until doubled in size, 1 to 2 hours.

4. Meanwhile, stir together the sugar, cinnamon, and salt in a medium bowl. Set aside.

5. Heat 3 in/7.5 cm canola oil to 375°F/190°C in a Dutch oven or countertop fryer. Begin by frying one test doughnut; after about 2 minutes per side, remove it from the fryer and break it open to check that it's cooked through. If it's browned on the outside but raw inside, it means the dough is underproofed and has not risen enough. Stop frying, re-wrap the doughnuts, let them continue to rise, and try again.

6. When the dough is ready, place each doughnut onto a spider, or other long-handled skimmer, and carefully lower it into the oil. Working in batches, fry three or four doughnuts at a time until they are a nice golden brown, about 2 minutes per side; then fry the holes all at once until golden.

7. Immediately toss the doughnuts in cinnamon-sugar and serve hot!

   These keep well for only a few hours.

jelly doughnuts

1 batch Brioche dough (page 105)

1½ cups/510 g Strawberry Jam (page 55)

1 tbsp cornstarch

Powdered sugar for tossing

1. Cut out the same size and shape from the dough as instructed on page 176, but do not cut holes in the dough; then fry for 1 to 2 minutes longer than directed.

2. Add the jam and cornstarch to a medium saucepan and whisk to combine. Cook over medium heat, stirring regularly, until the jam bubbles and thickens. Set aside to cool.

3. With a skewer, poke a hole in one side of the doughnut and wiggle it around inside to create a pocket. Do not puncture the opposite side. Fill a piping bag or turkey baster with jam and insert 1 to 2 tbsp of filling into the cavity. Immediately toss each doughnut in powdered sugar twice, until well coated.

Dip the top half of the cooled doughnut in the glaze. Transfer to a cooling rack to set up.

DOUGHNUT GLAZES

MAKES ENOUGH FOR 10 DOUGHNUTS AND 16 DOUGHNUT HOLES

vanilla glaze

2 cups/200 g powdered sugar

1 pinch kosher salt

¼ cup + 2 tbsp/90 ml crème fraîche

1 tsp vanilla extract

½ vanilla bean, split, seeds scraped out

2½ tbsp heavy cream

Sift the powdered sugar and salt into a large mixing bowl. With a wooden spoon, stir in the crème fraîche, vanilla extract, and vanilla seeds, stirring to work out any lumps. Whisk or stir in the cream.

nutella glaze

1¼ cups/370 g Nutella

½ cup/120 ml whole milk, plus 2 tbsp if needed

Spoon the Nutella into a large bowl. Gradually add the ½ cup/120 ml milk, a little at a time, whisking until smooth. Check the consistency and add 2 tbsp more milk if needed. This one won't really set up, so enjoy it in all its gooeyness.

strawberry glaze

½ cup/120 g puréed strawberries
4 cups/480 g powdered sugar

Combine the strawberries and powdered sugar in a blender. Blend until smooth.

sugar glaze

4 cups/480 g powdered sugar
1 vanilla bean, split, seeds scraped out
½ cup/120 ml water

Sift the powdered sugar into a large bowl and add the vanilla seeds. Gradually whisk in the water, working out any lumps.

peanut butter glaze

3 cups/360 g powdered sugar
2 tsp kosher salt
1 cup/260 g creamy peanut butter
½ cup/170 g honey
½ cup/120 g whole milk

Sift the powdered sugar and salt into a large mixing bowl. With a wooden spoon, stir in the peanut butter and honey and work out any lumps. Gradually stir or whisk in the milk.

It took me a long time to figure out how to make a good cake doughnut—I'm almost embarrassed to say how long. I found the two most important things to be almost undermixing your batter and the addition of cream cheese.

During the winter we also make a spiced version of these. Simply add 2 tsp cinnamon, 1 tsp nutmeg, ½ tsp cloves, and ¼ tsp ginger to the batter. When the doughnuts are done, coat them in a mixture of 2 cups/400 g sugar, 1½ tsp cinnamon, ⅛ tsp nutmeg, ⅛ tsp cloves, ⅛ tsp ginger, and ⅛ tsp salt.

These are also great glazed with Vanilla Glaze (page 178) or Sugar Glaze (page 179).

chocolate-glazed cake doughnuts

MAKES 10 LARGE DOUGHNUTS AND 16 DOUGHNUT HOLES

BATTER

4 tbsp/55 g unsalted butter, cubed, at room temperature

5 tbsp/65 g granulated sugar

5 tbsp/70 g brown sugar

1 tsp kosher salt

1 egg

1 egg yolk

3 tbsp canola oil

1 tbsp vanilla extract

1 tbsp maple syrup

1½ cups/190 g all-purpose flour

1¼ cups/150 g whole-wheat flour

¾ cup/100 g pastry flour

1½ tsp baking powder

1 tsp baking soda

5 tbsp/70 g cream cheese

¼ cup/60 ml buttermilk

Canola oil for frying

GLAZE

½ cup/60 g powdered sugar

¼ cup/60 ml heavy cream

1½ tbsp unsalted butter, cubed

2 cups/340 g chopped dark chocolate, 60 to 70% cacao

3 tbsp honey

⅛ tsp kosher salt

Cacao nibs for sprinkling

1. To make the batter: In a stand mixer fitted with the paddle attachment, cream the butter, granulated sugar, brown sugar, and salt. Add the egg and egg yolk and mix until incorporated. Add the canola oil, vanilla, and maple syrup and mix until combined. Add the all-purpose flour, whole-wheat flour, pastry flour, baking powder, baking soda, cream cheese, and buttermilk and mix until just barely incorporated.

2. Dump onto a floured surface and flatten to a ¾-in/2-cm thickness. Using a 2½-in/6-cm round cutter, cut 10 rounds and transfer to a lightly floured sheet pan. Using a ½-in/12-mm cutter, cut a small hole in each round and place them on the sheet pan, too. Press the scraps together, re-roll once, and cut more rounds. After that, throw away any scraps.

3. Wrap the rounds tightly in plastic and refrigerate for at least 1 hour, or overnight.

4. Heat 3 in/7.5 cm canola oil to 400°F/200°C in a Dutch oven or countertop fryer.

5. Place each doughnut onto a spider, or other long-handled skimmer, and carefully lower it into the oil. Working in batches, fry three to four doughnuts at a time, until they are a deep golden brown, about 45 seconds per side. Then fry the holes all at once, until golden. Allow to cool slightly on a cooling rack while you make the glaze.

6. To make the glaze: Sift the powdered sugar into a medium bowl. Add the cream and stir to combine. Add the butter, chocolate, honey, and salt. Create a double boiler by placing the bowl over a medium saucepan of hot water and heat the mixture over medium-low heat, stirring to combine, until everything is melted.

7. Immediately dip the top half of each doughnut in the glaze, sprinkle with cacao nibs, and serve.

Doughnuts keep well for only a few hours.

I grew up loving beignets. There was a place in the bowling alley by my house called Café Beignet, where every table started their meal with a huge basket of them. I vividly remember the beignets being so hot you'd pull your hand away after touching one, but you would immediately go back, fighting through a slight finger burn, and pop a hot one in your mouth. My family was always amazed at my ability, even back then, to eat burning-hot things.

These should be copiously dusted in powdered sugar. They're messy, so don't eat them when you have your best clothes on and please enjoy licking the powdered sugar off your fingers.

powdered sugar beignets

MAKES 45 BEIGNETS

1⅔ cups/230 g bread flour

½ cup/70 g pastry flour, sifted

½ cup/120 ml water

½ cup + 2 tbsp/150 ml whole milk

1 cup/225 g unsalted butter, cubed

2 tsp sugar

1½ tsp kosher salt

1 vanilla bean, split and seeds scraped out

9 eggs

Canola oil for frying

Powdered sugar for coating

1. Combine the bread flour and pastry flour in a medium bowl and set aside.

2. In a large saucepan, heat the water, milk, butter, sugar, salt, and vanilla seeds over medium-high heat. Bring to a boil, whisking occasionally. Add the flour mixture and stir vigorously with a wooden spoon until a shiny paste, free of lumps, forms, about 3 minutes.

3. Transfer the batter to the bowl of a stand mixer fitted with the paddle attachment and mix on medium-low speed. Add the eggs, one at a time, beating well after each addition. Continue mixing on medium speed until the batter cools to a warm room temperature.

4. Meanwhile, in a Dutch oven or countertop fryer, heat 3 in/7.5 cm canola oil to 375°F/190°C.

5. Using a soup spoon, scoop up 2 to 2½ tbsp of batter and ease it into the hot oil using another spoon. Don't crowd the pot. Fry in batches of four to eight depending on the size of your pot. Fry for about 5 minutes, agitating and flipping the beignets so they cook evenly. If any of the beignets fill with air and don't want to flip, use a spider, or other long-handled skimmer, to hold them under the oil for about 30 seconds. Repeat as needed until you can flip and fry them like the others.

6. You should see the beignets expand once almost right away and you might think they're ready soon after that, but they're not. They need to expand a second time, inflating so much that they tear on one side. After that second inflation, continue to brown them well. Remember, this is a wet, eggy dough and it really needs to cook! Once you get that double expansion and achieve a deep, dark color, only then are they ready to come out of the oil.

7. Transfer to a bowl lined with paper towels to drain any excess oil, then coat with powdered sugar. Serve hot! Continue frying in batches, but serve each batch moments after it comes out— don't wait to serve them!

These do not keep well at all—but why should they.

There's a great restaurant in San Francisco called Frances that makes something like this for dinner. It made me realize that savory doughnuts are fun to eat at any time of day, especially if you're drinking a glass of Champagne or Prosecco while doing so. This is another one of those recipes that you can play with: add ham, bacon, more spice, lots more herbs, etc. And, like almost everything in this chapter, eat these hot!

black pepper beignets

MAKES 20 BEIGNETS

1 cup/140 g bread flour

¼ cup/35 g pastry flour

¾ cup/180 ml water

¼ cup/60 ml whole milk

½ cup + 2 tbsp/140 g unsalted butter, cubed

1 tsp sugar

1¼ tsp kosher salt

5 eggs

1 cup + 2 tbsp/130 g grated Gruyère

1½ tsp freshly ground black pepper

¼ tsp cayenne pepper

Canola oil for frying

Fleur de sel for tossing

Chopped fresh parsley for sprinkling

1. Combine the bread flour and pastry flour in a medium bowl and set aside.

2. In a large saucepan, heat the water, milk, butter, sugar, and salt over medium-high heat. Bring to a boil, whisking occasionally. Add the flour mixture and stir vigorously with a wooden spoon until a shiny paste, free of lumps, forms, about 3 minutes.

3. Transfer the batter to the bowl of a stand mixer fitted with the paddle attachment and mix on medium-low speed. Add the eggs, one at a time, beating well after each addition. Continue mixing on medium speed until the batter cools to a warm room temperature. Add the Gruyère, black pepper, and cayenne and mix for 1 minute longer.

4. Meanwhile, in a Dutch oven or countertop fryer, heat 3 in/7.5 cm canola oil to 375°F/190°C.

5. Using a soup spoon, scoop up 2 to 2½ tbsp of batter and ease it into the hot oil using another spoon. Don't crowd the pot. Fry in batches of four to eight depending on the size of your pot. Fry for about 5 minutes, agitating and flipping the beignets so they cook evenly. If any of the beignets fill with air and don't want to flip, use a spider, or other long-handled skimmer, to hold them under the oil for about 30 seconds. Repeat as needed until you can flip and fry them just like the others.

6. You should see the beignets expand once almost right away and you might think they're ready soon after that, but they're not. They need to expand a second time, inflating so much that they tear on one side. After that second pop, continue to brown them well. Remember, this is a wet, eggy dough and it really needs to cook! Once you get that double expansion and achieve a deep, dark color, only then are they ready to come out of the oil.

7. Transfer to a bowl lined with paper towels to drain any excess oil; then toss with fleur de sel and sprinkle with parsley. Serve hot!

These do not keep well, but you won't need them to.

Fritters wait for no man. When they are ready they must be eaten right away. This is not the kind of thing you can set out in a bowl as part of a beautiful pastry display, for your guests to slowly enjoy. When you make these, everyone should be standing around looking over your shoulder, sipping mimosas, and waiting for the next batch to come out so they can quickly shove them into their mouths. It's way more fun that way anyway.

lemon ricotta fritters

MAKES 18 TO 20 FRITTERS

Canola oil for frying

2 eggs, separated

½ cup/125 g ricotta

Zest of 2 lemons

⅓ cup/80 ml whole milk

1 cup/130 g all-purpose flour

5 tsp sugar

¾ tsp kosher salt

½ tsp baking powder

2 tbsp unsalted butter, melted

Powdered sugar for sprinkling

1. In a Dutch oven or countertop fryer, heat 3 in/7.5 cm canola oil to 375°F/190°C.

2. Whisk together the egg yolks, ricotta, lemon zest, and milk in a small bowl.

3. In medium bowl, whisk together the flour, sugar, salt, and baking powder.

4. In the bowl of a stand mixer fitted with the whisk attachment, whisk the egg whites on high speed until soft peaks form, 3 to 4 minutes.

5. Meanwhile, add the egg yolk mixture to the flour mixture, followed by the melted butter. Stir until just combined. Gently fold in the egg whites.

6. Using a soup spoon, scoop up 2 to 2½ tbsp of batter and ease it into the hot oil using another spoon. Fry in batches until golden brown, 5 to 6 minutes.

7. Allow to cool just slightly on a cooling rack, then sprinkle with powdered sugar. Serve hot!

These do not keep well at all, so don't ask them to. Eat immediately.

8 A.M.

pancakes

The doors have just opened and the pancake police is here, my dad, Stephen Nathan. He orders his pancakes then saunters right into the kitchen, hugs me, kisses my forehead, and tells me how much he wishes he could stay here and work with me today. I laugh, knowing he probably has ten meetings lined up and his own set of problems running a successful television show, but I also know that he really means it. "I wish you could stay, too, Dad," I say, and then run off to pull out another batch of coffee cake from the oven.

My dad was my first official line cook when I started Saturday Morning Breakfast at Rustic Canyon. He came in every Saturday morning at 6 A.M. to prep ingredients for his two signature dishes: pancakes and frittatas. He certainly wasn't my fastest cook, but he has a great sense of taste and put a ton of love into every dish he made, which frankly I would take over speed any day. I used to want to kill him when he would make and then immediately run an order of pancakes out himself before a table of six had any of their other food close to being ready. I had to forgive him because I understood that he was so excited to make it and that it truly killed him to see a delicious plate of food wait an extra second before someone was enjoying it. Somehow he didn't find it ironic when he'd run back into the kitchen and tell us, "They're waiting on the rest of their food? Come on guys!"

My dad did not have the best kitchen timing, but every person who had his pancakes got to feel the love and attention to detail that he and my mom taught me growing up. They showed me that the way a meal is prepared can be a work of art and of love, and that the love comes from caring for the food and the process of making it. For my mom this was meticulously picking out our fruits and vegetables at the farmers' market, and for my dad it was spending his entire day off in the kitchen making Sunday Sauce because he simply thought it was fun and he knew how much we'd love it once it was ready.

Before I took the job at Rustic Canyon, I accepted a job offer at a much more prestigious restaurant than my soon-to-be husband's six-month-old startup. My parents were so happy and proud that I would be the next in line at this well-regarded place that had spawned so many famous cooks. Then I interviewed at Rustic and met Josh. Afterward, he called me every hour trying to convince me to take a chance on this heartfelt new kid on the block, and eventually I was sold. I called my parents crying, afraid they'd be disappointed that I was turning down the famous place and following my heart. But, of course, they supported me completely, reminding me that following my heart is all they have ever hoped for me.

I turn to Norberto as he begins to pour my dad's pancakes onto the griddle, "Super VIP. That griddle better be hot. It's got to be perfect, please."

My father used to make these almost every weekend when I was growing up, and then he proudly made them every weekend for Saturday Morning Breakfast at Rustic Canyon. They're so simple and so delicious and the perfect example of why we say color is flavor. If these pancakes aren't done on a super-hot griddle and they don't get that deep brown color, they become an entirely different, sadder animal. So please, cook these properly and make my Dad proud. Serve with butter and maple syrup or yogurt and fruit.

my dad's pancakes

MAKES ABOUT 12 PANCAKES

1 vanilla bean or 1½ tbsp vanilla extract

2 cups/480 ml whole milk

2 cups/250 g all-purpose flour

1 tbsp baking powder

4 tsp sugar

1¼ tsp kosher salt

1 cup/220 g unsalted butter, melted

4 eggs, separated

1. If using the vanilla bean, split lengthwise, scrape the seeds into the milk, and toss the pod in, too. Bring to a boil, whisking occasionally to help break up the vanilla bean. Allow to cool, or refrigerate overnight. Discard the pod before using.

2. Place the flour, baking powder, sugar, and salt in a large bowl. Add the butter, egg yolks, and vanilla milk (or milk and vanilla extract). Whisk to combine.

3. In a separate bowl, whip the egg whites to soft peaks with an electric beater on medium-high speed, 3 to 4 minutes. Fold the whites into the batter.

4. About 5 minutes before you're ready to make the pancakes, preheat a greased griddle or large skillet over medium-high heat; the griddle is ready when a few droplets of water sizzle and dance across the surface.

5. Drop ½ cup/120 ml of batter onto the hot griddle. When bubbles set on the surface of the pancake and the bottom is golden, flip and cook about 1 minute longer. Serve immediately, while hot.

These are best the moment they leave the griddle.

These pancakes are both satisfying and decadent; two qualities that can be hard to come by when you're eating gluten-free *and* vegan. My family and I eat these often and never feel deprived. Feel free to use different fruits in the compote and substitute homemade Almond Milk (page 206) for the coconut milk.

vegan gluten-free pancakes with maple blueberry compote

MAKES ABOUT 12 PANCAKES

COMPOTE
1 cup/150 g fresh blueberries

3 tbsp maple syrup

BATTER
1½ cups/125 g Huckleberry Gluten-Free Flour Mix (page 55)

¼ cup/20 g almond flour

¼ cup/20 g cornmeal

1½ tsp baking powder

1½ tsp baking soda

2 tbsp flax seed meal

2 tsp chia seeds or poppy seeds

1½ tsp kosher salt

½ tsp cinnamon

2¼ cups/540 ml coconut milk

½ cup + 2 tbsp/150 ml canola oil

¼ cup/60 ml maple syrup

1 tbsp vanilla extract

1. To make the compote: Combine the blueberries and maple syrup in a small saucepan over medium-high heat until the berries start to burst a little. Set aside over low heat.

2. To make the batter: Combine the flour mix, almond flour, cornmeal, baking powder, baking soda, flax seed meal, chia seeds, salt, and cinnamon in a large bowl.

3. Add the coconut milk, canola oil, maple syrup, and vanilla to the dry ingredients and whisk to combine.

4. About 5 minutes before you're ready to make the pancakes, preheat a greased griddle or large skillet over medium-high heat; the griddle is ready when a few droplets of water sizzle and dance across the surface.

5. Drop ⅓ cup/80 ml of batter onto the hot griddle. When bubbles set on the surface of the pancake and the bottom is golden, flip and cook for about 1 minute longer. Serve immediately, while hot, with a big spoonful of warm compote right on top.

These are best the moment they leave the griddle.

These are my family's absolute favorite pancakes. Every house has its go-to pancake recipe, and this is ours. I love all the grains and I find these keep you fuller and more satisfied for way longer then most pancakes.

If you don't have all these grains and flours on hand, don't let that stop you. Just substitute any one for another and in the process create your own special family recipe.

These pancakes are delicious with butter and maple syrup or yogurt and fruit.

multigrain pancakes
MAKES ABOUT 12 PANCAKES

½ cup + 2 tbsp/80 g cornmeal

⅓ cup/35 g rye flour

¼ cup/30 g all-purpose flour

¼ cup/30 g whole-wheat flour

¼ cup/25 g oat flour

4 tsp rolled oats

2 tsp flax seed meal or wheat germ

1 tsp chia seeds or poppy seeds

2 tbsp + 2 tsp/35 g brown sugar

1 tsp baking soda

1 tsp kosher salt

2 cup + 4 tsp/500 ml buttermilk

6 tbsp/85 g unsalted butter, melted and cooled

2 eggs

3 tbsp + 2 tsp/25 g grated Cheddar

1. Put the cornmeal, rye flour, all-purpose flour, whole-wheat flour, oat flour, rolled oats, flax seed meal, chia seeds, brown sugar, baking soda, and salt in a large bowl. Add the buttermilk, melted butter, eggs, and Cheddar and whisk to combine.

2. About 5 minutes before you're ready to make the pancakes, preheat a greased griddle or large skillet over medium-high heat; the griddle is ready when a few droplets of water sizzle and dance across the surface.

3. Drop ⅓ cup/80 ml of batter onto the hot griddle. When bubbles set on the surface of the pancake and the bottom is golden, flip and cook for about 1 minute longer. These should cook quickly. Serve immediately, while hot.

These are best the moment they leave the griddle.

Occasionally I make something I love so much that I literally want to eat it every day, and that's how I feel about these. I like them as straightforward pancakes cooked on a griddle, but they're also really good as a large baked pancake. Pour all the batter into a buttered cast-iron skillet, bake at 450°F/230°C for about 15 minutes, and serve immediately straight from the skillet slathered with butter and maple syrup. It's a fun way to eat a pancake with a group.

These should be your go-to breakfast anytime you have leftover rice. And if you're not up for cooking quinoa, you can always use all brown rice, but I will say if you choose to use just quinoa, the flavor can be a little overpowering.

It is mandatory to serve these with maple syrup, but, honestly, you don't even need butter these pancakes are so good.

brown rice quinoa pancakes

MAKES ABOUT 15 PANCAKES

½ cup/60 g whole-wheat flour

5 tbsp/50 g cornmeal

2 tbsp rolled oats

1 tbsp flax seed meal or wheat germ

2 tsp chia seeds or poppy seeds

1 tbsp millet

2 tbsp brown sugar

1½ tsp baking soda

1 tsp kosher salt

2 cups/480 ml buttermilk

½ cup/110 g unsalted butter, melted

3 eggs

1¼ cups/200 g cooked brown or wild rice

½ cup/100 g cooked quinoa

1. Put the whole-wheat flour, cornmeal, rolled oats, flax seed meal, chia seeds, millet, brown sugar, baking soda, and salt in a large bowl. Add the buttermilk, melted butter, and eggs and whisk to combine. Stir in the rice and quinoa.

2. About 5 minutes before you're ready to make the pancakes, pre-heat a greased griddle or large skillet over medium-high heat; the griddle is ready when a few droplets of water sizzle and dance across the surface. But once heated, lower the heat to medium to prevent burning.

3. Drop ⅓ cup/80 ml of batter onto the hot griddle. When bubbles set on the surface of the pancake and the bottom is golden, flip and cook for about 1 minute longer. Serve immediately, while hot.

These are best the moment they leave the griddle.

Let's talk bananas. Do not fear the black-spotted, super-soft banana—the uglier, the better. Spritely and green will be starchy and flavorless: don't use those. If you're worried that your bananas are not ripening fast enough, seal them in a brown paper bag and leave them in a warm spot in your kitchen to speed up their demise to ugly deliciousness.

This batter can be a bit heavy, so I find these pancakes cook better and more evenly when done in silver dollars. Also, set them over low heat to make sure they don't burn before they're cooked through. Slow and low is the way to go with these little guys.

For a gluten-free version, substitute brown rice flour for the whole-wheat. For a whole-grain version, add flax seeds, chia seeds, and/or poppy seeds.

Top with butter and syrup or, if you're feeling particularly inspired, with bananas warmed in maple syrup.

banana chocolate silver dollars

MAKES ABOUT 25 SMALL PANCAKES

¼ cup/15 g rolled oats

½ cup/50 g oat flour

¼ cup + 2 tbsp/45 g all-purpose flour

2 tbsp whole-wheat flour

2 tbsp sugar

1 tsp baking soda

1 tsp baking powder

¾ tsp kosher salt

½ cup/120 ml whole milk

5 tbsp/70 g unsalted butter, melted and cooled

1 egg

1 tbsp vanilla extract

3 bananas; 2 mashed, 1 coarsely chopped

Heaping ½ cup/85 g coarsely chopped dark chocolate, 60 to 70% cacao

½ cup/60 g finely chopped walnuts, toasted

1. Put the rolled oats, oat flour, all-purpose flour, whole-wheat flour, sugar, baking soda, baking powder, and salt in a large bowl. Add the milk, melted butter, egg, and vanilla. Whisk to combine. Fold in the mashed and chopped bananas, chocolate, and walnuts.

2. About 5 minutes before you're ready to make the pancakes, pre-heat a greased griddle or large skillet over medium-high heat; the griddle is ready when a few droplets of water sizzle and dance across the surface. But once heated, lower the heat to medium-low to prevent burning.

3. Drop about 2 tbsp of batter onto the hot griddle. When bubbles set on the surface of the pancake and the bottom is golden, flip and cook for about 1 minute longer. Serve immediately, while hot.

These are best the moment they leave the griddle.

These pancakes smell like pure heaven the moment they touch the griddle. The apples and cinnamon warm your house faster than any heater can. One of my favorite ingredients to add to any sweet pancakes is grated Cheddar cheese. It adds a savory depth that is so delicious and they still work perfectly covered with butter and maple syrup. I left that out of this recipe for simplicity, but if you want to try it, stir 3 to 4 tbsp grated Cheddar into the batter with the cooked apples and you will not be disappointed. If you have any caramel sauce lying around, you can turn these flapjacks into an incredibly decadent breakfast.

apple cinnamon flapjacks

MAKES ABOUT 12 FLAPJACKS

6 tbsp/85 g unsalted butter

2 small apples, unpeeled and diced, anything but Fuji

½ tsp ground cinnamon

Kosher salt

1 cup/120 g whole-wheat flour

½ cup/80 g cornmeal

3 tbsp sugar

½ tsp baking powder

½ tsp baking soda

1 cup + 2 tbsp/270 ml whole milk

½ cup/120 ml plain whole-milk yogurt

1 egg

2 tbsp canola oil

1 tsp vanilla extract

1. Melt the butter over medium heat in a medium sauté pan. Add the apples, cinnamon, and a pinch of salt and sauté until soft but not browned. Set aside.

2. Put the whole-wheat flour, cornmeal, sugar, baking powder, baking soda, and ½ tsp salt in a large bowl and whisk to combine.

3. In a separate bowl, combine the milk, yogurt, egg, canola oil, and vanilla and whisk to combine.

4. With a wooden spoon, stir the wet mixture into the dry ingredients. Stir in the cooked apples.

5. About 5 minutes before you're ready to make the pancakes, preheat a greased griddle or large skillet over medium-high heat; the griddle is ready when a few droplets of water sizzle and dance across the surface.

6. Drop ⅓ cup/80 ml of batter onto the hot griddle. When bubbles set on the surface of the pancake and the bottom is golden, flip and cook for about 1 minute longer. Serve immediately, while hot.

These are best the moment they leave the griddle.

I grew up eating blintzes at old dark Los Angeles delis with my grandparents. In fact, those are still some of my favorite food memories. These pancakes remind me of those blintzes. I often wish my Grandma Evelyn and Grandpa Irving were alive to see Huckleberry and taste my cooking. They would have gotten a real kick out of it, and let everyone within earshot know all about it. "Excuse me, she's our granddaughter!" they'd yell as they made their way to a table. And man, oh man, would they have loved being able to skip the line and get free food.

Serve these cakes with butter and maple syrup or yogurt, fruit, or homemade jam.

ricotta griddlecakes

MAKES ABOUT 14 GRIDDLECAKES

1¾ cups + 2 tbsp/240 g all-purpose flour

3 tbsp granulated sugar

1 tbsp brown sugar

1½ tsp baking powder

1 tsp kosher salt

3 eggs, separated

¾ cup/170 g ricotta

1¾ cups + 2 tbsp/450 ml whole milk

1 tbsp vanilla extract

1. Put the flour, granulated sugar, brown sugar, baking powder, and salt in a large bowl. Add the eggs yolks, ricotta, milk, and vanilla and whisk to combine.

2. In a separate bowl, whip the egg whites to soft peaks with an electric beater on high speed for 3 to 4 minutes. Fold the whites into the batter.

3. About 5 minutes before you're ready to make the pancakes, preheat a greased griddle or large skillet over medium-high heat; the griddle is ready when a few droplets of water sizzle and dance across the surface.

4. Drop ⅓ cup/80 ml of batter onto the hot griddle. When bubbles set on the surface of the pancake and the bottom is golden, flip and cook for about 1 minute longer. Serve immediately, while hot.

These are best the moment they leave the griddle.

I have tried to change the name of these to Cornmeal Pancakes many times, but Laurel refuses to allow it. She gets far too much enjoyment from hearing our customers order "hoecakes."

They are a perfect balance between butter, salt, honey, and cornmeal. But you can also make this batter both savory and sweet by adding ¼ cup/30 g grated Cheddar cheese. Or go completely savory and toss in sautéed broccoli, mushrooms, or whatever veggies you find kicking around your fridge that morning.

They're delicious served with butter and honey or maple syrup and fresh blueberries.

laurel's hoecakes

MAKES ABOUT 12 HOECAKES

1½ cups/240 g cornmeal

½ cup/60 g all-purpose flour

1 tbsp baking powder

1½ tsp kosher salt

2 tbsp honey

3 tbsp maple syrup

¾ cup/180 ml whole milk

¼ cup/60 ml buttermilk

½ cup/110 g unsalted butter, melted and slightly cooled

2 eggs

2 ears fresh corn, grated

1. Put the cornmeal, all-purpose flour, baking powder, and salt in a large bowl. Add the honey, maple syrup, milk, buttermilk, melted butter, eggs, and corn. Whisk to combine.

2. About 5 minutes before you're ready to make the pancakes, preheat a greased griddle or large skillet over medium-high heat; the griddle is ready when a few droplets of water sizzle and dance across the surface. But once heated, lower the heat to medium to prevent burning.

3. Drop ⅓ cup/80 ml of batter onto the hot griddle. When bubbles set on the surface of the pancake and the bottom is golden, flip and cook for about 1 minute longer. They should cook quickly. Serve immediately, while hot.

These are best the moment they leave the griddle.

Make this your let-your-tired-wife-sleep-in surprise. They're simple to make but appear very time-consuming and thoughtful. You'll get major brownie points here, I promise.

Normally, I would say substitute whatever fruit you like for the sauce, but the sourness of the cranberries is crucial to cutting the sweetness of the brown sugar and rounding out this dish.

I love to serve this French toast with whipped cream, salty bacon, and nice runny eggs. Now go show her how great you are!

vanilla french toast with brown sugar–cranberry sauce

SERVES 3

SAUCE

½ cup + 2 tbsp/140 g brown sugar

2 tbsp water

½ tsp kosher salt

¼ cup/60 ml heavy cream

6 tbsp/85 g unsalted butter

Peel of 1 orange, cut into 4 long pieces

2 cups/300 g frozen or fresh cranberries, whole

FRENCH TOAST

6 eggs

¾ cup/180 ml heavy cream

1½ tbsp sugar

¼ tsp vanilla extract

¼ tsp kosher salt

6 slices Brioche (page 105) or store-bought challah, cut 1 in/2.5 cm thick

1. To make the sauce: In a saucepan over high heat, cook the brown sugar, water, and salt until it bubbles furiously, 1 to 2 minutes. Turn off the heat and stir in the cream, butter, and orange peel. Then return to the heat and cook 1 minute longer. Add the cranberries and set aside.

2. To make the French toast: Whisk together the eggs, cream, sugar, vanilla, and salt in a large bowl. Soak the sliced bread in the custard until saturated but not falling apart, 1 to 2 minutes.

3. Preheat a greased griddle or large skillet over medium heat. Cook the French toast on each side until nice and brown.

4. While the French toast cooks, return the sauce to the stove. Cook over medium heat until heated through, about 3 minutes.

5. Plate the French toast immediately and pour two giant spoonfuls of the sauce over the top. Serve while good and hot.

The French toast is best the moment it leaves the griddle; the sauce keeps well, refrigerated, for up to 4 days.

8:30 A.M.

cereals

The place is in full swing, line out the door, down the ramp, almost to the parking lot. It's Saturday—we do this every week—and we're ready.

The expediter calls out tickets to the kitchen as fast as she can. "Order fire! One egg sandwich, easy . . . one green eggs and ham, no ham . . . one granola add berries . . ." One of the cooks calls me over to tell me he's out of granola. "Really, you're realizing this now or just remembering to tell me? Either way this is very, very annoying." I have steam coming off me like a cartoon character. Just at that moment my sleeping beauty of a morning baker walks in four hours late, smiling and looking like somehow I will think this is all very cute, "Sorrrrrrrry, it won't happen—" I cut her off, "Don't smile at me ever again. Make granola!" My cook seems pleased that I have found someone who screwed up worse than he did.

I yell over to the girl in front of the oven and tell her to turn it down and open the door so it can cool down enough to make the granola. Just then I turn around and bump right into my extremely tall husband's chest, "Hi, baby, having a rough morning?" he says with an understanding smirk.

He knows me better than I know myself and I rarely have to explain to him what's going on with me. He hands me a pint glass from home filled with a dark, and very thick, green liquid—his latest "healthy" smoothie creation. We're trying to get pregnant and the doctor told me to eat better and lead a less stressful lifestyle. I'm trying to follow at least some of this advice, but the smoothie looks foul at this moment and I'm feeling stressed.

People often ask me what it's like to work with my husband: It's challenging and annoying, but it's the best thing ever and I couldn't imagine it any other way. Many relationships implode when couples work together, but for me it creates the safe and loving atmosphere I need to thrive. Over the years, we have slowly learned not to take it all so personally and to simply, without too many questions, have each other's backs. But just because he has my back does not mean this smoothie looks appetizing right now, but man, oh man, do I want a baby. I close my eyes and guzzle it down.

There are a thousand variations when making granola, so mix in anything you like. Every house should have its own recipe. I like mine not too sweet, but if you like yours sweeter, add more honey to this recipe. If your family likes coconut, throw in sweetened toasted coconut. For a chocolate granola, omit the cinnamon, add an additional ½ tsp salt, use only toasted almonds, and instead of dried fruit toss in ¾ cup/100 g chopped dark chocolate. For a spiced granola, double the cinnamon and add ¼ tsp nutmeg, ¼ tsp ginger, and ¼ tsp cloves.

I always make sure we have a batch of granola around the house. My son takes it to the park, my husband takes it on runs, and I love it over ice cream.

granola

SERVES 4

4 cups/200 g rolled oats, not quick-cooking

½ cup/110 g unsalted butter, melted

½ cup/170 g honey

1 tsp kosher salt

⅛ tsp ground cinnamon (optional)

1 cup/150 g mixed toasted nuts, like walnuts, almonds, pecans, pumpkin seeds, hazelnuts, pistachios

1 cup/170 g mixed dried fruit, like sliced apricots, sour cherries, cranberries, currants, raisins

1. Preheat your oven to 325°F/165°C.

2. In a large bowl, toss together the rolled oats, melted butter, honey, salt, and cinnamon.

3. Spread the mixture on a sheet pan and bake until golden, about 25 minutes. Add the nuts and bake 5 minutes longer. Allow to cool. Toss with the dried fruit.

This keeps well, in an airtight container, at room temperature, for up to 2 weeks.

This is a very traditional way to make muesli and it's definitely the one I prefer. All the ingredients are mixed together the night before so the grains soften and the flavors come together to make a very creamy, earthy, sweet mixture. This recipe is incredibly versatile. You can use any fruit you like in any combination you wish. Feel free to trade out the grated apples for grated peaches, nectarines, or pears, or simply mix in whole blueberries and sliced strawberries. If you don't have dates, you can always use prunes or dried figs. Occasionally, I'll add toasted almonds or walnuts to the mix. Please make sure to grind the flax seeds, because whole flax seeds get very slimy after soaking.

muesli

SERVES 4 TO 6

3 cups/720 ml whole milk

2 cups/480 ml plain whole yogurt

2 apples, skin on, grated

1 ripe banana, sliced

¾ cup/125 g golden raisins

9 tbsp/110 g cracked wheat or bulgur

9 tbsp/110 g wheat germ, toasted

9 tbsp/50 g rolled oats, toasted

¼ cup/85 g honey

¼ cup/35 g chopped dates

2 tbsp millet

2 tbsp flax seeds, ground,
or 3¾ tbsp flax seed meal

1 tbsp chia seeds or poppy seeds

1 pinch kosher salt

Seasonal fresh fruit for topping

1. Stir together the milk, yogurt, apples, banana, raisins, cracked wheat, wheat germ, rolled oats, honey, dates, millet, flax seeds, chia seeds, and salt in a large mixing bowl. Cover tightly and refrigerate overnight.

2. In the morning, mound the mixture into bowls and top with sliced, chopped, or whole seasonal fruit.

This keeps well, refrigerated, for 2 or 3 days.

Though soaking the oats is not absolutely necessary, it does makes the oatmeal cook much faster. If you opt for store-bought almond milk, you'll have to adjust the sweetness of this recipe depending on the sweetness of your almond milk. If you prefer a sweeter oatmeal, slice 2 or 3 pitted dates, soak them with the oat mixture, and cook all together or just add more honey.

steel-cut oats with homemade almond milk

SERVES 2

2½ cups/600 ml Almond Milk (recipe follows)

1 large pinch kosher salt

½ cup/100 g steel-cut oats

1 cinnamon stick or 1 large pinch cinnamon

2 tbsp honey

2 tbsp sliced almonds, toasted

DAY ONE

1. Combine the almond milk, salt, steel-cut oats, and cinnamon in a small bowl. Cover with plastic wrap and refrigerate overnight.

DAY TWO

2. In the morning, cook the oat mixture in a small saucepan over medium heat until thickened, about 10 minutes. Portion into two bowls and top with honey and toasted almonds.

This keeps well, refrigerated, for up to 3 days. Add a little almond milk or water when reheating.

Josh loves to make shakes with almond milk in the morning, we put it in our coffee and tea, we use it to make oatmeal, and we love to make hot chocolate with it as well. You can use it anywhere you would think to use regular milk. I strongly recommend raw whole almonds with the skins on because they give it a much richer flavor.

almond milk

MAKES 3 CUPS/720 ML

¾ cup/100 g raw almonds, whole, skin on

4 dates, pitted

1 vanilla bean (optional)

½ tsp kosher salt

1. Combine the almonds, dates, and 1 cup/240 ml cold water. Refrigerate overnight.

2. Strain the mixture, discarding the water.

3. If using the vanilla bean, split lengthwise and scrape the seeds into a blender. Set the scraped pod aside. Add the almond mixture, salt, and 3½ cups/830 ml cold water. Blend until smooth, about two minutes.

4. Strain the mixture through a cheesecloth or fine-mesh strainer into a large canning jar. Add the vanilla pod, then refrigerate until needed.

This keeps well, refrigerated, for up to 4 days. It will separate as it sits, but just shake it back together.

It's very rare to have 40 minutes to make a weekday breakfast for yourself. If you don't have that kind of time in the morning, prepare this porridge the night before; then just reheat with a little additional water and it will be perfect. This dish is the perfect jump-start to a cold morning. It's so warming and soul-satisfying it'll give you that added boost you need to go out and greet the day. Feel free to play with different dried fruits in place of the raisins or switch out the maple syrup for honey or agave. Basically, figure out the combination that makes you feel loved in the morning and make it that way.

cinnamon-sugar bulgur porridge

SERVES 2 OR 3

PORRIDGE

3 cups/710 ml water

¾ cup/150 g bulgur wheat

2 tbsp millet

1 tbsp flax seed meal

1 tbsp chia seeds or poppy seeds

1 tbsp raisins, chopped

2 tsp maple syrup

½ tbsp unsalted butter

½ tsp kosher salt

TOPPING

3 tbsp sugar

¼ tsp ground cinnamon

1. To make the porridge: Combine the water, bulgur wheat, millet, flax seed meal, chia seeds, raisins, maple syrup, butter, and salt in a medium saucepan and simmer over medium heat until the bulgur is cooked through and the mixture is nice and creamy, about 15 minutes.

2. Meanwhile, make the topping: Mix the sugar and cinnamon in a small bowl and set aside.

3. Scoop the porridge into bowls and sprinkle liberally with the topping.

This keeps quite well, refrigerated, for up to 4 days. Add a little water when reheating.

This dish is simple to make but looks and tastes very exciting when it hits the table. I love it with blueberries, but it works just as well with red seedless grapes or blackberries because they get tender very quickly while still holding their shape. You can always pour plain cream over the top or serve with a dollop of unsweetened Whipped Cream (page 149), but it's not necessary. If you want to make this more wintry, cook the farro with a cinnamon stick, or if you have a scraped vanilla pod lying around, add that while you cook the farro for another layer of flavor.

hot farro porridge with blueberries and toasted walnuts

SERVES 2

1 cup/200 g farro

Kosher salt

3 tbsp unsalted butter

2 cups/480 ml water, plus 1 tbsp

1 cup/150 g fresh blueberries

2 tbsp brown sugar

¾ cup/180 ml whole milk

¼ cup/30 g walnuts, chopped and toasted

1. In a small saucepan over high heat, toast the farro with ⅛ tsp salt and 2 tbsp of the butter, until slightly fragrant, 1 to 2 minutes. Add the 2 cups/480 ml water and reduce the heat to low. Simmer, uncovered, until the water cooks off, about 25 minutes.

2. Meanwhile, in a small sauté pan over medium-high heat, combine the remaining 1 tbsp butter, the blueberries, 1 tbsp of the brown sugar, a pinch of salt, and the 1 tbsp water. Quickly sauté until the blueberries are tender but not bursting, about 2 minutes.

3. When the water has cooked off, add the milk and remaining 1 tbsp brown sugar. Increase the heat to medium-high and simmer until the liquid is absorbed, 5 to 10 minutes.

4. Portion the farro into two bowls and top with cooked blueberries and toasted walnuts.

This keeps well, refrigerated, for up to 3 days. Add a little milk when reheating.

If you're serving only two, I highly suggest making this whole porridge recipe anyway. Pour any leftovers onto a sheet pan, wrap in plastic, and refrigerate. It will set up firmly and you can cut it into squares or sticks. Lightly brush with olive oil and either roast in a 500°F/260°C oven, grill outside, or pan-fry in a little more oil. Cook until browned and crisp on the outside, but soft inside. Serve with sautéed mushrooms or spinach, lamb chops, Spicy Tomato Jam (facing page), or, if you happen to be having a little man named Milo over, just plain ketchup will do.

corn porridge with strawberry compote and greek yogurt

SERVES 4 TO 6

3 ears corn

4 qt/3.8 L water, plus ¼ cup/60 ml

2½ cups/380 g fresh strawberries, quartered

4 tbsp unsalted butter

3 tbsp brown sugar

Kosher salt

1 cup/160 g cornmeal

1 to 2 cups/240 to 480 ml Greek yogurt

4 to 6 fresh sage leaves, finely chopped

1. Begin 1 day ahead or first thing in the morning by making a corn stock. Shave the kernels from the cobs and set aside. In a large saucepan, simmer the 4 qt/3.8 L water and the bare cobs, until reduced to 5 cups/1.2 L, about 1½ hours. Discard the cobs and set the stock aside.

2. Combine the strawberries, 2 tbsp of the butter, 1 tbsp of the brown sugar, a pinch of salt, and the ¼ cup/60 ml water in a medium saucepan and simmer over medium-high heat, covered, for 2 minutes. Uncover and mash the strawberries. Continue cooking until the compote has thickened, stirring occasionally to keep it from burning, 1 to 2 minutes. Set aside.

3. In a medium saucepan, sauté the corn kernels in 1 tbsp butter over medium-high heat. Add the cornmeal and 1 tsp salt. Stir, lightly toasting, for 2 to 3 minutes. Whisk in 1 qt/960 ml of the corn stock. Bring to a boil, then reduce, whisking occasionally. Add the remaining 1 tbsp butter and 2 tbsp brown sugar. Continue cooking until thickened, 1 to 2 minutes. (You can keep the porridge warm over low heat, stirring occasionally and adding the remaining 1 cup/240 ml stock, 2 to 3 tbsp every 10 minutes, as needed.)

4. Portion into bowls and top with a spoonful of the strawberry compote, a big scoop of Greek yogurt, and the finely chopped sage.

The porridge and compote keep well, refrigerated, for up to 4 days. Reserve the extra 1 cup/240 ml corn stock for use in reheating the porridge.

I'm calling this jam but it could easily be a grown-up alternative to ketchup.

You can twist it a hundred different ways; add curry powder, spicy peppers, sweet peppers, beer. . . . Make it as crazy and interesting as you like. I chose to put cumin in this recipe because the flavor goes with many recipes in this book.

Try it on any sandwich, with any of the frittatas, beside the Butter and Herb Potatoes (page 172), or smeared on a biscuit. During the winter months, it's a great alternative to sliced tomato on a BLT.

spicy tomato jam

MAKES ABOUT 1 CUP/130 G

2 lb/900 g large tomatoes, sliced into eighths or left whole

1½ cups/270 g cherry tomatoes

2 tbsp sugar

½ tsp kosher salt

½ tsp ground cumin

½ tsp chile flakes

1. Combine the tomatoes, cherry tomatoes, sugar, salt, cumin, and chile flakes in a medium saucepan and cover with water by about ½ in/12 mm. Simmer over medium-high heat until more than half of the water has cooked off, 1½ to 2 hours.

2. Blend in a blender or food processor until smooth. Return to the stove and simmer over medium-high heat until thickened and cooked down to a little less than half, about 1½ hours. Refrigerate until needed.

This keeps well, refrigerated, for up to 2 weeks.

The first time I made this dish, my husband and I were in Big Sur early in our marriage, so this holds a special place in my heart. Obviously this is a breakfast book, but I must confess I've eaten this for dinner plenty of times and it's incredibly satisfying. If you can't find spring onions, use yellow onions. Try shaved Brussels sprouts, collard greens, or sprouting broccoli instead of kale, and bacon or mushrooms instead of sausage. This can also be made with just about any grain, from brown rice to quinoa, so don't feel you have to use barley.

I know for some the maple syrup might seem odd, but in its own sweet way it brings the dish together, so trust me, don't leave it out. This recipe calls for veggie stock, but if you have a good homemade chicken or beef stock in your fridge, feel free to use that. This stock recipe is just enough for this dish, but when I make stock at home, I always make extra to freeze, so make a bigger batch of stock if you're game, but keep in mind it may take a longer time to reduce.

barley porridge with spring onions, kale, and sausage

SERVES 4

VEGGIE STOCK

2 carrots, cut into 1-in/2.5 cm chunks

½ onion, rough chopped

1 spring onion, green tops only

2 garlic cloves

1 bay leaf

12 cups/2.8 L water

BARLEY PORRIDGE

½ onion, finely diced

1 carrot, finely diced

1 garlic clove, minced

1½ tbsp chopped fresh savory

1 tbsp extra-virgin olive oil

1¾ tsp kosher salt

1 cup/200 g barley

1 cup/240 ml white wine

2 tbsp unsalted butter

¼ cup/25 g grated Parmesan

TOPPINGS

4 to 8 large raw breakfast sausages or your favorite sausage

2 tbsp extra-virgin olive oil

2 spring onions, thinly sliced, white and light green parts only

½ tsp kosher salt

4 cups/145 g chopped kale

1 pinch chile flakes

2 tbsp unsalted butter

4 eggs

4 to 6 tbsp/60 to 90 ml maple syrup

CONTINUED

DAY ONE

1. To make the veggie stock: Simmer the carrots, onion, spring onion, garlic, bay leaf, and water in a stock pot until reduced to 1 qt/960 ml liquid, about 1½ hours. Remove from heat and bring to room temperature. Strain into a large bowl, pressing on the solids with a spoon to extract the liquid. Discard the solids. Refrigerate until using, up to 1 week.

DAY TWO

2. To make the porridge: In a medium saucepan, sauté the onion, carrot, garlic, and savory in the olive oil until beginning to soften, 5 to 8 minutes. Add 1½ tsp of the salt and the barley. Sauté for 1 minute longer. Add the white wine and cook down by half.

3. When the wine in the porridge mixture is reduced, add the veggie stock, reduce the heat to medium-low, and simmer gently, stirring occasionally, until the barley is cooked through and most of the liquid has been absorbed, about 45 minutes. Stir in the butter and Parmesan.

4. To prepare the toppings: Preheat your oven to 400°F/200°C. Put the sausages on a sheet pan, toss with 1 tbsp of the olive oil, and roast until browned and cooked through. The cook time will depend on the size of your sausages, about 15 minutes.

5. Meanwhile, in a large sauté pan, heat the remaining 1 tbsp olive oil. Add the spring onions and the remaining ¼ tsp salt. Sauté until softened, about 5 minutes. Add the kale and chile flakes. Sauté until wilted, about 3 minutes. Set aside.

6. When it comes to frying the eggs, you may need to either work in batches or have two pans going at once. Heat 1 tbsp of the butter in a nonstick sauté pan over high heat. Crack 2 eggs into a small bowl and gently slide them into the butter. (If you break a yolk, discard the egg and try again.) Reduce the heat to medium and cook until the whites are set but the yolks are runny, about 2 minutes. When ready, give the pan a gentle shake to loosen the eggs. Repeat with the remaining 2 eggs.

7. Spoon the barley into bowls, top with the kale-onion mixture, a sausage or two, and a fried egg. Drizzle each serving with about 1 tbsp maple syrup.

This dish is best served immediately, but the components keep well, refrigerated, for up to 3 days.

This is a grown-up chocolate breakfast—it's not super-sweet and the mocha glaze is loaded with coffee. Despite that, it should be enjoyed with a tall glass of ice-cold milk. Make this for your special someone as a Valentine's Day breakfast in bed or just as a fun treat on a cold Sunday morning.

warm chocolate rice pudding

SERVES 4

PUDDING

1 cup/200 g short grain white rice

¼ cup/50 g sugar

½ tsp kosher salt

2 tbsp Dutch process cocoa powder

1 vanilla bean, split, seeds scraped out, or 2 tsp vanilla extract

4½ cups/1 L whole milk

GLAZE

¾ cup/125 g chopped dark chocolate, 60 to 70% cacao

¼ cup + 2 tbsp/90 ml hot coffee

1 batch Whipped Cream (page 149)

3 tbsp cocoa nibs or chopped toasted hazelnuts (optional)

1. To make the pudding: In a small saucepan, whisk the rice, sugar, salt, cocoa powder, and vanilla to break up the cocoa powder and distribute the vanilla seeds. Add the milk and bring to a boil over medium-high heat, stirring occasionally. Once boiling, immediately reduce the heat to medium-low and simmer, stirring regularly to keep the bottom from burning. Cook until the rice is soft and the mixture is thick and creamy, about 30 minutes.

2. Cover, remove from heat, and set aside while you make the glaze.

3. To make the glaze: Put the chocolate in a small bowl and pour the hot coffee over it. Allow to sit and melt for a couple of minutes, then stir until homogenous.

4. Spoon the pudding into bowls, drizzle with glaze, and top with whipped cream and cocoa nibs.

This is best the day it's made but keeps, refrigerated, up to 3 days. Add a little milk when reheating.

9 A.M.

sandwiches

The guys on the line have their heads down, full speed ahead. I'm in the front of the kitchen watching as the servers take people through the line and get their orders. I'm looking out at the people enjoying all our hard work when I overhear one customer ordering a fried egg sandwich, "I would like one egg poached and one egg scrambled." I roll my eyes. Are you seriously asking for that on the same sandwich?! I watch in shock as the server turns around and starts to head into the kitchen to ask if we can accommodate this insane request. I say No as nicely as possible as the server enters the kitchen because it is an open kitchen and I don't want to look like a jerk. I have a line of forty people and thirty-five tickets on my board, and I know if I even said yes to this for sure it would not come out as the woman has envisioned, and it's not fair to throw this curveball at my line cooks. Not to mention that it's simply an annoying request and she should be ashamed that she asked for it!

On the average Saturday at Huckleberry, we have about a thousand different customers and three line guys, who have been with me since almost the beginning, making all the food. I'm not sure if it's me, but for some reason Huckleberry attracts a very unique kind of line cook. Ours aren't the kind of guys who stay out blowing lines of coke and drinking all night or check out the bodies of our various pastry girls and make comments. Our line guys are sweet, tough, talented, and sensitive. They put out hundreds of dishes each day seemingly unfazed by the stress of tickets piling up, server mistakes that they need to re-fire, and people yelling at them from each direction. Yet, every month I have to have a sit-down talk with one of them because their feelings were hurt that they weren't consulted on where we moved the soup warmer. And they're genuinely upset! Norberto has been with me the longest, and when he started off he was certainly not the fastest line cook, but everything he made was delicious and had tons of love and care behind it. Now he's ahead of even the nastiest of rushes, and his food still comes out with love and care each time. These guys are our family.

I watch the server go back to tell the woman that she can't have her crazy order "her way" and see the woman grow angrier and start to lay into the server. Then the server heads back, and before I can get out of the way I hear, "That woman in line would like to talk to you."

"My pleasure," I say as I drop my knife and head out to talk to her. My girls all crane their necks to see out of the kitchen, and I know that they're thankful I didn't take my knife with me. Laurel pretends to fill pastries in front so she can get closer to my impending rant. I know she loves and cherishes a good Zoe rant—and this one is going to be gold. Right as I'm just about to approach the woman, Joel swoops in. "Zoe, back to the kitchen, you know better than that. Let me handle this." Intercepted! No rant and all our fun ruined. Sometimes I really hate that Joel is good at his job. At least my girls and I have a good laugh about what could have been.

This is another one of those things that we've been making since Saturday Morning Breakfasts at Rustic. It never changes because people wouldn't stand for it, but between you and me, this would be awesome with a slice of fresh tomato in the height of summer.

It's such a simple sandwich, so it has to be the best bacon and organic eggs, and it really does make a difference if you make the aioli from scratch. Everything has to be in balance. At Huckleberry, we make our own country bread, so please be sure to get your hands on some artisan bread for this sandwich.

huck's fried egg sandwich

SERVES 4

12 to 16 slices thick-cut bacon

8 slices sourdough bread

4 oz/115 g Gruyère, grated

1 batch Aioli (page 224)

4 tbsp/55 g unsalted butter

8 eggs

3 cups/110 g arugula

Fleur de sel for sprinkling

1. Preheat your oven to 375°F/190°C.

2. Arrange the bacon on a sheet pan and bake until golden brown, about 15 minutes.

3. Increase the oven temperature to 450°F/230°C and toast the bread. When the bread is mostly toasted, distribute the Gruyère on four of the slices and return them to the oven to melt, 3 to 4 minutes. Remove the four bare slices of bread and spread each with about 2 tbsp aioli and top with 3 or 4 slices of bacon. Remember to keep one eye on your cheesy bread in the oven. When the cheese is melted, remove the bread, slice in half, and set aside.

4. When it comes to frying the eggs, you may need to either work in batches or have two pans going at once. Heat 1 tbsp of the butter in a nonstick sauté pan over high heat. Crack 2 eggs into a small bowl and gently slide them into the butter. (If you break a yolk, discard the egg and try again.) Reduce the heat to medium and cook until the whites are set but the yolks are runny, about 2 minutes. When ready, give the pan a gentle shake to loosen the eggs.

5. Slide the eggs onto a bacon-covered toast. Top with a handful of arugula and a sprinkle of fleur de sel. Slice that half, being careful not to slice into the yolk, before topping with the cheese-bread halves. (We cut the two sides of the sandwich separately to avoid breaking the yolks, which would spoil the fun of eating this sandwich.) Repeat for the remaining sandwiches, unless you have multiple pans going!

This is best eaten the moment it's made.

If you've gone through the trouble of making Maple Bacon Biscuits, it's mandatory to make at least one of these. Hence this recipe serves only one; but by all means multiply this by as many as you want, and eat up. We run these as an off-the-menu special at Huckleberry and most people don't know about them; those who do, love them.

The hard thing about having a "secret" off-menu item and so many employees is that there is always mass confusion when it's ordered. Everyone in the kitchen has a different idea of how it should be made. So here it is, once and for all, the way it was intended. If you come to Huckleberry and see it prepared differently, please let me know. Although, wedging fried chicken inside would not be a bad decision either.

egg huck muffin
SERVES 1

3 slices bacon

2 eggs

2 tsp heavy cream or crème fraîche

1 big pinch kosher salt

1 Maple Bacon Biscuit (page 60)

1 tsp unsalted butter

Fleur de sel for topping

Maple syrup for drizzling

1. Preheat your oven to 375°F/190°C.

2. Arrange the bacon on a sheet pan and bake for about 15 minutes, until golden brown.

3. Increase the oven temperature to 400°F/205°C.

4. In a small mixing bowl, whisk together the eggs, cream, and salt.

5. Toss the biscuit in the oven to heat while you scramble the eggs. In a small sauté pan over medium heat, melt the butter. Add the eggs and scramble until soft-set.

6. Once heated, carefully slice the biscuit in half with a serrated knife. On the bottom half of the biscuit, layer half the bacon, then the scrambled eggs, followed by the remaining bacon. Drop the biscuit top on, drizzle it with a healthy dose of maple syrup, and dig in!

This does not keep, don't ask it to.

At about the same time as I began holding Saturday Morning Breakfast at Rustic, our friend, and former Rustic Canyon chef, Evan Funke, came in to take over the kitchen. He got a big kick out of the fact that the pastry chef of the place took over the restaurant every weekend to run her own breakfast place. He loved my fresh-baked English muffins so much that he helped me create this dish, and we've been making it at Huckleberry ever since.

It's quintessential Huck, because it's simple, but everything is made from scratch in-house, which is what takes this simple dish to the next level.

I suggest you make a big batch of English muffins and freeze a bunch. Then you can have this anytime you like.

green eggs and ham

SERVES 4

4 English Muffins (page 102)

¾ cup/170 g unsalted butter, melted or at room temperature

4 oz/115 g thinly sliced prosciutto

8 eggs

1 batch Pesto (page 225)

4 cups/145 g arugula

Fleur de sel for sprinkling

1. Preheat your oven to 500°F/260°C.

2. Fork-split the English muffins, lightly butter both sides, and toast in the oven until nice and crispy, 5 to 10 minutes.

3. Begin building the open-face sandwiches by layering each English muffin half with 2 slices of the prosciutto.

4. When it comes to frying the eggs, you may need to either work in batches or have two pans going at once. Heat 1 tbsp of the butter in a nonstick sauté pan over high heat. Crack 2 eggs into a small bowl and gently slide them into the butter. (If you break a yolk, discard the egg and try again.) Reduce the heat to medium and cook until the whites are set but the yolks are runny, about 2 minutes. When ready, give the pan a gentle shake to loosen the eggs.

5. Slide an egg onto each English muffin half. Top with a very large spoonful of pesto, a big handful of arugula, and a sprinkle of fleur de sel. Repeat for the remaining sandwiches, unless you have multiple pans going!

This does not keep.

Homemade aioli is so easy to make, and once you try it you'll never want to buy mayonnaise again. We use it on almost all the breakfast sandwiches in this book, but there are tons of things that aioli is good for, including dipping for the Butter and Herb Potatoes (page 172), or tossing with pieces of roasted chicken for a homemade chicken salad sandwich. This aioli recipe is also super-versatile. Feel free to add cayenne pepper, curry powder, or your favorite relish.

aioli

MAKES ¾ CUP/165 G

2 egg yolks

1 tbsp Dijon mustard

½ tsp kosher salt

2 tbsp extra-virgin olive oil

1 tsp lemon juice

1 tsp Champagne vinegar

¼ cup + 2 tbsp/90 ml canola oil

1 tbsp chopped fresh parsley

1. In a medium bowl, whisk together the egg yolks, mustard, and salt until combined.

2. Slowly stream in the olive oil, whisking constantly. It helps to set the bowl on a kitchen towel to steady it. Add the lemon juice and vinegar and whisk to combine.

3. Now, very slowly, stream in the canola oil, whisking constantly. If it shows signs of separating, slow down the oil a little. When you have a nice even emulsion, stir in the parsley. Wrap or transfer to a jar and refrigerate until needed.

This keeps well, refrigerated, for up to 1 week.

Pesto is insanely versatile, so I always make a double batch, and at Huckleberry we make it by the boatload. It will elevate almost every savory recipe in this book. I love putting it on the Poached Eggs, Pesto, and Snap Peas (page 266) or serving it as a dipping sauce alongside frittatas, or the Butter and Herb Potatoes (page 172). It's also good served with the Braised Brisket and Fingerling Potato Hash (page 262).

This is the way I like my pesto, but you should feel free to make it to your own liking. Make it more garlicky, more lemony, use different herbs like parsley, mint, tarragon, even arugula. A good variation is to substitute cilantro for the basil and finish it in the blender with 1 oz/30 g goat cheese or cream cheese; serve it this way as a condiment for our beer-braised pork (see page 230).

pesto

MAKES ABOUT 1½ CUPS/300 G

¼ cup/20 g fresh basil leaves, tightly packed

⅔ cup/160 ml extra-virgin olive oil

2 garlic cloves

¼ cup/25 g grated Parmesan

1 tbsp chopped fresh parsley

1 tbsp pine nuts, lightly toasted

½ tsp kosher salt

Zest and juice of ½ lemon

1. Fill a medium saucepan with water and bring to a boil. Beside it, set up a medium bowl with ice water.

2. Blanch the basil leaves in the boiling water for 30 to 45 seconds. Remove with a strainer or slotted spoon and immediately plunge in the ice water to stop the cooking. Shake off the water and set aside in a blender.

3. Combine ⅓ cup/80 ml of the olive oil and 1 garlic clove in a small saucepan and cook over medium heat until fragrant and lightly browned. Refrigerate until cooled completely.

4. In a blender or food processor, combine the cooled garlic and oil, blanched basil, Parmesan, parsley, pine nuts, the remaining ⅓ cup/80 ml olive oil, the remaining garlic clove, and the salt. Blend until smooth. Add the lemon zest and juice and stir in by hand. Refrigerate until needed.

This keeps well, refrigerated, for up to 1 week.

I make this exactly the way my mom made it. It's the same perfectly salty and sweet sandwich that fed me on so many mornings and helped make my taste buds the way they are today. I love you, mom.

A fun variation on this would be using our Fresh Blueberry Brioche (page 108). I think it would taste amazing with the egg and butter and brown sugar. Or for a savory version, substitute 1 tbsp grated Parmesan for the brown sugar and serve it with a little mustard. But if you're making it for me, make it the original way, or you'll get an earful.

my mom's egg in a hole

SERVES 1 OR 2

2 slices thick-cut Brioche (page 105)
1 tbsp unsalted butter
2 eggs
2 tbsp brown sugar
Fleur de sel for sprinkling

1. Preheat your oven to 475°F/245°C.

2. Make a 1-in/2.5-cm hole in the center of each slice of bread.

3. In a large ovenproof sauté pan, melt the butter and add the bread; cook until brown. Flip the bread and carefully crack an egg into each hole. Quickly sprinkle each slice of bread, not the egg, with 1 tbsp brown sugar.

4. Immediately transfer to the oven to bake. Don't try to brown the second side on the stove, that will happen all by itself in the oven. Bake until the egg white sets, but the yolk is quite runny, 6 to 8 minutes. But check your egg at 5 minutes, as a firm yolk ruins the pleasure of this simple dish.

5. Sprinkle lightly with fleur de sel.

This is best the moment it emerges from the oven. Does not keep well.

This is a great summertime dish because that's when all these vegetables are at their best. It's also one of those dishes that generally tastes better if it's made the day before you serve it to give the flavors time to come together, although it still tastes great if you throw it all together the day of.

I leave the garlic cloves whole with the veggies because I love the surprise bites that contain the soft, sweet garlic cloves; but if you're offended by such things, pull them out of the vegetables after they cook and discard.

If you have leftover ratatouille, it makes a great lunch or dinner served over pasta, polenta, farro, or any delicious grain. I've even smeared it on a turkey sandwich and it was fantastic.

Make sure you use farm eggs so that beautiful, rich yellow yolk pops against the deep red of the ratatouille.

ratatouille on toast
with over-easy eggs

SERVES 4

⅔ cup/160 ml extra-virgin olive oil, plus more for drizzling

5 garlic cloves

2 cups/340 g chopped tomatoes (cut into ¾-in/2-cm pieces)

Kosher salt

2 or 3 pinches chile flakes

2 cups/275 g chopped onions (cut into ¾-in/2-cm pieces)

2 cups/290 g chopped zucchini (cut into ¾-in/2-cm pieces)

2 cups/275 g chopped red bell pepper (cut into ¾-in/2-cm pieces)

2 cups/150 g chopped eggplant (cut into ¾-in/2-cm pieces)

⅓ cup/80 ml water

About 30 fresh basil leaves, plus ½ cup/40 g torn fresh basil leaves

1 bay leaf

4 slices thick-cut country bread

2 to 4 tbsp unsalted butter

4 to 8 eggs

Fleur de sel for sprinkling

1. In a large sauté pan over medium-high, heat 2 tsp of the olive oil and 1 garlic clove until fragrant and beginning to color. Add the tomatoes, ¼ tsp salt, and season with the chile flakes. Sauté until softened, occasionally shaking the pan to avoid burning, about 4 minutes. Transfer to a medium saucepan and set aside.

2. In the same pan, over medium-high heat, sauté 1 garlic clove in 2 tsp olive oil until fragrant. Add the onions and ¼ tsp salt and sauté until slightly soft and a light golden brown. Transfer to the saucepan with the tomatoes and set aside.

3. Repeat, sautéing 1 garlic clove in 2 tsp olive oil. This time add the zucchini and ¼ tsp salt and cook over high heat, until browned. Transfer to the saucepan with the tomatoes and onions. Set aside.

4. Repeat again with 1 garlic clove in 2 tsp olive oil. Now add the bell peppers and ¼ tsp salt and cook over medium-high heat, until browned. Transfer to the saucepan with the rest of the veggies. Set aside.

5. And finally, repeat one last time, with the pan on medium-high heat. Add the remaining garlic, olive oil, and now the eggplant and ¼ tsp salt. Sauté until browned and cooked through. If the eggplant sucks up all the oil and the pan looks dry, add a splash of water. Add the eggplant to the saucepan of veggies, too.

6. Preheat your oven to 500°F/260°C.

7. To the saucepan of vegetables, add the water, 8 to 10 whole basil leaves, and the bay leaf. Cook the vegetable mixture, covered, over medium heat for 20 minutes. Remove the lid and cook for 2 to 5 minutes longer to reduce the juices slightly.

8. Remove from the heat and stir in the torn basil leaves. (If refrigerating overnight, do so now. In the morning, preheat your oven to 500°F/260°C and warm up the ratatouille in a medium saucepan, covered, over medium heat.)

9. Drizzle the bread with olive oil, sprinkle with a few pinches of salt, and toast in the oven until crisp. Spoon the warm ratatouille over the toast.

10. When it comes to frying the eggs, you may need to either work in batches or have two pans going at once. Heat 1 tbsp of the butter in a nonstick sauté pan over high heat. Crack 2 eggs into a small bowl and gently slide them into the butter. (If you break a yolk, discard the egg and try again.) Reduce the heat to medium and cook until the whites are set but the yolks are runny, about 2 minutes. When ready, give the pan a gentle shake to loosen the eggs.

11. Repeat with any remaining butter and eggs. Slide the eggs onto the ratatouille, drizzle with olive oil, sprinkle with fleur de sel, and garnish with a few whole basil leaves.

This should be eaten the moment the eggs hit the bread. The ratatouille keeps well, refrigerated, for up to 3 days.

It's best to braise the pork the day before you serve it so it can absorb all the wonderful flavors in the sauce. The key to this dish is cooking the sauce down by more than half, so you get a really nice concentration of pork, beer, onions, and spices. What you lose in volume, you'll more than make up for in rich, intense flavor. Watercress works really well here because it freshens up the dish, but if you don't have watercress, use any light green that you see at your farmers' market, such as arugula, baby spinach, or young lettuces.

beer-braised pork on toast with an egg on top

SERVES 3 OR 4

DRY RUB

1 tbsp kosher salt

1 tbsp sugar

1 tsp ground cumin

¼ tsp ground coriander

¼ tsp ground cardamom

¼ tsp ground paprika

¼ tsp curry powder

3 onions, sliced ¼ in/6 mm thick

5 tbsp + 1 tsp/80 ml extra-virgin olive oil

Kosher salt

2 to 2½ lb/910 g to 1.2 kg pork butt

2 garlic cloves

2 bay leaves

3 bottles very light beer or 1½ bottles white wine

4 slices country bread or Brioche (page 105)

3 to 4 tbsp unsalted butter

6 to 8 eggs

Fleur de sel for sprinkling

2 bunches watercress, trimmed

DAY ONE

1. Preheat your oven to 500°F/260°C.

2. To make the dry rub: Toss the salt, sugar, cumin, coriander, cardamom, paprika, and curry powder together in a small bowl.

3. Toss the onions with 2 tbsp of the olive oil and 1 tsp of salt and spread onto a sheet pan. Roast until nicely seared, about 20 minutes. Lower the oven temperature to 300°F/150°C.

4. Liberally sprinkle the dry rub over the pork, coating all sides well and using all the rub. Heat 2 tbsp olive oil in a Dutch oven over high heat. Sear the pork until very dark on all sides.

5. Add the roasted onions, garlic, bay leaves, and beer to the pot, cover, and bake for 4 to 5 hours, until very soft. You should be able to easily pull the meat with a fork.

6. Refrigerate the pork in the sauce overnight.

DAY TWO

7. In the morning, skim off any fat from the braise, then transfer the meat to a cutting board. Simmer the sauce over medium heat, cooking it down by half.

8. Meanwhile, pull the pork with your hands into rustic hunks and preheat your oven to 500°F/260°C.

9. When the sauce has cooked down, return the pork to the pot and simmer for 10 minutes.

10. Drizzle each slice of bread with 1 tsp olive oil, sprinkle with salt, and toast in the oven on a sheet pan.

11. Dollop a big messy scoop of saucy pork onto the toast and set aside while you fry the eggs.

CONTINUED

12. When it comes to frying the eggs, you may need to either work in batches or have two pans going at once. Heat 1 tbsp of the butter in a nonstick sauté pan over high heat. Crack 2 eggs into a small bowl and gently slide them into the butter. (If you break a yolk, discard the egg and try again.) Reduce the heat to medium and cook until the whites are set but the yolks are runny, about 2 minutes. When ready, give the pan a gentle shake to loosen the eggs.

13. Slide the eggs onto the pork sandwiches, liberally sprinkle with fleur de sel, and top with a big handful of watercress. Repeat for the remaining sandwiches, unless you have multiple pans going!

   The braised pork keeps well, covered, refrigerated, for up to 3 days.

If you're avoiding carbs and happen to be torturing yourself by reading this book, you can make a wonderful salad out of this recipe, too. Omit the bread, maybe add a little arugula or radicchio, and serve with the eggs on top just the same. We love using saba in this dish because it's thick, sweet, and vinegary and the flavor is a perfect balance for ripe figs. For those of you not familiar with it, saba is the cooked-down must of wine grapes. It can be hard to find and really expensive, so feel free to use a good aged balsamic in its place or even cook down some not-so-great balsamic until it's sweet and syrupy. If figs are out of season, ripe pears are delicious in this dish, too.

figs, frisée, bacon, and egg on toast

SERVES 2

5 or 6 slices thick-cut bacon

2 tbsp extra-virgin olive oil, plus more for drizzling

1 tsp whole cumin seeds

Kosher salt

2 slices country bread, cut 1 in/2.5 cm thick

1 head frisée, washed, dried, and chopped

2 tsp saba or high-quality balsamic vinegar

5 ripe figs, carefully quartered

1 to 2 tbsp unsalted butter

2 to 4 eggs

Fleur de sel for sprinkling

1. Preheat your oven to 375°F/190°C.

2. Arrange the bacon on a sheet pan and bake until golden brown, about 15 minutes. Allow to cool, and then chop the bacon into 1-in/2.5-cm pieces. Set aside.

3. Increase the oven temperature to 500°F/260°C.

4. In a small sauté pan over high heat, combine 1½ tbsp of the olive oil, the cumin seeds, and a large pinch of salt and sauté for about 1 minute, until the cumin is fragrant. Set aside.

5. Drizzle the bread with olive oil, sprinkle with salt, and toast in the oven until crisp.

6. In a large bowl, toss the frisée, bacon, saba, ½ tbsp olive oil, and a pinch of salt. Add the figs and gently toss just until dispersed.

7. Evenly distribute the salad onto both slices of toast.

8. When it comes to frying the eggs, you may need to either work in batches or have two pans going at once. Heat 1 tbsp of the butter in a nonstick sauté pan over high heat. Crack 2 eggs into a small bowl and gently slide them into the butter. (If you break a yolk, discard the egg and try again.) Reduce the heat to medium and cook until the whites are set but the yolks are runny, about 2 minutes. When ready, give the pan a gentle shake to loosen the eggs.

9. Repeat with any remaining butter and eggs. Slide the eggs onto the salad, liberally spoon the cumin oil over the eggs, and sprinkle with a pinch of fleur de sel.

This must be eaten the moment it's made. Does not keep well at all.

My husband and I share a favorite easy snack of smashed avocado on a good piece of toast with a little salt. This dish is a slightly more evolved version of that. I use hard-boiled eggs because, first of all, I love them, and second, I wanted to give you an alternative to all the fried egg sandwich recipes in case you don't want to get stuck in your kitchen frying eggs à la minute. The anchovy dressing pairs perfectly with the eggs and adds a healthy amount of much-needed acidity to the rich fattiness of the avocado and the eggs.

smashed avocado toast with hard-boiled eggs and anchovy dressing

SERVES 4

8 eggs

DRESSING
½ cup/120 ml extra-virgin olive oil
3 tbsp red wine vinegar
6 or 7 anchovy fillets
4½ tsp Dijon mustard
4½ tsp capers in brine, drained
¼ tsp kosher salt
¼ tsp freshly ground black pepper
2 tsp honey
4 tsp chopped fresh chives

4 very ripe avocados
Kosher salt
2 lemons; 1 juiced, 1 cut into quarters
4 slices of your favorite bread
Extra-virgin olive oil for drizzling
1 head butter lettuce,
washed and hand torn

1. Put the eggs in a medium saucepan with water to cover by about 2 in/5 cm. Bring to a boil, then immediately turn off the heat, cover, and allow to sit for 12 minutes. Remove the eggs from the pan and refrigerate on a dish until cool.

2. To make the dressing: Combine all the ingredients except the chives in a blender or food processor. Blend until homogenous, transfer to a small bowl, and fold in the chives. Set aside.

3. Preheat your oven to 500°F/260°C.

4. When the eggs have cooled, peel off the shells. I find this easiest to do under a little running water. Slice the eggs into ¼-in/6-mm rounds and set aside.

5. Scoop the flesh from the avocados and transfer to a bowl with ¾ tsp salt and the lemon juice. Using a fork or a potato masher, lightly smash the avocados.

6. Arrange the bread on a sheet pan, drizzle with olive oil, sprinkle with salt, and toast in the oven. When the bread is toasted, drizzle 1½ tbsp of dressing over each slice. Top with the smashed avocado, the more the better, followed by 2 sliced hard-boiled eggs. Drizzle with ½ to 1 tbsp more dressing, to taste. Top with a small handful of the lettuce and squeeze 1 lemon quarter over each.

This must be eaten the moment it's made. Does not keep well.

Tartine is a fancy French word for "open-faced sandwich." This tartine is perfect for you if you're a slightly challenged gardener like myself and end up with a vine of tomatoes that don't quite come to maturity. This would be awesome with an egg on top but it is not necessary, and the same goes for adding sliced ripe avocado. I've also used big ripe red tomatoes and tested it with tomatillos; both work well, but ripe tomatoes do cause it to get soggier faster, so eat fast.

fried green tomato, bacon, and spicy slaw tartine

SERVES 4

SLAW

About ½ head cabbage, shredded

½ jalapeño, sliced into thin coins (seeds removed if you prefer it mild)

¼ cup/40 g thinly sliced red onion

½ cup/8 g chopped fresh cilantro

¼ cup/60 ml extra-virgin olive oil

2 tbsp Champagne vinegar

1 tbsp sherry vinegar

2 tbsp brown sugar

1 tsp kosher salt

½ tsp dried mustard

TARTINE

12 slices thick-cut bacon

4 slices country bread or Comfort Food Biscuits (page 62)

4 tsp extra-virgin olive oil

Kosher salt

4 large green tomatoes

1 cup/125 g flour, all-purpose or whole-wheat

4 eggs, beaten

1½ cups/160 g breadcrumbs (homemade or unseasoned store-bought)

Canola oil for frying

1 batch Aioli (page 224)

1. To make the slaw: Combine the cabbage, jalapeño, red onion, and cilantro in a large bowl.

2. In a small bowl, whisk together the olive oil, Champagne vinegar, sherry vinegar, brown sugar, salt, and mustard. Pour the vinaigrette over the cabbage mixture, toss thoroughly to coat, and set aside at room temperature, tossing occasionally while you prepare the rest.

3. Preheat your oven to 400°F/200°C.

4. To make the tartine: Arrange the bacon on a sheet pan and roast until golden brown and crisp, about 10 minutes.

5. Arrange the bread on a sheet pan, top each slice with 1 tsp of the olive oil and a pinch of salt, and toast in the oven with the bacon. (Skip this step if using biscuits.)

6. Slice the tomatoes into ½-in/12-mm rounds and transfer to paper towels to drain for a few minutes.

7. Set up three medium bowls for a breading station. Place the flour in one bowl, the eggs in another, and the breadcrumbs in the third. Add ¼ tsp salt to each bowl. Set a cooling rack over a sheet pan.

8. Dip each tomato round into the flour, then the eggs, and finally the breadcrumbs. Then transfer to the prepared cooling rack.

9. Heat 3 tbsp of canola oil in a large sauté pan over high heat. When the oil is hot, reduce the heat to medium and cook each tomato round until brown and crisp, 1 to 2 minutes per side. Transfer back to the cooling rack. You'll most likely need to replenish the oil after each batch. Sprinkle the tomatoes with a little salt and transfer to the oven to cook through, 8 to 10 minutes.

10. Spread 2 tsp aioli on each slice of toast, followed by 3 bacon slices, 2 or 3 tomato slices, and a healthy handful of slaw.

These are best the moment they're made; they do not keep well.

When I make this dish, I make it really spicy. I love the kick from the chile flakes with the sweetness of the squash and the earthiness of the kale. But if you don't like heat, use less chile flakes or even omit them altogether. Also feel free to substitute bacon for pancetta if you'd like, or make this a great vegetarian dish with no meat at all.

spicy butternut squash, kale, pancetta, and egg tartine

SERVES 2

1 small butternut squash, halved and seeded

3 tbsp/45 ml extra-virgin olive oil

¾ tsp kosher salt, plus more if needed

6 to 8 slices thick-cut pancetta

5 large fresh sage leaves

2 garlic cloves

2 slices country sourdough bread

½ tsp brown sugar, plus more if needed

4 cups/145 g finely chopped kale

Chile flakes for seasoning

1 tbsp unsalted butter

2 eggs

Fleur de sel for sprinkling

1. Preheat your oven to 425°F/220°C.

2. Put the squash on a sheet of aluminum foil, drizzle with 1 tbsp of the olive oil, and ½ tsp of the salt. Seal in the foil and roast until very soft, 45 to 55 minutes. The cook time varies with squash size, so poke it with a fork to test doneness before removing it from the oven. Set aside to cool, or refrigerate overnight.

3. Lower the oven temperature to 375°F/190°C. Spread out the pancetta on a sheet pan and bake until nice and crisp, about 15 minutes.

4. While the squash cools, heat 1 tbsp olive oil, the sage leaves, and 1 garlic clove in a small sauté pan over medium heat, until fragrant. Discard the garlic and sage. Allow the oil to cool.

5. Increase the oven temperature to 500°F/260°C and toast the bread on a sheet pan until crisp. It's fine to start toasting while the oven temperature is still rising.

6. When the squash has cooled, scoop out the flesh and drop it into a blender with the infused oil, brown sugar, and salt. Purée until smooth. Taste, adjust for sugar and salt, and set aside. You should have about 2 cups/240 g.

7. In a large sauté pan over medium-high heat, sauté the kale with 1 tbsp olive oil, the remaining garlic, ¼ tsp salt, and lots of chile flakes, until soft, 2 to 3 minutes.

8. Spread about ¾ cup/90 g of the butternut squash on each slice of toast. Top with the pancetta and sautéed kale. Set aside.

9. Heat the butter in a nonstick sauté pan over high heat. Crack the eggs into a small bowl and gently slide them into the butter. (If you break a yolk, discard the egg and try again.) Reduce the heat to medium and cook until the whites are set but the yolks are runny, about 2 minutes. When ready, give the pan a gentle shake to loosen the eggs.

10. Slide the eggs onto the sandwiches and liberally sprinkle with fleur de sel.

This must be eaten the moment it's made. Does not keep well at all.

This is an old-school, traditional, salty-sweet breakfast sandwich, so obviously I think it's amazing. A Monte Cristo is naughty but delicious, so you really shouldn't have it too often and you should really enjoy it when you do. Monte Cristo eating is not a passive sport, it's an event. When inviting your friends over to eat this sandwich, do not invite them over for brunch; you need to be much clearer than that. Invite them over to "eat a Monte Cristo," then commit to spending the rest of the afternoon together watching movies or playing board games because there are very few activities you can do after eating a sandwich like this.

    The best approach to any Monte Cristo party is to build the sandwiches, mix up the custard, and make a batch of jam the night before. Then in the morning, all you have to do is soak, sauté, and make a nice green salad—though Laurel is sitting beside me suggesting that when a person is eating a Monte Cristo they don't want to waste their time eating a salad. We rarely disagree, so salad or no salad, up to you.

monte cristo

SERVES 3

3 tbsp/45 ml heavy cream

3 fresh sage leaves

¼ tsp kosher salt

1 pinch freshly ground black pepper (optional)

3 eggs

1 tsp sugar

9 slices Brioche (page 105) or store-bought challah

4 tbsp/60 g dijon mustard

6 tbsp/100 g mayonnaise or Aioli (page 224)

12 thin to medium slices of ham

1½ cups/125 g grated Gruyère

½ cup/120 g Blueberry Jam (page 241)

1 tbsp butter

1 tsp extra-virgin olive oil

Powdered sugar for dusting

1. In a small sauté pan, bring the cream to a boil with the sage, salt, and pepper (if using). Allow to cool completely. Then whisk in the eggs and sugar. Refrigerate until needed.

2. Build the sandwiches by laying out all nine slices of bread on a clean work surface. On three slices, spread the mustard. Set aside. On the six remaining slices, spread the mayonnaise, then divide the ham and Gruyère evenly among the bread slices. Place the three mustard-covered bread slices on top of three of the ham-and-cheese slices; invert those onto the last three ham-and-cheese slices. You should now have three triple-decker sandwiches with mustard slices in the middle, surrounded by ham and cheese.

3. Cut off the crusts in order to help seal the layered sandwiches. Wrap tightly in plastic and refrigerate for at least 1 hour, or up to 12 hours. When ready to cook, put your jam in a small saucepan on a back burner and warm it on low. Remove the egg batter from the fridge.

4. In a large sauté pan, heat 1 tbsp butter and 1 tsp olive oil over medium heat. Dip each sandwich in the egg batter until coated and place together in the pan.

5. Brown the top, bottom, and all four sides of the sandwiches, until the entire outside is a deep golden brown and the cheese is melted. Serve immediately, with a dusting of powdered sugar and a dollop of warm blueberry jam.

    No one will ever know how well these keep because they will be eaten in seconds. But I suspect not well.

This is the jam I always have around for Milo. It's my favorite jam to make because it's free of processed sugars and it goes with absolutely everything. You can sub maple syrup for the honey if you like; and though fresh are always tastier, you can use frozen berries for this; but keep in mind, they will leak more liquid and take a little longer to cook down, so adjust accordingly.

blueberry jam

MAKES ABOUT 1 CUP/320 G

3½ to 4 cups/525 to 600 g
fresh blueberries

¼ cup/85 g honey

¼ tsp kosher salt

¼ cup/60 ml water

Combine the blueberries, honey, salt, and water in a medium stainless-steel pot. Simmer over medium heat until jammy, about 15 minutes. Refrigerate until needed.

This keeps well, refrigerated, for up to 2 weeks.

The great thing about this sandwich is that you can assemble it the night before. If you're having people over for breakfast, relax and sleep in. All you need to do is throw the sandwiches in a super-hot oven and within 25 minutes you'll have a killer hot breakfast and all you've been doing is chatting and sipping your coffee. Heaven!

If you want to shake things up, you can use cooked sausage or bacon instead of ham and/or top it with fried eggs. I always serve these with Dijon mustard, a simple green salad, and pickles.

traditional croque monsieur

SERVES 6

6 slices good sourdough bread,
cut 1 in/2.5 cm thick

1 batch Béchamel (facing page)

12 slices ham (I love Niman Ranch)

3 cups/350 g grated Gruyère

1. Preheat your oven to 475°F/240°C.

2. Arrange the bread on a rack over a sheet pan. Spread ¼ cup/60 ml of the béchamel on each. Layer with 2 slices of ham and sprinkle liberally with the Gruyère.

3. Bake until browned and crispy, about 20 minutes.

   Uncooked, the croque keeps well, tightly wrapped, refrigerated, for up to 1 day. After baking, it keeps well for a couple of hours at room temperature.

Occasionally when I step away from the kitchen at Huck, a recipe will change without my knowing. I'll come into work, stick my finger into something, and pause, thinking, *That's new.* Shortly afterward an investigation will ensue and everyone will point their fingers in the other direction, afraid of getting in trouble with the boss. Well, whoever made this unconventional béchamel by adding jalapeño should probably step up and take credit. It's awesome and it made it into the book. The jalapeño is left whole in here so that it doesn't overpower the béchamel, instead just giving it a subtle but more complex flavor.

béchamel

MAKES 2 CUPS/480 ML

4 tbsp/55 g unsalted butter
¼ cup/40 g chopped onion
1 jalapeño
2 sprigs fresh thyme
1 tsp kosher salt
⅛ tsp freshly ground black pepper
⅓ cup/40 g all-purpose flour
1½ cups/360 ml whole milk, at room temperature

1. Set a mesh strainer over a bowl and set aside.

2. Melt the butter in a medium sauté pan over medium-high heat. Add the onion, jalapeño, thyme, salt, and black pepper and sauté until the onion is softened but not browned. Add the flour and cook, stirring continuously, for 1 minute, to cook out that floury taste. Slowly add the milk, about ¼ cup/60 ml at a time, while whisking constantly to maintain the emulsion, and continue cooking until slightly thickened, 2 to 3 minutes.

3. Strain the sauce into the bowl. Use a silicone spatula or wooden spoon to help work the sauce through the mesh. It will take some elbow grease. You should end up with about 2 cups/430 ml of sauce. Discard the onion, thyme, jalapeño, and any lumpy bits. Immediately cover with plastic wrap, pressing the plastic directly to the surface of the béchamel in order to prevent a skin from forming. Refrigerate until cool.

This keeps well, refrigerated, for up to 1 week.

I almost like these better than the traditional ham version, and there are endless variations. Here we use leeks and spinach, but they're also great with fresh or sun-dried tomatoes, sautéed mushrooms, asparagus and leeks, roasted squash and sautéed kale, or even sautéed Brussels sprouts.

The key to any good croque is making sure the cheese is brown and bubbly and the bread is crispy, while the inside stays nice and moist. That's the reason we want you to bake it on a rack, because it allows the hot air to circulate and brown both the top and bottom of the bread, while the abundant amount of béchamel keep it delicious and moist inside. Serve with a large salad.

vegetarian croque

MAKES 4

4 large leeks, white and light green parts only

3 cups/340 g grated Gruyère

2 tsp fresh thyme leaves

2 tbsp unsalted butter

Kosher salt

1 tsp water

4 cups/120 g fresh spinach

Freshly ground black pepper

4 slices good sourdough bread or Brioche (page 105)

1 batch Béchamel (page 243)

1. Preheat your oven to 475°F/240°C. Slice the leeks into ¼-in/6-mm coins; wash thoroughly and drain.

2. Put the Gruyère and thyme leaves in a medium bowl and toss to combine. Set aside.

3. Melt the butter in a large sauté pan over high heat. Add the leeks and 1 tsp salt and sauté until just starting to brown. Add the water, lower the heat to medium, and continue cooking until the leeks are soft, about 4 minutes. Allow to cool completely. Then, toss with the spinach and season with salt and pepper.

4. Arrange the bread on a rack over a sheet pan. Spread ¼ cup/60 ml of béchamel on each. Evenly distribute the spinach-leek mixture on the béchamel. Top each with about ¾ cup/85 g of the Gruyère mixture.

5. Bake until browned and crispy, about 20 minutes.

Uncooked, the croque keeps well, tightly wrapped, refrigerated, for up to 1 day. After baking, it keeps well for a couple of hours at room temperature.

hearty plates
with an egg
on top

It's only 9:30 A.M. and we're already starting to prep tomorrow's brisket. We have to. It roasts for 6 hours and marinates overnight. But it's worth it. I never get sick of seeing lovely West Los Angeles ladies taking down big hearty plates of brisket hash topped with eggs over-easy.

On any given week, we go through 200 lb/91 kg of brisket, 300 lb/136 kg of bacon, and 7,000 eggs. The line guys face the minute-to-minute pressure of getting orders out on time, but none of this is possible without our amazing team of prep cooks whose sole job is to do all the nitty-gritty—like cutting the right amount of fat off of a pork shoulder so it'll braise correctly, or making soup, or forming hundreds of turkey meatballs in order to make the customers happy and make me and the line cooks look good. If the prep cooks do their job well, then 85 percent of the work on most dishes is done before it reaches the guys on the line. Well-cooked meat and properly roasted vegetables mean those line cooks don't have to be so perfect all the time, although most often they are.

I go back to check on how the prep's going, and there's Eva simultaneously lining thin slices of ham on béchamel-covered country bread for Croque Monsieurs, slicing butternut squash to roast for a new salad, and regulating the new prep guy and the dishwasher at the same time. She's my picture of perfection. Eva's been with us since the beginning of Rustic Canyon and I insisted when we opened Huckleberry that she come with me. She's a single mom with four kids and she's not afraid to work hard and certainly not too shy to lay down the law, even if it means putting me in my place. She's the kind of person who gives you the cold shoulder until she trusts you, and then she opens up with the sweetest smile reserved only for those who have worked their way into her inner circle. She gets there early, at 4 A.M. with the bakers, and does her savory prep with care throughout her shift. She gets mad if the menu feels stagnant and she doesn't have enough new stuff to do. She understands that if the squash she's roasting doesn't have the right color on it, then some customer is going to have a subpar salad, and that pains her as much as it pains me. I love her so much.

She's just finished her multitasking and is ready for her break. She eases into a cup of coffee with her girl, Eli, who's been with us equally as long and is just as amazing. If we had more Evas and Elis throughout our restaurants, our jobs would be a lot easier.

This is one of the most straightforward recipes in this chapter, but its no less beautiful and satisfying. If you want to do a little more, it would be great with a little Pesto (page 225) on the eggs and even a sprinkle of breadcrumbs. And if you want to substitute out the potatoes, roasted carrots or squash would be great. People have all different goat cheese thresholds, so add or subtract to taste.

roasted potato, spinach, and goat cheese with an egg on top

SERVES 2

1½ lb/680 g fingerling potatoes, cut into ¼-in/6-mm coins

3 tbsp extra-virgin olive oil

1½ tsp kosher salt

¼ cup/40 g finely diced shallots or yellow onions

6 cups/180 g tightly packed spinach

1 to 2 tbsp unsalted butter

2 to 4 eggs

Fleur de sel for sprinkling

¼ cup/55 g goat cheese, crumbled

¼ cup/15 g sliced fresh chives, cut into ½-in/12-mm pieces

1. Preheat your oven to 425°F/220°C.

2. Toss the potatoes with 2 tbsp of the olive oil and 1¼ tsp of the salt. Roast on a sheet pan for about 35 minutes, until browned and crisp but not dry.

3. When the potatoes are roasted, sauté the shallots with the remaining 1 tbsp olive oil in a large sauté pan over medium-high heat until soft and translucent. Add the potatoes, spinach, and the remaining ¼ tsp salt and sauté for about 30 seconds, until wilted. Set aside.

4. When it comes to frying the eggs, you may need to either work in batches or have two pans going at once. Heat 1 tbsp of the butter in a nonstick sauté pan over high heat. Crack 2 eggs into a small bowl and gently slide them into the butter. (If you break a yolk, discard the egg and try again.) Reduce the heat to medium and cook until the whites are set but the yolks are runny, about 2 minutes. When ready, give the pan a gentle shake to loosen the eggs.

5. Mound the potato mixture into bowls. Slide the eggs onto the potatoes. Sprinkle each serving with fleur de sel and top with the goat cheese and chives. Repeat with any remaining butter and eggs.

This is best enjoyed immediately.

I thought I didn't like turnips, and neither did Laurel, until we made this. So if you think you don't like turnips, put them in anyway. Roasted like this, they're actually really good. On the other hand, I tested this with rutabaga, and it is not good at all. The flavor is just too strong.

Roasting the beets the day before makes a lot of sense. It's a long process, so you might want to roast a bunch and save some for a salad or to eat with fresh burrata or on the Smashed Avocado Toast with Hard-Boiled Eggs and Anchovy Dressing (page 234), thinly sliced, instead of the eggs.

roasted root vegetables with eggs

SERVES 2

2 or 3 small beets, plus 3 cups/110 g beet greens, washed and chopped

4 tbsp/60 ml extra-virgin olive oil

Kosher salt

1 apple, unpeeled, sliced into eighths

2 small turnips

2 cups sliced carrots, cut into ½-in/12-mm coins

1 tbsp chopped fresh rosemary

1 garlic clove

1 tbsp capers in brine, drained and coarsely chopped

1 tbsp Dijon mustard

1 tbsp chopped fresh parsley

1 to 2 tbsp unsalted butter

2 to 4 eggs

Fleur de sel for sprinkling

1. Preheat your oven to 425°F/220°C.

2. Put the beets, 1 tbsp of the olive oil, and ⅛ tsp salt on a sheet of aluminum foil and wrap thoroughly. Roast for about 1 hour and 30 minutes.

3. Meanwhile, toss the apple, turnips, and carrots with 2 tbsp olive oil, 1 tsp salt, and the rosemary. Place on a sheet and roast beside the beets until browned, 15 to 20 minutes longer, and the beets are fork-tender. While warm, but not hot, rub the skin off the beets with a paper towel or clean kitchen towel. Slice the beets.

4. When everything is roasted, heat the remaining 1 tbsp olive oil and the garlic in a large sauté pan over medium-high until browned and fragrant. Discard the garlic. Add the beet greens and capers and sauté until wilted. Add the roasted vegetables and sauté until heated through. Taste for salt and adjust as needed. Remove from the heat, toss with the mustard and parsley, and set aside.

5. When it comes to frying the eggs, you may need to either work in batches or have two pans going at once. Heat 1 tbsp of the butter in a nonstick sauté pan over high heat. Crack 2 eggs into a small bowl and gently slide them into the butter. (If you break a yolk, discard the egg and try again.) Reduce the heat to medium and cook until the whites are set but the yolks are runny, about 2 minutes. When ready, give the pan a gentle shake to loosen the eggs.

6. Meanwhile, mound the roasted vegetables onto two plates. Slide the eggs onto the vegetables, and sprinkle with fleur de sel. Repeat with any remaining butter and eggs.

The roasted vegetable mixture keeps well, refrigerated, for up to 2 days.

After we opened our pizzeria Milo & Olive, my son developed a deep obsession with the wood-fired oven. So I began to think of fun foods we could cook in our fireplace at home. One of our favorites is roasting spaghetti squash by wrapping each half in foil and burying them in the hot coals. It adds an amazing smoky flavor, and my young son is amazed that although his tiny fireman jacket won't fit me, I'm actually a fire woman. Depending on the size of your squash it should take 1 to 1½ hours to roast in the fireplace; check by piercing it with a butter knife.

roasted spaghetti squash with parmesan and eggs

SERVES 4

3 medium spaghetti squash

4 tbsp/60 ml extra-virgin olive oil

¾ tsp kosher salt

2 garlic cloves

½ tsp chile flakes, plus more for topping

½ cup/40 g fresh basil leaves, torn

2 to 4 tbsp unsalted butter

4 to 8 eggs

½ cup/50 g coarsely chopped Parmesan, cut into ¼-in/6-mm pieces

Fleur de sel for sprinkling

1. Preheat your oven to 425°F/220°C.

2. Slice the squash in half lengthwise and remove and discard the seeds. Transfer to a sheet pan, drizzle with 2 tbsp of the olive oil, and sprinkle with the salt. Wrap tightly with foil and roast for 50 minutes to 1 hour, until soft. The cook time varies with squash size, so poke with a fork to test doneness before removing from the oven. Set aside to cool, or refrigerate overnight.

3. When the squash is cool, use a fork to scrape the flesh from the skin in long strands into a bowl and set aside. It should feel like al dente spaghetti. Do not use a spoon.

4. Heat the remaining 2 tbsp olive oil and the garlic in a sauté pan over medium heat until the garlic is aromatic and slightly browned, 1 to 2 minutes. Discard the garlic. Add the squash and chile flakes. Sauté until warmed through, occasionally tossing with a fork, not a spoon. Remove from the heat, toss with the basil, and set aside.

5. When it comes to frying the eggs, you may need to either work in batches or have two pans going at once. Heat 1 tbsp of the butter in a nonstick sauté pan over high heat. Crack 2 eggs into a small bowl and gently slide them into the butter. (If you break a yolk, discard the egg and try again.) Reduce the heat to medium and cook until the whites are set but the yolks are runny, about 2 minutes. When ready, give the pan a gentle shake to loosen the eggs.

6. Meanwhile, mound the squash onto three or four plates and top with Parmesan. Slide the eggs onto the squash and sprinkle with fleur de sel and a tiny pinch of chile flakes. Repeat with any remaining butter and eggs.

This is best enjoyed immediately.

If blanching and roasting the asparagus feels like too much trouble, this would be delicious with roasted carrots, sautéed spinach, sautéed mushrooms, or quickly sautéed peas and pea shoots. I added the crispy prosciutto because I like the crunch with the soft polenta, but if you don't have prosciutto or you don't like eating meat, feel free to substitute salted, hand-torn breadcrumbs in its place to get that nice contrast.

polenta with roasted asparagus, crispy prosciutto, and eggs

SERVES 4

Kosher salt
2 bunches medium asparagus, trimmed
2 tbsp extra-virgin olive oil
Freshly ground black pepper
8 to 12 slices prosciutto
1 garlic clove, chopped
1 cup/160 g cornmeal
4 tbsp/55 g unsalted butter
½ cup/50 g grated Parmesan
4 eggs
Fleur de sel for sprinkling

1. Preheat your oven to 500°F/260°C.

2. Bring a large pot of water with a small handful of salt to a boil. Cook the asparagus until just tender but not soft, 3 to 4 minutes.

3. Meanwhile, set up a large bowl of ice water. When the asparagus is done, immediately drop it into the ice bath to cool for 2 to 3 minutes. Lightly towel-dry the asparagus and spread out, in a single layer, on one or two sheet pans. If the spears are too crowded, they won't brown properly. Toss with the olive oil, ¼ tsp salt, and season with pepper; roast until browned, about 15 minutes.

4. Arrange the prosciutto on a sheet pan and roast until crisp, about 12 to 15 minutes. Transfer to a cooling rack and set aside.

5. Combine 1 qt/960 ml water, the garlic, and 2 tsp salt in a medium saucepan. Bring to a boil and slowly whisk in the cornmeal. Reduce the heat to medium and cook for about 3 minutes. When the cornmeal has absorbed most of the liquid and has a nice creamy texture, add 2 tbsp of the butter and the Parmesan and season with pepper. Whisk to combine and set aside.

6. When it comes to frying the eggs, you may need to either work in batches or have two pans going at once. Heat 1 tbsp of the butter in a nonstick sauté pan over high heat. Crack 2 eggs into a small bowl and gently slide them into the butter. (If you break a yolk, discard the egg and try again.) Reduce the heat to medium and cook until the whites are set but the yolks are runny, about 2 minutes. When ready, give the pan a gentle shake to loosen the eggs.

7. While the eggs finish, dollop the polenta onto serving plates, followed by a large helping of asparagus. Slide the eggs onto the asparagus, sprinkle with fleur de sel, and top with shards of crispy prosciutto. Repeat with any remaining butter and eggs.

The polenta keeps well, refrigerated, for up to 4 days.

Quinoa and eggs is a Huck staple. We always have it on the menu, though the veggies change with the seasons. It might be squash and kale, or corn and shallots, or roasted cherry tomatoes and spring onions depending on the month. Many things seem to work well with quinoa, so play with this recipe as much as you like.

quinoa, baby carrots, sprouting broccoli, and eggs

SERVES 2

2 tbsp finely chopped shallots or yellow onion

1 leek, finely diced

2½ tbsp extra-virgin olive oil

1 cup/200 g quinoa, rinsed

1 tsp kosher salt

2 cups/480 ml water or stock, plus 2 tbsp

Zest of 1 lemon

2 bunches whole baby carrots

Freshly ground black pepper

1 garlic clove

1 bunch sprouting broccoli, stem ends trimmed

1 to 2 tbsp unsalted butter

2 to 4 eggs

Fleur de sel for sprinkling

1. Preheat your oven to 425°F/220°C.

2. In a saucepan, sauté the shallots and leek in 1 tbsp of the olive oil over medium heat until nice and soft, 3 to 4 minutes. Add the quinoa and ½ tsp of the salt and sauté for 1 minute longer. Add the 2 cups/480 ml water and simmer over medium heat until the water is absorbed. Remove from the heat, fold in the lemon zest, and set aside.

3. Meanwhile, toss the carrots with ½ tbsp olive oil and ¼ tsp salt and season with pepper. Spread out on a sheet pan and roast until brown and soft, about 35 minutes.

4. When the quinoa and carrots are both done, heat the remaining 1 tbsp olive oil and the garlic in a large sauté pan over medium-high heat, until fragrant and slightly browned. Discard the garlic. Add the broccoli, the 2 tbsp water, and ¼ tsp salt to the pan. Cover and sauté until tender, shaking the pan occasionally, about 4 minutes. Lower the heat to medium-low, add the quinoa and carrots to the pan, toss to combine, and cook for about 2 minutes. Remove from the heat and set aside.

5. When it comes to frying the eggs, you may need to either work in batches or have two pans going at once. Heat 1 tbsp of the butter in a nonstick sauté pan over high heat. Crack 2 eggs into a small bowl and gently slide them into the butter. (If you break a yolk, discard the egg and try again.) Reduce the heat to medium and cook until the whites are set but the yolks are runny, about 2 minutes. When ready, give the pan a gentle shake to loosen the eggs.

6. While the eggs finish, scoop the quinoa mixture onto two dishes. Slide the eggs onto the quinoa. Sprinkle with fleur de sel. Repeat with any remaining butter and eggs.

The quinoa mixture keeps well, refrigerated, for up to 3 days.

Just like in baking, I equate color with flavor, so the browner the grain the better the flavor. Grains like wild rice or bulgur add depth of flavor and nuttiness to whatever you're cooking. You can swap out grains in pretty much any recipe that calls for them in this book.

This is a soul-satisfying, deeply flavored, but simple breakfast. So much so that you could easily serve it for dinner. A nice variation on this dish would be adding ½ to ¾ lb/225 to 350 g sliced Brussels sprouts to the leeks, with ¼ tsp salt and black pepper—they would work beautifully with the leeks, mushrooms, and raisins.

mushrooms, leeks, and fried eggs over wild rice

SERVES 4

2 tbsp extra-virgin olive oil

1½ cups/240 g chopped onion

2 garlic cloves, chopped

1 tbsp chopped fresh rosemary

2¾ tsp kosher salt

Freshly ground black pepper

1¼ cups/200 g wild rice

5 to 7 tbsp unsalted butter

2¾ cups/650 ml water

2 leeks, white and light green parts only, chopped

1½ lb/680 g fresh mushrooms, any kind you fancy, lightly rinsed and sliced

1 tbsp chopped fresh oregano, plus torn fresh oregano leaves for garnish

1 tbsp chopped fresh thyme

¼ cup/40 g raisins

4 to 8 eggs

Fleur de sel for sprinkling

1. In a medium saucepan, combine 1 tbsp of the olive oil, the onion, garlic, rosemary, ¼ tsp of the salt, and a pinch of pepper and sauté over medium heat until soft, 10 to 15 minutes. Add the rice and 1 tbsp of the butter and sauté for 1 to 2 minutes. Add the water and 1½ tsp salt and stir to combine. Bring to a boil, then immediately reduce the heat to medium-low, cover, and simmer gently for 45 minutes to 1 hour, until the rice is tender and the liquid is absorbed.

2. Meanwhile, heat the remaining 1 tbsp olive oil in a large sauté pan over a medium-high heat. Add the leeks, ½ tsp salt, and a pinch of pepper and sauté, stirring frequently, until soft, about 5 minutes. Set aside in a small bowl.

3. When the rice is done, remove it from the heat and keep it covered while you sauté the mushrooms.

4. In the same sauté pan, melt 1 tbsp butter over high heat. When the pan is good and hot, add the mushrooms, the remaining ½ tsp salt, a pinch of pepper, the chopped oregano, and thyme. Sauté, stirring as little as possible, until browned and tender, about 10 minutes. Add the leeks and raisins to the pan and toss to combine. Remove from the heat, add 1 tbsp butter, and toss to combine. Set aside.

5. When it comes to frying the eggs, you may need to either work in batches or have two pans going at once. Heat 1 tbsp of the butter in a nonstick sauté pan over high heat. Crack 2 eggs into a small bowl and gently slide them into the butter. (If you break a yolk, discard the egg and try again.) Reduce the heat to medium and cook until the whites are set but the yolks are runny, about 2 minutes. When ready, give the pan a gentle shake to loosen the eggs.

6. While the eggs finish, mound the rice onto plates and top with the mushroom mixture. Slide the eggs onto the mushrooms. Sprinkle with fleur de sel. Top the dish with a few torn oregano leaves. Repeat with any remaining butter and eggs.

The rice and mushrooms keep well, refrigerated, for up to 3 days.

The key to this recipe is the last 2 tbsp of vinegar at the end. It brings this dish together and brightens it up at the same time. I love to eat this dish with sausages on the side, but crumbled sausage or chopped bacon cooked in with the lentils is really good as well. Serve it with nice crusty bread and butter.

lentils with roasted cherry tomatoes and sunny-side-up eggs

SERVES 4

4 cups/720 g whole cherry tomatoes

1 tbsp chopped fresh thyme

3 garlic cloves; 1 whole, 2 chopped

¼ cup/60 ml extra-virgin olive oil, plus 1 tbsp

1¾ tsp kosher salt

¼ tsp chile flakes

1 cup/160 g chopped onion

1 cup/120 g chopped carrots

1 cup/160 g chopped fennel

1 tbsp chopped fresh rosemary

1 cup/190 g dried lentils, washed

1 cup/240 ml dry white wine

3½ cups/830 ml water

Freshly ground pepper

2 tbsp red wine vinegar

2 tbsp unsalted butter

4 eggs

Fleur de sel for sprinkling

1. Preheat your oven to 450°F/230°C.

2. Combine the cherry tomatoes, thyme, whole garlic clove, ¼ cup/ 60 ml olive oil, ½ tsp of the salt, and the chile flakes in a medium sauté pan. Roast until the tomatoes are dark brown, bursting, and beginning to cook down, about 30 minutes.

3. In a medium saucepan, sauté the onion, carrots, fennel, chopped garlic, and rosemary in the remaining 1 tbsp olive oil with ¼ tsp salt over medium-high heat until the vegetables begin to soften, about 10 minutes.

4. Stir in the lentils, add the wine, and cook down by about two-thirds. Add the water and simmer, uncovered, for 45 minutes to 1 hour, until the lentils are tender, stirring occasionally.

5. Stir in the remaining 1 tsp salt and season with pepper. Gently fold in the roasted tomatoes and their juices, and cook for 5 minutes. Remove the pan from the heat and stir in the vinegar; set aside.

6. When it comes to frying the eggs, you may need to either work in batches or have two pans going at once. Heat 1 tbsp of the butter in a nonstick sauté pan over high heat. Crack 2 eggs into a small bowl and gently slide them into the butter. (If you break a yolk, discard the egg and try again.) Reduce the heat to medium and cook until the whites are set but the yolks are runny, about 2 minutes. When ready, give the pan a gentle shake to loosen the eggs.

7. While the eggs finish, scoop the lentil mixture into bowls. Slide the eggs onto the lentils. Sprinkle with fleur de sel. Repeat with the remaining butter and eggs.

The lentil mixture keeps well, refrigerated, for up to 3 days.

If you've spent some time reading through this book, you probably have some understanding of my deep and obsessive love of corn. It is the perfect salty-sweet vegetable. For that reason, this dish is my hands-down favorite in this chapter. However, please make this recipe only in the height of summer when both corn and tomatoes are at their best.

corn, cherry tomato, and spinach hash

SERVES 2

About ¼ loaf unsliced bread, whatever you have around

3 tbsp extra-virgin olive oil

1 tsp kosher salt

2 cups/330 g cherry tomatoes

⅛ tsp chile flakes

2 cups/245 g fresh corn kernels

3 cups/90 g spinach

¼ cup/20 g thinly sliced fresh basil, plus a few whole basil leaves for topping

1 to 2 tbsp unsalted butter

2 to 4 eggs

Fleur de sel for sprinkling

1. Preheat your oven to 500°F/260°C.

2. Scoop out the soft insides from the loaf of bread. Discard the crusty shell. Tear the bread into bite-size pieces. You should have about ½ cup/50 g. Scatter on a sheet pan, drizzle with 1 tbsp of the olive oil, and ¼ tsp of the salt. Toast in the oven until nicely browned and crunchy, 4 to 5 minutes.

3. In a medium sauté pan, combine 1 tbsp olive oil, the cherry tomatoes, ½ tsp salt, and the chile flakes. Sauté over high heat, covered, until the tomatoes burst, 3 minutes. Remove the lid and allow the tomato juices to cook down and thicken for another 3 to 4 minutes. Don't stir too often, because you don't want the tomatoes to break up into a sauce; you want whole tomatoes. Set aside in a small bowl.

4. In the same pan, over high heat, combine the remaining 1 tbsp olive oil, the corn, and ¼ tsp salt and sauté until tender, but not browned, 1 to 2 minutes. Add the tomatoes back to the pan and toss to combine and reheat. Add the spinach and sliced basil and sauté until just barely wilted, about 30 seconds. Remove from the heat and set aside.

5. When it comes to frying the eggs, you may need to either work in batches or have two pans going at once. Heat 1 tbsp of the butter in a nonstick sauté pan over high heat. Crack 2 eggs into a small bowl and gently slide them into the butter. (If you break a yolk, discard the egg and try again.) Reduce the heat to medium and cook until the whites are set but the yolks are runny, about 2 minutes. When ready, give the pan a gentle shake to loosen the eggs.

6. While the eggs finish, mound the hash onto two plates. Slide the eggs onto the hash, sprinkle with fleur de sel, and top with the breadcrumbs and basil leaves. Repeat with any remaining butter and eggs.

The corn and tomato mixture keeps well, refrigerated, for up to 3 days.

I created this dish one morning when I wanted to make something really special for breakfast and happened to have a ton of leftover brisket from the night before. So feel free to follow suit and make this brisket one night for dinner alongside some beautiful roasted carrots and mashed potatoes, then serve it the next day for breakfast as a hash.

Be sure to start this recipe at least one day ahead, as brisket really needs time to absorb the flavor from the sauce. In fact, it probably tastes best on day three. The key to braising a good brisket is to keep as much fat on the meat as possible when you braise it, then cut it off the next day after the meat is cooked. So please be very stern with your butcher and make him leave all that fat on.

Bread is a natural with this saucy dish, either big hunks of crusty bread served on the side or torn breadcrumbs right on top. Either way you want something to soak up this luscious sauce. I love piling a big handful of arugula on top because it makes it taste fresher and lighter, but no less hearty. At Huckleberry we serve two eggs per person, but at home, with such a hearty dish, I fry only one.

braised brisket and fingerling potato hash

SERVES 6

DRY RUB

1 tbsp brown sugar

½ tbsp kosher salt

½ tsp freshly ground black pepper

½ tsp ground cinnamon

½ tsp chile flakes

2 lb/1.2 kg beef brisket, untrimmed

2 tbsp extra-virgin olive oil

2 onions, cut into ¾-in/2-cm dice

2 carrots, cut into ¾-in/2-cm dice

1 fennel bulb, cut into ¾-in/2-cm dice

1 tbsp chopped fresh thyme

1 garlic clove, chopped

One 750-ml bottle red wine

One 28-oz/800-g can whole tomatoes

HASH

1¼ lb/570 g fingerling potatoes, sliced into ¼-in/6-mm coins

2 tbsp extra-virgin olive oil

1½ tsp chopped fresh rosemary

1½ tsp kosher salt

3 to 6 tbsp/45 to 85 g unsalted butter

6 to 12 eggs

Fleur de sel for sprinkling

3 cups/110 g arugula

DAY ONE

1. To make the dry rub: In a small bowl toss together the brown sugar, salt, pepper, cinnamon, and chile flakes.

2. Preheat your oven to 300°F/150°C. Spread the rub evenly over the brisket. Do not trim any fat.

3. Heat the olive oil in a Dutch oven over high heat. When the pan is quite hot, sear the meat on all sides until each is a very deep, dark brown. Remove the brisket from the pan and set aside.

4. Immediately, with the pot still over high heat, add the onions, carrots, fennel, thyme, and garlic. The bottom of the pan will be very dark, but don't be scared, it will only add depth of flavor. Sauté the veggies while scraping the dark bits from the bottom of the pan until beginning to brown, about 4 minutes. Add the wine and scrape the last bits from bottom. Lower the heat to a simmer, cooking down the liquid for 2 minutes. Add the tomatoes, crushing them with your hands into the pot. Stir together and cook for 1 minute longer.

5. Return the meat to the pan and ladle the sauce over it. Cover and bake until insanely tender, 4½ to 5 hours. Check doneness by poking with a fork. If the fork goes through easily, then it's done.

6. Refrigerate overnight.

CONTINUED

7. To make the hash: In the morning, preheat your oven to 425°F/220°C.

8. Toss the potatoes with the olive oil, the rosemary, and salt. Roast on a sheet pan for 35 to 40 minutes until browned and crisp but not dry.

9. Meanwhile, remove the brisket from the sauce and place it on a cutting board. Skim any fat from the sauce and discard the fat. Over medium-high heat, cook the sauce down by about half, about 30 minutes.

10. Trim the fat from the brisket and cut the meat into 1-in/2.5-cm cubes. Add the brisket back to the sauce and cook until heated through, 5 to 10 minutes.

11. By now the potatoes should be ready. Add them to the sauce just before frying the eggs to prevent them from getting soggy. Set aside over low heat.

12. When it comes to frying the eggs, you may need to either work in batches or have two pans going at once. Heat 1 tbsp of the butter in a nonstick sauté pan over high heat. Crack 2 eggs into a small bowl and gently slide them into the butter. (If you break a yolk, discard the egg and try again.) Reduce the heat to medium and cook until the whites are set but the yolks are runny, about 2 minutes. When ready, give the pan a gentle shake to loosen the eggs.

13. While the eggs finish, mound the hash into bowls. Slide the eggs onto the hash and sprinkle with fleur de sel. Top with a big handful of arugula. Repeat with any remaining butter and eggs.

The brisket keeps very well, refrigerated, for up to 3 days.

This dish was inspired by my mom's Spider-Man Eggs. When we were kids, my brother wouldn't eat anything Spider-Man wouldn't eat, so according to my mother, this was Spider-Man's favorite breakfast. It consisted of toasted buttered white bread cubes tossed with smashed soft-boiled eggs and lots of salt. Even now in our thirties, my brother and I still go to our mom's house sometimes and ask for Spider-Man Eggs.

But this is a very grown-up version. I call for rye bread, but I think a whole-wheat or a yummy sourdough would be a great substitute. I go with chard here, but kale, dandelion greens, beet greens, and collards would all work well instead.

warm breakfast panzanella a.k.a. grown-up spider-man eggs

SERVES 2 TO 4

3 cups/170 g cubed rye bread, cut into ½-in/12-mm pieces

3 tbsp + 1 tsp extra-virgin olive oil, plus more for drizzling

1⅛ tsp kosher salt

1 chopped yellow onion

1 tbsp chopped fresh thyme

1 garlic clove

1 pinch chile flakes

2 apples, unpeeled, sliced

3 to 5 tbsp/45 to 55 g unsalted butter

6 cups/215 g chopped Swiss chard

10 oz/285 g bulk sausage

4 to 8 eggs

Fleur de sel for sprinking

1. Preheat your oven to 500°F/260°C.

2. Scatter the bread on a sheet pan and drizzle with 1 tbsp of the olive oil and ½ tsp of the salt. Toast in the oven for 5 to 6 minutes, or until browned.

3. Meanwhile, sauté the onion in a large sauté pan over medium heat with 1 tbsp olive oil, ¼ tsp salt, the thyme, garlic, and chile flakes until soft and golden, 10 to 15 minutes. Set aside in a large bowl.

4. In the same pan, over high heat, cook the apples in 1 tbsp of the butter and ⅛ tsp salt until soft and golden, 4 to 5 minutes. Set aside with the onion.

5. In the same pan, over high heat, cook the chard in 1 tbsp olive oil and the remaining ¼ tsp salt, until wilted, 4 to 5 minutes. Set aside with the onion and apples.

6. In the same pan, over high heat, cook the sausage in 1 tsp olive oil, breaking it up with the back of a spoon, until browned, but not quite cooked through.

7. Add the onion, apples, chard mixture, and bread cubes to the pan. Toss to combine into a panzanella and heat through. Remove from the heat and set aside.

8. When it comes to frying the eggs, you may need to either work in batches or have two pans going at once. Heat 1 tbsp of the butter in a nonstick sauté pan over high heat. Crack 2 eggs into a small bowl and gently slide them into the butter. (If you break a yolk, discard the egg and try again.) Reduce the heat to medium and cook until the whites are set but the yolks are runny, about 2 minutes. When ready, give the pan a gentle shake to loosen the eggs.

9. While the eggs finish, mound the panzanella onto plates. Slide the eggs onto the panzanella, drizzle with olive oil, and sprinkle with fleur de sel. Repeat with any remaining butter and eggs.

Spider-Man says this is best the moment it's made.

This is a very bright-green dish. Instead of having green juice in the morning and feeling hungry an hour later, make this. If you can't find pea shoots, you can always use arugula or spinach. If you are avoiding bread, toasted pine nuts would be lovely instead of breadcrumbs. And finally, if you're feeling lazy, use ¼ cup/25 g store-bought breadcrumbs—just be sure they're unseasoned.

   This is a very simple dish that's all about timing. The veggies don't need long and neither do the poached eggs, but you want them to come together at once. So have that game plan in mind and be sure to set out everything you need so you're not caught doing something like searching for a slotted spoon when the eggs are ready.

poached eggs, pesto, and snap peas
SERVES 2

2 slices good-quality stale bread

2 tsp extra-virgin olive oil, plus 1 tbsp

Kosher salt

2 tbsp white vinegar

4 eggs

3 cups/160 g snap peas, ends trimmed by hand

Freshly ground black pepper

3 cups/50 g pea shoots

1½ cups/300 g Pesto (page 225), at room temperature

Fleur de sel for sprinkling

1. Preheat your oven to 350°F/180°C.

2. Dice the bread and toss with the 2 tsp olive oil and a large pinch of salt. Toast on a sheet pan until dry, crisp, and golden brown, about 30 minutes, depending on the bread.

3. Meanwhile bring 6 qt/5.7 L water and the vinegar to a simmer in a Dutch oven or large saucepan.

4. Allow the bread to cool, then grind until fine in a food processor or crush by hand. You should have about ¼ cup/25 g. Set aside.

5. Now we're going to work back and forth between our eggs and our veggies. Be sure your water is gently simmering, not vigorously boiling, and have a slotted spoon and a paper towel–covered plate nearby.

6. Heat the remaining 1 tbsp olive oil in a large sauté pan over high heat.

7. Meanwhile, start the eggs poaching, two at a time, unless you're a pro. Crack 1 egg into each of two teacups. Give the water a swirl with a spoon and slip an egg into the little vortex you created. This will help the bulk of the white take a compact shape, while whisking away any webby tendrils. Repeat, carefully adding the second egg. Poach for 3 minutes.

8. While the eggs poach, add the snap peas to the heated pan, season with salt and pepper, and sauté for about 1 minute. You want them to be al dente. Add the pea shoots to the pan and sauté until just barely wilted, 1 to 2 minutes.

9. By now the eggs should be ready. Lift them out of the water with a slotted spoon and drain for a moment over the paper towels. Drop your second round of eggs into the water and poach as before.

10. Pile the veggies into two bowls, top with the poached eggs, spoon very, very large spoonfuls of pesto over the eggs, sprinkle with fleur de sel, and top with breadcrumbs.

Enjoy immediately. Does not keep well.

This is the quintessential California breakfast-by-the-beach dish. It should be eaten outside with a nice cold beer or some iced tea. You want to be nursing a hangover, or somehow sunning your legs while eating this. If a meal without meat is not complete to you, serve this dish with a side of sausages.

beer-baked eggs with peppers and onions

SERVES 2 TO 4

2 tbsp extra-virgin olive oil

1 large onion, sliced

1 garlic clove, diced

¾ tsp kosher salt

½ tsp ground ancho chile

½ tsp ground coriander

½ tsp cumin seeds

3 or 4 red bell peppers, sliced

1 jalapeño, sliced into thin coins (seeds removed if you prefer it mild)

One 12-oz/350-ml bottle or can light-colored beer

4 to 8 eggs

8 corn tortillas, best quality available

Fleur de sel for sprinkling

3 tbsp chopped fresh cilantro

2 limes, quartered

1. Preheat your oven to 500°F/260°C.

2. In a large ovenproof sauté pan over medium-high heat, combine the olive oil, onion, garlic, salt, ancho chile, coriander, and cumin seeds. Sauté, stirring often, until dark brown, about 5 minutes. Add the bell peppers and jalapeño and toss. Add the beer and cook down by about half. Reduce the heat to medium-low, cover, and cook until the peppers and onion are very soft, 12 to 15 minutes longer.

3. Uncover, reduce the heat to low, and make four to eight wells in the sauce. Gently crack the eggs into each well. Cover and simmer for 2 to 3 minutes, until the whites begin to set.

4. Quickly transfer to the oven. Bake, uncovered, until the whites set but the yolks remain very runny, 2 to 3 minutes.

5. Meanwhile, toast the tortillas with tongs over an open medium flame, about 10 seconds per side. Consider working with all four burners at once. Wrap the tortillas in a clean kitchen towel to keep warm.

6. Sprinkle each egg with fleur de sel and the entire dish with cilantro. Serve immediately with the warm tortillas and lime wedges.

This dish does not keep well, so just eat it all.

coffee and other beverages

Coffee is backed up. Actually it's at a standstill. Rosemary has decided to recalibrate the espresso machine because she feels the shots aren't coming out perfectly. Now everyone has to wait ten minutes for a latte, maybe longer. This is certainly not the first time she has done this during a rush, so I immediately start having our servers give out free cups of drip coffee. That's what happens at Huck: Things may go wrong, but generally when they do it's because we're trying to make something better, and at least we always give out free things to make up for it. It's a real human-run business.

Rosemary runs our coffee program and our catering program, is assistant general manager, buys the wine, and handles about a dozen other things. I'm pretty sure she works around 80 hours a week and stays for hours after we tell her to go home, but the girl has heart and energy for days and I've never seen her tired. She is also hilarious and occasionally wears the craziest outfits to work, clothes that I would immediately send someone else home to change out of, but which somehow just work for her. When she started as a server, she and I got into a confrontation on the line because she was moving too fast for her own good and confusing the line guys. I told her to slow down in the way I say everything in the kitchen, directly, and she got defensive and started to cry. I told her to stop crying, in pretty much the same tone, and she cried some more. Once we both calmed down, we made up; mostly because I realized in that moment how much she cared and how much of a fool I would be if I pushed that kind of person away. When we felt the need to take our coffee program to the next level, we put Rosemary in charge.

She trained extensively, became a total coffee geek, and even introduced several new drinks to the coffee menu. It doesn't make sense to bend over backward to make our food the best it can be—training line cooks for months, sourcing the best ingredients from the farmers' market—and then have mediocre beverages. We want everything at Huckleberry to be the best of its kind, and that goes for the coffee and for the people who put their heart and soul into it.

The espresso machine is now recalibrated and Rosemary and another barista are doing their best to catch up with tickets. She pulls a beautiful shot, medium length, sweet and creamy, but with just enough earthiness and grittiness to round it out and give it complexity. We may have given away a few dozen cups of coffee, but now we are back on track.

As I go back into the kitchen, my last morning baker is done and heading out. I thank her for a good day of work and tell her to enjoy a good, long nap. There's nothing better than the "baker's nap." I rarely take them now because I don't have to come in at 3 A.M. any longer, and having a young child and four businesses to look over makes it difficult to steal away for a couple of hours in the middle of the day. But I used to love that nap. It's the great reward for starting your day so early. You get to go home when everyone else is still at work, when the world is bustling, close your shades, get under your covers, and sleep the sleep of the dead for a couple of solid hours, so you actually have enough energy for that early dinner with your boyfriend or to go out for happy hour with one of your girlfriends. A sweet reward for a job well done.

At Huckleberry, we take our hot chocolate very seriously. It's made with whole milk, heavy cream, and rich Valrhona chocolate and topped with Shiho's Sweet Rose Marshmallows (page 272). It cannot be ordered nonfat or low fat, but we hope once people taste it, they realize there's a method to our madness. This is not the kind of hot chocolate that you'll drink every day, but when you do drink it, the satisfaction is huge. Sometimes I like to add a vanilla bean to this recipe to add another dimension. From the bottom of my heart I say, have your kids grow up on this decadent treat instead of the watery substitute we were all raised on.

hot chocolate

SERVES 4 TO 6

1½ cups/260 g chopped dark chocolate, 65% cacao or higher

4 cups/950 ml organic whole milk

3 cups/720 ml heavy cream

1 tbsp sugar

1 pinch kosher salt

1. Put the chocolate in a large bowl and set aside.

2. In a medium saucepan, bring the milk, cream, sugar, and salt to a boil. Pour the hot milk mixture over the chocolate. Allow it to sit for a moment undisturbed to melt. Then whisk until homogenous. Serve immediately or refrigerate until needed.

This keeps very well, refrigerated, for up to 1 week. It might even get better after the flavors have time to come together, so don't hesitate to make this well in advance or to make big batches to keep on hand. When ready to serve, just whisk to ensure it hasn't settled, and warm it in a saucepan over medium heat.

Shiho Yoshikawa is one of the most talented women I know. She and I have worked together since Tartine, working side by side on almost every station in that kitchen. When I opened Huckleberry, she came down from San Francisco to help for the first few months, living in our guest room and working from 3 A.M. to 7 P.M. almost every day. When it was time for her to go home, Josh and I couldn't imagine our lives, or our restaurants, without her. I knew she always wanted to make ice cream and we knew she was amazing at anything she put her mind to, so we decided to open Sweet Rose Creamery with her. She makes artisanal, farmers' market–driven ice creams and sorbets that change weekly, daily, and sometimes hourly. She is crazy in the most perfect way. Well, these are her marshmallows; we use them on our Hot Chocolate (page 271) at Huckleberry, and I assure you, they are well worth the trouble.

shiho's sweet rose marshmallows

MAKES 4 CUPS/190 G

½ cup/60 g powdered sugar
½ cup/65 g cornstarch
½ cup/120 ml water
1 envelope gelatin
1 tbsp + 1 tsp agave syrup
⅔ cup/135 g granulated sugar
Pinch of kosher salt
¾ tsp vanilla extract

1. Stir together the powdered sugar and cornstarch in a small bowl until well combined. Set aside.

2. Place ¼ cup/60 ml of the water in the bowl of a stand mixer fitted with the whisk attachment and sprinkle the gelatin over it to bloom.

3. Combine the agave syrup, granulated sugar, salt, and remaining ¼ cup/60 ml water in a small saucepan. Simmer over medium-high heat until the temperature reaches exactly 249°F/120°C on a digital thermometer.

4. Immediately remove from the heat, begin mixing the gelatin mixture on low speed, and slowly pour the sugar syrup down the side of the mixer bowl into the gelatin.

5. Once all the syrup has been added, increase the mixer speed to high and whip until tripled in volume.

6. After you achieve full volume, reduce the speed to low, add the vanilla, and continue to whip until cooled to a warm room temperature.

7. Meanwhile, dust two sheet pans evenly with ¼ cup/30 g of the powdered sugar mixture by tapping it through a mesh strainer.

8. Place a ½-in/12-mm round tip in a piping bag.

9. Once the marshmallow mixture has cooled, fill the piping bag and pipe long cylinders onto the dusted sheet pans. Allow about ½ in/12 mm between marshmallow cylinders.

10. Allow to dry for 30 minutes to 1 hour.

11. Dust the top of the marshmallows generously with the remaining powdered sugar mixture and gently roll the cylinders back and forth to coat the sides as well.

12. Transfer the marshmallow cylinders to a cutting board and cut into ½-in-/12-mm-long pieces.

13. Toss in the powdered sugar mixture to coat the cut sides, shaking off any excess.

These keep well, in an airtight container, refrigerated, for up to 1 week.

A mocha is only as good as the chocolate, the milk, and the espresso you put into it. We make our mochas with dark Valrhona chocolate, the best organic milk, and our favorite espresso. Of course, not everyone has access to espresso at home. Not to worry, you can make a pretty delicious version of this using ⅔ cup/160 ml drip coffee instead of the espresso. Just reduce the milk to ⅓ cup/80 ml to make up for the increased water content of the coffee, and add the same amount of chocolate syrup.

This chocolate syrup is super-versatile and can be used throughout this book. You'll have plenty left over and it would be great on top of Chocolate Chocolate Teacake (page 94), Gluten-Free Vegan Banana Chocolate Muffins (page 53), or as a topping for ice cream.

mocha

SERVES 1

CHOCOLATE SYRUP

½ cup + 2 tbsp/150 ml water

¼ cup + 3 tbsp/85 g sugar

¼ cup + 1 tbsp/35 g Dutch processed cocoa powder

1 cup/170 g chopped dark chocolate, 60 to 70% cacao

1 tbsp + 2 tsp agave syrup

SIMPLE SYRUP

½ cup/120 ml water

½ cup/100 g sugar

¼ cup/60 ml hot espresso

1 cup/240 ml organic whole milk

1. To make the chocolate syrup: Combine all the ingredients in a small saucepan and melt gently over medium-low heat, stirring frequently, 2 to 4 minutes. Set aside.

2. To make the simple syrup: Combine the water and sugar in a small saucepan and heat, stirring occasionally, until dissolved, 1 to 2 minutes. Set aside.

3. Combine 1 tbsp of the chocolate syrup and 1 tbsp of the simple syrup in a mug and top with the hot espresso, stirring to combine. (Reserve the remaining syrups for another use.)

4. If you have an espresso machine, heat and froth the milk with the steam wand. If you are not so fortunate, simply heat the milk in a small saucepan over medium heat until hot—if we're getting technical, to 150°F/65°C to prevent the milk from scalding and losing its sweetness.

5. Pour the hot milk into the coffee mixture and stir until it comes together.

The chocolate sauce keeps well, refrigerated, for up to 2 weeks but will thicken when cold. To liquefy, warm gently over low heat, as needed. The simple syrup keeps well, refrigerated, for up to 1 month.

This is a great drink that works well with pretty much any kind of dairy or dairy substitute. Make it with whole milk, almond milk, or organic soymilk. The vanilla simple syrup here is a wonderful recipe in its own right. Make a big batch and keep it in your fridge for iced or hot tea or iced coffee. Homemade syrups are night and day compared to any of the overly processed store-bought alternatives, and they are super-simple to make. This recipe makes about 2 cups/480 ml of syrup, so you'll have plenty left over.

If you don't have an espresso machine at home, you can still make a pretty delicious latte using use ⅔ cup/160 ml drip coffee and ⅓ cup/80 ml warm milk, instead of the espresso and milk quantities below.

vanilla latte

SERVES 1

VANILLA SYRUP

2 cups/400 g sugar

2 cups/480 ml water

1 vanilla bean, split, seeds scraped out, pod reserved

¼ cup/60 ml hot espresso

1¼ cups/300 ml organic whole milk

1. To make the vanilla syrup: Combine the sugar, water, and vanilla seeds and pod in a small saucepan and heat, whisking occasionally, until the sugar dissolves and the seeds are dispersed. Set aside.

2. Combine 2 tbsp of the vanilla syrup and the hot espresso in a mug and stir to combine. (Reserve the remaining syrup for another use.)

3. If you have an espresso machine, heat and froth the milk with the steam wand. If you are not so fortunate, simply heat the milk in a small saucepan over medium heat until hot—if we're getting technical, to 150°F/65°C to prevent the milk from scalding and losing its sweetness.

4. Pour the hot milk into the coffee mixture and stir until it comes together.

The vanilla syrup keeps well, refrigerated, for up to 1 month.

When I'm having a hard day, I make one of these. It's the kind of drink that makes everything right in the world for a few moments. It works really well hot, but shaken over ice with the salty sweetness of the homemade caramel makes a fun and slightly frothy version of those overly sweet drinks that everyone is used to. The caramel sauce recipe below makes way more than you'd need for a few drinks (about 2 cups/430 ml), but make it anyway; the sauce is fantastic over bread pudding, pancakes, ice cream, hot cereals, and sometimes best right off your finger for a few quick seconds of bliss.

When making the caramel, be sure to use a medium saucepan instead of a small one, even though it doesn't look like a lot of ingredients. When you add the cream to the hot caramel, it bubbles up a ton and I don't want anyone getting burned.

If you don't have an espresso machine at home, you can still make a pretty delicious latte using the same amount of caramel sauce, but ⅔ cup/160ml drip coffee and ⅓ cup/ 80 ml warm milk, instead of the espresso and milk quantities below.

iced shaken caramel latte

SERVES 1

CARAMEL SAUCE

2 cups/400 g sugar

1¼ tsp kosher salt

1 vanilla bean, split, seeds scraped out, pod reserved

3 tbsp water

2 cups/480 ml heavy cream, at room temperature

¾ cup + 2 tbsp/200 g unsalted butter, cubed, at room temperature

1 to 2 generous handfuls of ice

¼ cup/60 ml espresso, at room temperature

1¼ cups/300 ml whole organic milk

1. To make the caramel sauce: Cook the sugar, salt, vanilla seeds and pod, and water in a medium saucepan over medium-high heat, stirring with a wooden spoon occasionally. Cook until all the sugar is melted and has turned a deep brown. Be sure to have the cream close at hand.

2. Turn the heat to low and add the cream and butter. It will bubble like crazy; be careful to stay out of its way. Increase the heat to medium and stir until smooth and thickened, about 2 minutes.

3. Set aside at room temperature, stirring every so often to make sure it doesn't separate, and allow to cool.

4. Fill a cocktail shaker three-quarters full with ice. Add the espresso, 2 tbsp of the cooled caramel sauce, and the milk. Shake vigorously for about 15 seconds. Drizzle some caramel sauce around the rim of a tall glass and pour the contents of the shaker into it. (Reserve the rest of the sauce for another use.)

The caramel sauce keeps well, refrigerated, for up to 2 weeks but will thicken when cold. To liquefy, warm gently over low heat, as needed.

We didn't serve chai lattes at Huckleberry for a long time because we pride ourselves on making everything from scratch and didn't want to use one of those overly sweet prepackaged powders that most places use. We were a bit intimidated by making our own chai until we started playing with it and came up with this simple but super-flavorful recipe. Make the chai in advance so you always have it in your fridge as an easy treat to throw together. The vanilla syrup here lends a rich sweetness to the drink, and by adding it to each drink separately, you are always in control of how sweet you make it. And you can always substitute honey or agave instead. This recipe makes about 4 cups/960 ml of chai tea, so you'll have plenty left over.

chai latte

SERVES 1

CHAI TEA
5 cinnamon sticks
3 tbsp + 1 tsp whole allspice berries
3 tbsp cardamom pods
2 tbsp fennel seeds
1 tbsp + 1 tsp whole cloves
1 tbsp + 1 tsp black peppercorns
6 star anise pods
One 1-in/2.5-cm piece/20 g fresh ginger
8 cups/2 L water
6 good-quality black tea bags

¾ cup/180 ml whole organic milk
1 to 2 tbsp Vanilla Syrup (see page 274)

1. Preheat your oven to 300°F/150°C.

2. Toast the cinnamon, allspice, cardamom pods, fennel, cloves, peppercorns, and anise on a sheet pan until fragrant, 5 to 10 minutes.

3. Combine the toasted spices, ginger, and water in a medium sauce-pan and simmer over high heat until reduced by half. Remove from the heat, add the tea bags, and steep for 3 minutes. Immediately strain, discarding the whole spices and tea bags.

4. Heat the milk and ¾ cup/180 ml of the chai tea in a small sauce-pan over medium-high heat, stirring occasionally. (Reserve the remaining chai tea for future servings.)

5. Pour in a mug and add the vanilla syrup to taste.

The chai tea keeps very well, refrigerated, for up to 2 weeks.

my apologies

DEAR JOEL:

I'm sorry you felt it was inappropriate when we posted your mostly naked, spread-eagle, Ray-Ban-wearing Facebook profile picture on the office desktop. And I'm sorry you lost your eyebrows for two months, but we appreciated you lighting the pilot for us. I'm also sorry you thought it was best to get a facial peel the day before Thanksgiving, our busiest catering day of the year. You've made us smile continuously since the day we opened, and Huckleberry would be nothing without you. I love you.

DEAR ROSEMARY:

I'm sorry that guitar riffs and brunch don't go together. And I'm sorry I made fun of your earth nature mama shawl. I'm also sorry I told you to "F*#^ off and get the f*#^ out of my kitchen!" so many times. I obviously didn't mean it and I'm glad you stuck around. Every day for one reason or another I am so grateful you are on this team. I love you.

DEAR NICOLE:

I am sorry you keep getting mistaken for me. No one should have to deal with that but me.

DEAR CATERER WHO PASSES OUR DESSERTS OFF AS HERS:

I'm sorry we couldn't make the cherry tarts you promised your client during winter when cherries were out of season.

DEAR LONGTIME REGULAR:

Rosemary is very sorry she told you to "F*#^ off" because you wouldn't get up from your table that she had promised to someone else and she didn't know who you were. I'm pretty sure she has picked up a few bad habits from me so I'm sorry, too. We hope the piece of chocolate cake we sent to you made up for it.

DEAR ARTHUR:

I'm sorry you pocket-dialed me from the bar at 11 p.m. the night before you called in sick. I'm sorry cilantro and parsley look so much alike, it really is confusing. But I'm not sorry that we played Beyoncé's "If I Were a Boy" every time you walked in late and hungover at 4 a.m. to work side by side with the all-girl bakery team. It's still funny. I know whatever you choose to create will be amazing; you have more courage and heart than anyone I know.

DEAR GRUMPY OLD MAN:

I'm sorry you don't like our granola. Fortunately, there are dozens of other granola options available to you around town. You never have to buy ours again, but we'd appreciate it if you stopped telling us how much you dislike it.

DEAR MATT:

I'm sorry Huckleberry is such a hen house, in which we spend the first thirty minutes of every meeting talking about Joel's love life, Rosie's new cape, Anastasia's preferred juice of the day, Laurel's new dye job, or with Josh and me watching a video of Milo on our phones. We're sorry we're never going to be more efficient. Thanks for putting up with us, because it just wouldn't be the same without you. You are incredibly talented.

DEAR GIRLS:

I'm sorry I blow through the kitchen, throw half your things out, tell Laurel everything that's wrong, and just walk out. I really do appreciate you and everything you do. You are the A team. You're the best team we've ever had and we're blessed to have you.

DEAR ANASTASIA:

I'm sorry that I've turned you into a sous chef's assistant, a baker's assistant, and an organizer of my sometimes rough-around-the-edges kitchen staff. I guess I took the term *director of operations* a little too liberally, but you're just so damn good at keeping things together and making them run. I believe you can fix anything and you generally do.

DEAR BANANA LADY:

I'm sorry you don't like bananas and we do. And I'm sorry that all our muffins don't weigh the exact same amount, but I have to say that's so weird that you took them home and weighed them.

DEAR ETHAN:

Laurel's sorry for all the dinners served way too late, or not at all, and that virtually every one of them consisted of fried eggs over various cereals, sandwiches, and plates. She is sorry that she rendered every countertop in the kitchen unusable for 4 months straight due to the stacks of dry ingredients and proofing breads that covered them. Thanks for putting up with it all. She loves you so much.

DEAR RECIPE TESTERS:

Aaron Ranf, Alex Nishizawa, Amber Banks, Amy Bray, Amy Wruble, Anastasia Smith, Ayala Chocron, Betty Urban, Caitlin Coyne, Callie Rogers, Cathy Bunin, Coco Kislinger, Colby Goff, Colleen Higgins, Courtney Sheils,

Daina Donovitch, David Katz, Deanne Ecklund, Debbie Irving, Drew Steinberg, Emily Roth, Esther Hillebrand, Grace Bush-Vineberg, Heather Ferguson Sperry, Heather Taylor, Jaclyn Rosenson, Jake Pushinsky, Jenny Levin, Jesse Nathan, Joel Dixon, Joseph Capponi, Kara Corwin, Karen Thomsen, Kate Farrell, Katherine Kurtz, Kathryn Weil, Kathy Katz, Kelsey Brito, Leo Pollock, Lily Sais, Linda Goff, Lucas Nathan, Mary Farrell, Megan D'Amour, Melissa Levin, Melissa Park, Nigel Briand, Nina Rubin, Shari Call, Sheila Kleinknecht, Stephan Nathan, Stevan Goff, Stu Bloomberg, Ted Pushinsky, Tessa Perliss, Tracy Erland Zehnder, Xenia Zampolli.

I'm sorry for those crazy only-partially written recipes, with ingredients missing and crazy bake times. Thank you for being willing to trash your kitchens and eat too many pastries and even more fried eggs for us. Your feedback made this book so much better.

DEAR KAREN:

So sorry for all the last-minute calls in the dead of winter begging for out-of-season fruits from the Southern Hemisphere. If we weren't testing these recipes a week before the book was due, we would never even think of it. We know it was hard to find and that, as always, you did it with love and care.

DEAR HUCKLEBERRY INVESTORS:

I'm sorry you still wait in long breakfast lines to order your fried egg sandwiches, but we hope you enjoy seeing how crowded Huckleberry has become. I can't tell you how grateful I am that you believed in my crazy plan and helped make it a reality.

DEAR FRENCH LADY:

I'm sorry we had to ban you from the bakery, although you are lucky because I was seconds away from performing a citizen's arrest. There's another bakery down the street that you will be much happier at, I promise.

DEAR BEN:

Josh and I are sorry for calling you a million times over the past few years and asking you to do the impossible like fix a flooding water heater in less than an hour or help us open our bakery on a budget and timeline that most people would laugh at. Your smile and enthusiasm make us so happy every time you walk in the door. We're also sorry to Maggie that we often replaced your healthful meal plan with a BBQ pork sandwich, but we do so get a kick out of watching you enjoy yourself while you eat it. You truly are the best contractor in L.A. and we're so happy to have you as a part of our family.

DEAR MELISSA:

I'm sorry for all the unintelligible scrawled recipes you were forced to decipher and type. I am sorry for all the calls at 6 a.m. or midnight asking you how to use my printer or to remind me what time we're meeting the next day. I am sorry for sending you to four or five markets to gather all the ingredients I needed for testing. I am not sorry that I found you to help with the book, which wouldn't have gotten done without you. Thank you, thank you, thank you!

DEAR JOURNALISTS AND FOOD CRITICS OF THE L.A. BASIN:

I'm sorry that I often can't think before speaking.

DEAR COLBY:

I'm sorry I grill you about your love life everytime I see you. I'm also sorry that I never change out of my PJs whenever you come over for a budget meeting; it's a real testament to how comfortable I feel around you. You're the best partner in the world and I thank you for taking Josh and my crazy dreams and helping ground them in reality. You have an amazing ability to do this without making us compromise any specialness along the way.

DEAR LAUREL:

I'm sorry I can be such an annoying person to work with. I can't believe you spend as much time working with me as you do and still come back for more. I'm not sorry that I chose you to be my sous chef a few years back. It was one of the best decisions of my life. You are an insanely talented, generous, funny, beautiful, brilliant woman. You are, and always will be, my family.

DEAR SHIRLEY:

I'm sorry I refused to bring back the Rocky Road Bread Pudding, but luckily I know you love a strong woman that holds her ground. I'm not sorry for my mother meeting you and your strong will to bring Josh and me together. Thank you for raising such an amazing man and loving your grandson so much.

DEAR GABE AND RACHEL:

I'm sorry I like to eat dinner around the same time you guys like to finish lunch but I will say the few meals we can actually sync up are always filled with the best conversation and the most love. You guys are simply the greatest.

DEAR LETTIE:

I'm sorry I still have such a hard time leaving Milo every day. If I didn't know he was being fed and loved by you with as much care as I do, then I couldn't do it at all. Thank you for loving my son as if he were your own, and for making this book and any continuation of my career possible. My family is blessed to have you in our lives.

DEAR OLIVER:

I'm sorry that I forced you to eat my cooking school final project. Pan-fried lemon chicken breast with avocado sauce and mango chutney. That was gross. I will never forget you saying how much you loved it, and you showing up at my graduation, and for always being one of my biggest supporters. There is no better feeling than when your big brother tells you he's proud of you—thank you for saying it so many times. You're the greatest.

DEAR LUKE:

I am sorry I made fun of you for being so very slow in the kitchen and complaining about your arm hurting when you made aioli. You're one of the most talented, insightful people I know and your taste is always spot-on. The way you look and act in the world is a thing of beauty and is an inspiration to be around.

DEAR GRANDPA IRV AND GRANDMA EVELYN:

I'm sorry you weren't here to see me open Huckleberry. I know you would have been so proud. I know you would have been in the dining room regularly screaming "That's my granddaughter, she owns this place. Isn't she beautiful!" I'm also sorry that Grandpa didn't get a chance to sit at the end of the communal table and motion to everyone's unfinished plates yelling "Pass it over here, I'll finish it." You were the first people to show me that life is about talking too much, laughing too loud, and hugging just a little too tightly.

DEAR MOM AND DAD:

I am sorry for the millions of calls during the first year of opening Huckleberry when I told you it was too much and I needed to quit and sell the place immediately. Thank you for listening, not taking anything too seriously, and always being willing to show up any time of day to help. I know other people may say this, but I truly think you are the greatest parents on Earth; you always make me feel loved and supported and have always been there to remind me to work hard but never too much so I don't have time to laugh at myself. Love and gratitude is an understatement for what I feel when I'm with my family.

DEAR JOSH:

I am sorry that writing this book meant that I could justify skipping every manager meeting. I think we both know it was sometimes for the book, but more often for a playdate with Milo. I love you and you are the greatest partner in the world. I would truly be nothing without your love and support, and there is no greater gift I could receive than being able to walk through this life next to you.

DEAR MILO:

I'm sorry that as the book dragged on, you began to associate the sight of Laurel, Melissa, or me putting on an apron at home as going to work, and had to make it very clear that you did not approve. I know that it may have been confusing, but the last six months of working primarily from home and always being a few steps from you have been the best six months of my life. I'm sorry that you will be getting dragged to work with me again soon. Luckily with all your new egg-cracking skills you'll be super-helpful. I am so blessed to have a front-row seat to the movie of your life; every day I wake up more excited than the last to see what will happen next. Watching you in the world is an inspiration. I love you.

DEAR BABY TALLULA:

I write this on my last day of edits as your little 6-week-old self lies in my arms. I waited what felt like forever for you, but now that you're here I can't remember a world without you. I love you. I'm counting the days until you, me, and Milo are all in the kitchen baking cookies, with the two of you fighting over who gets to lick the bowl just like I did with my brothers.

index